Stevenson University Library
Stevenson MD 21153

The Counterculture Reader

WITHDRAWN

D1056329

Other readers featured in the Longman Topics series include:

Issues of Gender
Ellen Friedman and Jennifer Marshall

Language and Prejudice
Tamara Valentine

Translating Tradition
Karen E. Beardslee

Citizenship Now
Jon Ford and Marjorie Ford

Considering Cultural Difference
Pauline Uchmanowicz

A Longman Topics Reader

The Counterculture Reader

E. A. SWINGROVER
University of Nevada, Reno

PEARSON
Longman

New York   San Francisco   Boston
London   Toronto   Sydney   Tokyo   Singapore   Madrid
Mexico City   Munich   Paris   Cape Town   Hong Kong   Montreal

Senior Vice President and Publisher: Joseph Opiela
Acquisitions Editor: Susan Kunchandy
Marketing Manager: Deborah Murphy
Senior Supplements Editor: Donna Campion
Media Supplements Editor: Nancy Garcia
Managing Editor: Bob Ginsberg
Production Manager: Joseph Vella
Project Coordination, Text Design, and Electronic Page Makeup:
    Sunflower Publishing Services
Senior Design Manager/Cover Designer: Nancy Danahy
Cover Photo: © Getty Images Inc./Image Bank
Manufacturing Manager: Dennis J. Para
Manufacturing Buyer: Alfred C. Dorsey
Printer and Binder: R.R. Donnelley & Sons Company
Cover Printer: Phoenix Color Corp.

For permission to use copyrighted material, grateful acknowledgment is made to the copyright holders on pp. 231–233, which are hereby made part of this copyright page.

Library of Congress Cataloging-in-Publication Data

The counterculture reader / [edited by] E. A. Swinger.
    p. cm. — (Longman topics)
    ISBN 0-321-14562-3
    1. United States—Social life and customs—1945–1970.
    2. United States—Social conditions—1960–1980.
    3. Counterculture—United States—History—20th century.
    4. Radicalism—United States—History—20th century. 5.
    Radicals—United States—Biography. 6. Youth—United States—
    Social life and customs—20th century. 7. Youth—United States—
    Social conditions—20th century. I. Swingrover, E. A. (Elizabeth
    A.) II. Series.

    E169.02C656 2004
    306'.1—dc22   2003062347

Copyright © 2004 by Pearson Education, Inc.

All rights reserved. No part of this publication may be reproduced, stored in a retrieval system, or transmitted, in any form or by any means, electronic, mechanical, photocopying, recording, or otherwise, without the prior written permission of the publisher. Printed in the United States.

Please visit our website at http://www.ablongman.com

ISBN 0-321-14562-3

3 4 5 6 7 8 9 10—DOH—06 05

This reader is for all those who survived the Counterculture, those who perished, those who flourished, and those who would like to know what happened. And for all the generations of my family.

CONTENTS

CHAPTER 3
Drugs and Bombs 77

CHAPTER 4
"Why the Counterculture Loves Indians, Black People, and Everybody": AIM, Indian National Literature, and Black Power 127

RHETORICAL CONTENTS

PREFACE

The personal is political.

I am not a child *of* the sixties because I was a child *in* the 1960s. My high school and college years were spent in the 1970s and 1980s, in the aftermath of Counterculture revolutions, Vietnam, Watergate, the oil embargo, and the Iran-Contra hostage crisis. We were not rebelling, but putting together our lives with the pieces left to us. I see my generation's fears for *their* children's future in the face of random violence, terrorist attacks, and war as of this writing that reminds me of what I have read about the atmosphere of the Cold War.

Most writers about the 1960s were students and often activists "in the day." Their interests remain in the political movements of the times. As scholars, they examine manifestoes, letters, newspapers, position papers, political analyses, protests, and marches, reliving golden moments along with the horrors they experienced or watched on television. The Counterculture is often identified as "the hippies," and usually merits only a brief glance as one is returned to more serious subjects like the politics of the Left. I believe, however, that the true Counterculture encompasses both the Beats who came before the hippies and the punks who came after. True, most of the Counterculture's participants were too busy *living* to write much down. Tom Wolfe's *Electric Kool-Aid Acid Test* is often used in sixties courses, but it is an observer's account, not a participant's. Still, a few rambling memoirs, poems, song lyrics, and scrapbooks remain. From these I have selected a sampling for *The Counterculture Reader,* as well as commentaries and reflections by observers. Not intended to be all-inconclusive, *The Counterculture Reader* should be viewed as a starting point from which to explore the last forty years of American culture. Students should be encouraged to read longer works, view films, look through newspaper and magazines archives, and gather oral histories from the era.

Many survivors of those years saw the Counterculture as a passing fad and only dabbled for awhile, moving on to "regular" jobs and families. Others never participated but watched (often in amusement, some, in horror) from the sidelines. Some teach at universities and continue agendas they began in that era, or if younger, write academic articles about those days such as those in *Imagine Nation* (2002). Others, such as Peter Collier and David Horowitz, have seriously recanted their former political views, and write books critiquing the legacies they helped to begin. Parents who raised teenagers (particularly in the 1960s but through the 1970s) tell tales of cults, drug addiction and abuse, their children taken from them by forces they could not comprehend at the time. Participants are now grandparents who may hide their past or speak openly of their experiences. Frequently, I speak to people who view the Counterculture as mostly entertaining but believe that the 1950s Cold War, Vietnam, and the 1970s are best forgotten. Contemporary college students are often intrigued by the nostalgic aspects of the times—sex, drugs, and rock and roll— which they view as somehow freer, less repressive, than our own times.

While the Beats retain their *cachet* because of their literary credentials (despite numerous scathing biographies and autobiographies from spouses and children), and the punks for their connection to pop music, snow- and skate-boarding, the hippies' legacy is a bit shakier and easier to parody. The Beats and punks are cool, the hippies, lame. However we want to categorize, eulogize, and demonize the Counterculture, its predecessors and its aftermath, and although often relegated to the sideshow and the carnivalesque, it remains the most recognizable part of the period from the 1950s to the 1970s in American society.

Although the Counterculture is often viewed as *the* cultural revolution of the 1960s, we can say that, as soon as World War II ended, a few Americans were already rejecting the mainstream with its promises of peace and prosperity. Indeed, the "starving artist" phenomenon can trace its roots back to the beginning of the Industrial Revolution in England with Romantic poets such as Shelly, Keats, Wordsworth, and Coleridge. Rimbaud, Baudelaire, and the French Decadents of late nineteenth century France would inspire countless beatniks and Jim Morrison of the 1960s rock group The Doors, who took their name from Aldous Huxley's 1954 drug odyssey *The Doors of Perception*. Living on leftovers, the discards of a "post-scarcity" society, the twentieth century Counterculture looked back before the twentieth century to what they imagined was a purer world. In 1966 the Diggers started serving the starving hordes who had come to San Francisco for the Summer of Love. Taking their name from a seventeenth century group of poor people who wanted free land to work, the Diggers set the Counterculture squarely in the history of Western civilization. Before there were hippies, there were Quakers, pacifists, bohemians, free thinkers, and free love advocates. The difference is that as soon as the Counterculture began its move against the establishment or mainstream, it became a part of it, absorbed into what would become, by the late 1960s, the biggest explosion of youth advertising in American history. Richard Goldstein, of New York's bohemian newspaper *Village Voice* commented that "The last laugh belongs to the media-men who chose to report a charade as a movement. In doing so, they created one." A Death of the Hippie mock funeral was held in San Francisco where the name "hippie" was officially disowned by its *true* denizens. Perhaps the most glaring result of the Counterculture's *revolution* is in its *commodification*. Although the hippies allegedly eschewed money, "bread" in the parlance of the times, the fashions they wore, the music they listened to, and, more darkly, the drugs they consumed generated a lot of "dough."

Several strains run through from the Beats through the hippies to the punks, and you can read this in their literature, hear it in their music. Rejecting nationalism and private property, the Beats went "on the road"; the hippies tried communal living, preached love, and sought bliss; and the punks coveted anarchy and its discontents. Nearly all of them took drugs with their alcohol; many perished from substance abuse. Some Counterculture types (a hundred groups and a few million individuals) were out to change the system (alternately known as the Establishment), which they saw as irreparably damaged. Rebelling against the Establishment (through violence or more peaceful means) appeared to them to be their only solution. As White Panther leader John Sinclair said, paraphrasing Beat writer William Burroughs, by partying down in "a total assault on the culture," the world would follow. Remembered most not for their politics but rather for their fashions, music, drugs, and sexuality, these legacies are with us still. Even more pressing is the backlash that the Counterculture has inspired, for although organic supermarkets and coffee houses have become ubiquitous reminders of the past, the Counterculture has been blamed for everything from the AIDS epidemic to low test scores in our children's schools. With international terrorism at its height, and the attacks of September 11th still fresh in our minds, *The*

Counterculture Reader brings back those "days of hope, days of rage" and the reactions to them, for better or for worse.

MAJOR COUNTERCULTURE THEMES

Fashion

The early Beats' lack of fashion sense—wrinkled shirts and rumpled suits—soon became fashionable. And although none of the Beat writers featured here has been photographed wearing a beret, the Counterculture they inspired was soon seen donning Breton hats and carrying bongo drums.

The "flower children" and freaks dressed to enhance their freakishness, appropriating and eventually commodifying clothing from every time period and culture imaginable—Edwardian suits and pointy boots; Buddhist robes; pirate shirts and headwraps; Davy Crockett buckskins; miners' blue jeans; Indian headbands; feathers; silver *conchas;* turquoise and beads; cowboy boots and hats. And that was just the *males.* Men had not worn their hair this long since the late eighteenth century. In his book *Hippies: A Study of Their Drug Habits and Sexual Customs,* researcher Tribhuwan Kapur finds it puzzling that hippies—Americans and Europeans from middle-class families—are dressed more ragged than the street people of New Delhi, India. Women wore variations of costumes once donned by Russian peasants, dumped their girdles and brassieres for a freer look, and wore trousers. Androgyny was in, and the term "uni-sex" appeared in fashion magazines. Of course, the high fashion world remained oblivious to women's demands for comfort and equality, and stuck females in micro-mini skirts that featured models such as reed-thin Twiggy, just as the communes featured earth mothers who resembled solid tree trunks, not broken branches.

Punks took clothes and tore them apart, deconstructed them, wore them inside out, and fastened them (and their body parts, a pre-cursor to the piercing fad) with safety pins. Razor blades became jewelry, and the hair was only long enough to be swept up into a Mohawk—*not* as a tribute to American Indians, but just to scare people.

Sex

Long before the Stonewall "Gay" Riots, Beat poets and writers were promoting the free love and sexual experimentation that had sent Oscar Wilde to prison in the 1890s. The hippies were sensationalized in the media for promiscuity. Free love was a bit more so with the invention of the birth control pill (1961), but it remained far too one-sided to some women, as they had just begun their fight for sexual equality and reproductive freedoms. Some communes adopted strict rules about sexuality, others were laissez-faire. Cults and their charismatic leaders often exploited their members financially and sexually.

Underground comix such as *Zap* and *Rat* promoted images of transgressive sexuality that were lewd, crude, and absolutely offensive to women and most ethnic groups. Now they are expensive collector's items. As commentators lament the selling of sex in music and films in the twenty-first century, we should recall such gems as the original cover of musician Jimi Hendrix's album *Electric Ladyland* (1968), which featured numerous naked women surrounding the guitar god. And we wonder why there was a "feminist" movement?

Music

Modern jazz, particularly the type known as bebop, with its complex harmonies and rhythms, is inextricably linked to the Beats. In his "Essentials of Spontaneous Prose," Jack Kerouac even tries to emulate the music's improvisational nature in language, at times producing poetry, at others, incomprehensibility. You will often hear the phrase "You had to be there" in Counterculture narratives of the 1950s through the 1970s.

If the politicos liked folk and protest music, the hippies and the Counterculture at large throughout the 1960s chose blues-based rock as their soundtrack of choice. Returned to the America of its roots by British bands such as the Rolling Stones, what had once been termed "race music" (black music not played on white radio until Elvis Presley crossed the line and recorded the songs early in his career) was transformed by bands like the Grateful Dead and the Jefferson Airplane who created a free-form improvisational rock that claimed to take its inspiration from a drug called Acid (LSD-25).

As White Panther leader John Sinclair remarked of the MC5's proto-punk rock concerts:

> So you listen to the band . . . you just go crazy and have a good time. Throw away your underwear, smoke dope, fuck. . . . Rather than go up there and make some speech about our moral com-

mitment in Vietnam, you just make 'em so freaky they'd never
want to go into the army in the first place. . . .'

(JOHN SINCLAIR AND D.A. LATIMER,
UNTITLED, *EAST VILLAGE OTHER,* JUNE 4, 1969, 3.)

Drugs

For the Beats, cigarettes, marijuana, amphetamines, and alcohol
were king. Kerouac suffered much from his alcoholism, in the
harrowing tradition of literary forebears such as Ernest Hemingway and F. Scott Fitzgerald. William Burroughs documented "the
sickness" of heroin addiction and ran off to South America in
search of yage, a potent hallucinogen. The darkness of his "drug
comedies" pay homage to the medieval poet Dante and set the
tone for gonzo journalist Hunter S. Thompson's sagas of chemical
dependency.

As the 1950s became the 1960s, marijuana and alcohol remained popular, but the Counterculture became defined by a
drug once considered for its chemical weapons potential by the
U. S. Government. (The military considered dropping it in the enemy's water supplies.) In 1965, a University of California–
Berkeley dropout named Augustus Owsley Stanley III began to
make LSD (lysergic acid diethylamide) in a home lab. Originally
called "psychodelics" for good reason, psychedelics remove the
filters that the brain uses to function normally. The flood of stim-
uli that is unleashed produces results that range from a terrifying
simulation of insanity and "having the shit beat out of you" to entering a new reality. Some people living on communes and others
thought psilocybin, or "magic mushrooms," offered a natural
form of high or sought peyote medicine in the American Indian
culture, and the Native American Church was formed.

Having a "mindblowing" experience came with higher risks
as more and harder drugs began to flood the Counterculture market. Cocaine, derived from coca leaves—chewed by some
Amerindians and used by Sigmund Freud, father of psychoana-
lytic theory in the late nineteenth century—had been outlawed in
the United States for years but found a niche in the waning years
of the Counterculture and the beginning of the disco 1970s.
(Disco was not a Counterculture phenomenon and thus not included in this book.) Punks rejected the hippies' love and bliss,
and their music, but kept most of their illicit drugs. Utilizing alco-

hol and heroin (immortalized in films such as *Sid and Nancy* (1986)) for their "downer" qualities, the punk ethos of nihilism knew booze was cheap, heroin dangerous and addictive, and never claimed drugs would bring any kind of enlightenment. They "rediscovered" William Burroughs, but neglected to heed his advice concerning "junk" (heroin). If drugs are the answer, what was the question?

THE COUNTERCULTURE, THEN AND NOW

Item One: In the 1960s, radical leader Abbie Hoffman tried to "levitate" the Pentagon (*Steal this Book* (1971)).

In 2001, the Pentagon was nearly levelled by terrorists who hijacked an American airliner and crashed it into the building.

Item Two: In *The Sixties Papers*, Albert and Albert describe America in the 1950s as "dominated by fear, repression, and cultural superficiality . . . political conformity, political paranoia, and cold war. Government leaders and newspaper editorialists encouraged Americans to believe that Russia was preparing for a nuclear conquest of the United States."

In 2003, the U.S. Government is passing laws influencing individuals and organizations in the interest of Homeland Security. Criticism of these laws is viewed by some Americans as unpatriotic and paranoid.

We would do well to consider some of the cultural trends of the last forty years or so as we examine our personal lives and relationships, critique images from the media, look at the United States' role on the world stage, and discuss ways to protect our planet and its inhabitants.

E. A. SWINGROVER

CHAPTER 1

Beats and Commentators

*From Founding Fathers to Martyred
Mothers, Zen Boys, Beatnik Chicks, and
Patron Saints*

Like the Romantic poets of the early nineteenth century who came before them, Beat writers never referred to themselves as such. The term "Beat" meant everything from beatific, according to Jack Kerouac, to down and out, according to many others. The sheer variation in the subjects and styles of Beat should not let us forget the similarities, as you will see in the readings that follow in Chapter 1. The original Beats, including Kerouac and William Burroughs, were actually members of what is now called "the Greatest Generation," those born in the 1920s who served in World War II. The first stirrings of the American Counterculture are a response to World War II, not Vietnam. We also catch glimpses of other writers who captured the Beat aesthetic, from West Coast poet Lawerence Ferlinghetti, owner of San Francisco's City Lights bookstore, to Beatnik "chick" Diane di Prima's poetic that the revolution begins with the individual. Although women Beat writers such as Joyce Johnson (one of Jack Kerouac's girlfriends and the mother of Daniel Pinchbeck, whose essay "Children of the Beats" is reprinted here in Chapter 6) were mainly viewed as life-support systems for the males, in recent years these women have been recognized as artists in their own right. Kerouac's interest in the transcendental is viewed here in an excerpt from *Dharma Bums* where we meet a thinly fictionalized Gary Snyder ("Japhy" in the novel), the poet who introduced him to Buddhism. Snyder's "Note on the Religious Tendencies" and poem "I Went into the Maverick Bar" reflect the range of his interests, which continue to this day. To say that the Beats are an eclectic group, however, is an understatement, as this sampling of readings demonstrates. Choosing a piece from William Burroughs' extensive catalogue of strangeness is not easy. For this chapter, a 1963 Paris interview gives us a sense not only of what he sounded like back then but what he looked like. No reading of hipness is complete without comparing the burgeoning Counterculture with the mainstream. Frank Conroy is decidedly *not* a part of this early version of the Counterculture, but he gives us a sense of what most people were thinking about in the 1950s—and it was not Beat, thus demonstrating what oddballs these people were once considered to be.

---

from *Dharma Bums*

JACK KEROUAC

Although known as the founding father of the Beats, Kerouac, more than any other of the core group, is one of the most varied and problematic. Growing up in Canada as a devout French Catholic, haunted by the death of his twin brother Gerard, he remained close to his mother all his life and sought the beatific vision that he believed determined the word "beat." His first and most successful novel *On the Road* (1955), a thinly disguised portrait of Neal Cassady and a band of bohemians, has caused Kerouac to be classified as a kind of Cassady character or *roué*, when most of his writings reveal him to be a deeply religious, troubled soul. *Dharma Bums* (1958) is full of the dark humor of the down and out, and the promise that Saint Teresa will shower "roses from heaven, forever, on all living creatures." The character of Japhy Ryder, student of Buddhism and True Meaning or *Dharma*, is a portrait of poet Gary Snyder, a sample of whose works appear in this chapter. Kerouac's writing philosophy, inspired by both his spiritual and earthly pursuits, is outlined in "Essentials of Spontaneous Prose" (1958) and "Belief & Technique for Modern Prose" (1958). You could read these pieces as a template for Counterculture living, for they inspired the next generation of hippies and freaks as well.

✦

Hopping a freight out of Los Angeles at high noon one day in late September 1955 I got on a gondola and lay down with my duffel bag under my head and my knees crossed and contemplated the clouds as we rolled north to Santa Barbara. It was a local and I intended to sleep on the beach at Santa Barbara that night and catch either another local to San Luis Obispo the next morning or the firstclass freight all the way to San Francisco at seven p.m. Somewhere near Camarillo where Charlie Parker'd been mad and relaxed back to normal health, a thin old little bum climbed into my gondola as we headed into a siding to give a train right of way and looked surprised to see me there. He established himself at the other end of the gondola and lay down, facing me, with his head on his own miserably small pack and said nothing. By and by they blew the highball whistle after the eastbound freight had smashed through on the main line and we pulled out as the air got colder and fog began to blow from the sea over the warm valleys of the coast. Both the little bum and I, after unsuccessful attempts to huddle on the cold steel in wraparounds, got up and paced back and forth and jumped and flapped arms at each our end of the gon. Pretty soon we headed into another siding at a small railroad town and I figured I needed a poorboy of Tokay wine to complete the cold dusk run to Santa Barbara. "Will you watch my pack while I run over there and get a bottle of wine?"

"Sure thing."

I jumped over the side and ran across Highway 101 to the store, and bought, besides wine, a little bread and candy. I ran back to my freight train which had another fifteen minutes to wait in the now warm sunny scene. But it was late afternoon and bound to get cold soon. The little bum was sitting crosslegged at his end before a pitiful repast of one can of sardines. I took pity on him and went over and said, "How about a little wine to warm you up? Maybe you'd like some bread and cheese with your sardines."

"Sure thing." He spoke from far away inside a little meek voice-box afraid or unwilling to assert himself. I'd bought the cheese three days ago in Mexico City before the long cheap bus trip across Zacatecas and Durango and Chihuahua two thousand long miles to the border at El Paso. He ate the cheese and bread and drank the wine with gusto and gratitude. I was pleased. I reminded myself of the line in the Diamond Sutra that says, "Practice charity without holding in mind any conceptions about charity, for charity after all is just a word." I was very devout in those days and was practicing my religious devotions almost to perfection. Since then I've become a little hypocritical about my lip-service and a little tired and cynical. Because now I am grown so old and neutral. . . . But then I really believed in the reality of charity and kindness and humility and zeal and neutral tranquil-lity and wisdom and ecstasy, and I believed that I was an oldtime bhikku in modern clothes wandering the world (usually the im-mense triangular arc of New York to Mexico City to San Fran-cisco) in order to turn the wheel of the True Meaning, or Dharma, and gain merit for myself as a future Buddha (Awakener) and as a future Hero in Paradise. I had not met Japhy Ryder yet, I was about to the next week, or heard anything about "Dharma Bums" although at this time I was a perfect Dharma Bum myself and considered myself a religious wanderer. The little bum in the gon-dola solidified all my beliefs by warming up to the wine and talk-ing and finally whipping out a tiny slip of paper which contained a prayer by Saint Teresa announcing that after her death she will return to the earth by showering it with roses from heaven, for-ever, for all living creatures.

5   "Where did you get this?" I asked.

"Oh, I cut it out of a reading-room magazine in Los Angeles couple of years ago. I always carry it with me."

"And you squat in boxcars and read it?"

"Most every day." He talked not much more than this, didn't amplify on the subject of Saint Teresa, and was very modest about his religion and told me little about his personal life. He is the kind of thin quiet little bum nobody pays much attention to even in Skid Row, let alone Main Street. If a cop hustled him off, he hustled, and disappeared, and if yard dicks were around in big-city yards when a freight was pulling out, chances are they never got a sight of the little man hiding in the weeds and hopping on in the shadows. When I told him I was planning to hop the Zipper firstclass freight train the next night he said, "Ah you mean the Midnight Ghost."

"Is that what you call the Zipper?"

10   "You musta been a railroad man on that railroad."

"I was, I was a brakeman on the S.P."

"Well, we bums call it the Midnight Ghost cause you get on it at L.A. and nobody sees you till you get to San Francisco in the morning the thing flies so fast."

"Eighty miles an hour on the straightaways, pap."

"That's right but it gits mighty cold at night when you're flyin up that coast north of Gavioty and up around Surf."

15   "Surf that's right, then the mountains down south of Mar-garita."

"Margarity, that's right, but I've rid that Midnight Ghost more times'n I can count I guess."

"How many years been since you've been home?"

"More years than I care to count I guess. Ohio was where I was from."

But the train got started, the wind grew cold and foggy again, and we spent the following hour and a half doing everything in our power and will power not to freeze and chatterteeth too much. I'd huddle and meditate on the warmth, the actual warmth of God, to obviate the cold; then I'd jump up and flap my arms and legs and sing. But the little bum had more patience than I had and just lay there most of the time chewing his cud in forlorn bitterlipped thought. My teeth were chattering, my lips blue. By dark we saw with relief the familiar mountains of Santa Barbara taking shape and soon we'd be stopped and warm in the warm starlit night by the tracks.

I bade farewell to the little bum of Saint Teresa at the cross-   20
ing, where we jumped off, and went to sleep the night in the sand in my blankets, far down the beach at the foot of a cliff where cops wouldn't see me and drive me away. I cooked hotdogs on freshly cut and sharpened sticks over the coals of a big wood fire, and heated a can of beans and a can of cheese macaroni in the redhot hollows, and drank my newly bought wine, and exulted in one of the most pleasant nights of my life. I waded in the water and dunked a little and stood looking up at the splendorous night sky, Avalokitesvara's ten-wondered universe of dark and diamonds. "Well, Ray," sez I, glad, "only a few miles to go. You've done it again." Happy. Just in my swim shorts, barefooted, wildhaired, in the red fire dark, singing, swigging wine, spitting, jumping, running—that's the way to live. All alone and free in the soft sands of the beach by the sigh of the sea out there, with the Ma-Wink fallopian virgin warm stars reflecting on the outer channel fluid belly waters. And if your cans are redhot and you can't hold them in your hands, just use good old railroad gloves, that's all. I let the food cool a little to enjoy more wine and my thoughts. I sat crosslegged in the sand and contemplated my life. Well, there, and what difference did it make? "What's going to happen to me up ahead?" Then the wine got to work on my taste buds and before long I had to pitch into those hotdogs, biting them right off the end of the stick spit, and chomp chomp, and dig down into the two tasty cans with the old pack spoon, spooning up rich bites of hot beans and pork, or of macaroni with sizzling hot sauce, and maybe a little sand thrown in. "And how

many grains of sand are there on this beach?" I think. "Why, as many grains of sand as there are stars in that sky!" (chomp chomp) and if so "How many human beings have there been, in fact how many living creatures have there been, since before the *less* part of beginningless time? Why, oy, I reckon you would have to calculate the number of grains of sand on this beach and on every star in the sky, in every one of the ten thousand great chilicosms, which would be a number of sand grains uncomputable by IBM and Burroughs too, why boy I don't rightly know" (swig of wine) "I don't rightly know but it must be a couple umpteen trillion sextillion infideled and busted up unnumberable number of roses that sweet Saint Teresa and that fine little old man are now this minute showering on your head, with lilies."

Then, meal done, wiping my lips with my red bandana, I washed up the dishes in the salt sea, kicked a few clods of sand, wandered around, wiped them, put them away, stuck the old spoon back in the salty pack, and lay down curled in my blanket for a night's good and just rest. Waking up in the middle of the night, "Wa? Where am I, what is the basketbally game of eternity the girls are playing here by me in the old house of my life, the house isn't on fire is it?" but it's only the banding rush of waves piling up higher closer high tide to my blanket bed. "I be as hard and old as a conch shell," and I go to sleep and dream that while sleeping I use up three slices of bread breathing. . . . Ah poor mind of man, and lonely man alone on the beach, and God watching with intent smile I'd say. . . . And I dreamed of home long ago in New England, my little kitkats trying to go a thousand miles following me on the road across America, and my mother with a pack on her back, and my father running after the ephemeral uncatchable train, and I dreamed and woke up to a gray dawn, saw it, sniffed (because I had seen all the horizon shift as if a sceneshifter had hurried to put it back in place and make me believe in its reality), and went back to sleep, turning over. "It's all the same thing," I heard my voice say in the void that's highly embraceable during sleep.

Essentials of Spontaneous Prose
JACK KEROUAC

Set-Up The object is set before the mind, either in reality, as in sketching (before a landscape or teacup or old face) or is set in the memory wherein it becomes the sketching from memory of a definite image-object.

Procedure   Time being of the essence in the purity of speech, sketching language is undisturbed flow from the mind of personal secret idea-words, *blowing* (as per jazz musician) on subject of image.

Method   No periods separating sentence-structures already arbitrarily riddled by false colons and timid usually needless commas—but the vigorous space dash separating rhetorical breathing (as jazz musician drawing breath between outblown phrases)— "measured pauses which are the essentials of our speech"—"divisions of the *sounds* we hear"—"time and how to note it down." (William Carlos Williams)

Scoping   Not "selectivity" of expression but following free deviation (association) of mind into limitless blow-on-subject seas of thought, swimming in sea of English with no discipline other than rhythms of rhetorical exhalation and expostulated statement, like a fist coming down on a table with each complete utterance, bang! (the space dash)—Blow as deep as you want—write as deeply, fish as far down as you want, satisfy yourself first, then reader cannot fail to receive telepathic shock and meaning-excitement by same laws operating in his own human mind.

Lag in Procedure   No pause to think of proper word but the infantile pileup of scatalogical buildup words till satisfaction is gained, which will turn out to be a great appending rhythm to a thought and be in accordance with Great Law of timing.

Timing   Nothing is muddy that *runs in time* and to laws of *time*— Shakespearian stress of dramatic need to speak now in own unalterable way or forever hold tongue—*no revisions* (except obvious rational mistakes, such as names or *calculated* insertions in act of not writing but *inserting*).

Center of Interest   Begin not from preconceived idea of what to say about image but from jewel center of interest in subject of image at *moment* of writing, and write outwards swimming in sea of language to peripheral release and exhaustion—Do not afterthink except for poetic or P. S. reasons. Never afterthink to "improve" or defray impressions, as, the best writing is always the most painful personal wrungout tossed from cradle warm protective mind—tap from yourself the song of yourself, *blow!—now!—your* way is your only way—"good"—or "bad"—always honest, ("ludicrous"), spontaneous, "confessional" interesting, because not "crafted." Craft *is* craft.

Structure of Work Modern bizarre structures (science fiction, etc.) arise from language being dead, "different" themes give illusion of "new" life. Follow roughly outlines in outfanning movement over subject, as river rock, so mindflow over jewel-center need (run your mind over it, *once*) arriving at pivot, where what was dim-formed "beginning" becomes sharp-necessitating "ending" and language shortens in race to wire of time-race of work, following laws of Deep Form, to conclusion, last words, last trickle—Night is The End.

10 **Mental State** If possible write "without consciousness" in semi-trance (as Yeats' later "trance writing") allowing subconscious to admit in own uninhibited interesting necessary and so "modern" language what conscious art would censor, and write excitedly, swiftly, with writing-or-typing-cramps, in accordance (as from center to periphery) with laws of orgasm, Reich's "beclouding of consciousness." *Come* from within, out—to relaxed and said.

Belief & Technique
for Modern Prose

JACK KEROUAC

List of Essentials

1. Scribbled secret notebooks, and wild typewritten pages, for yr own joy
2. Submissive to everything, open, listening
3. Try never get drunk outside yr own house
4. Be in love with yr life
5. Something that you feel will find its own form
6. Be crazy dumbsaint of the mind

7. Blow as deep as you want to blow
8. Write what you want bottomless from bottom of the mind
9. The unspeakable visions of the individual
10. No time for poetry but exactly what is   10
11. Visionary tics shivering in the chest
12. In tranced fixation dreaming upon object before you
13. Remove literary, grammatical and syntactical inhibition
14. Like Proust be an old teahead of time
15. Telling the true story of the world in interior monolog   15
16. The jewel center of interest is the eye within the eye
17. Write in recollection and amazement for yourself
18. Work from pithy middle eye out, swimming in language sea
19. Accept loss forever
20. Believe in the holy contour of life   20
21. Struggle to sketch the flow that already exists intact in mind
22. Dont think of words when you stop but to see picture better
23. Keep track of every day the date emblazoned in yr morning
24. No fear or shame in the dignity of yr experience, language
    & knowledge
25. Write for the world to read and see yr exact pictures of it   25
26. Bookmovie is the movie in words, the visual American form
27. In praise of Character in the Bleak inhuman Loneliness
28. Composing wild, undisciplined, pure, coming in from under,
    crazier the better
29. You're a Genius all the time
30. Writer-Director of Earthly movies Sponsored & Angeled in   30
    Heaven

Burroughs After Lunch

WILLIAM BURROUGHS

Undoubtedly the elder statesman of the Beats (the longest living, he died at 83), William S. Burroughs' life and works defies most standard definitions. His darkly comic satires of heroin addiction, *Junky* (1953) and the practically unreadable *Naked Lunch* (1959) were marketed with lurid covers that appealed to the mass market for pulp fiction in the 1950s and 1960s. Admired by modern bands like Sonic Youth, he was featured on record albums in the 1990s. This 1963 interview captures the elusive

nature of the man who spent a lifetime traveling the world—
Mexico, Morocco, Paris—in his words, trying to "shit out my
Missouri roots." Never without a tweed suit and hat, Burroughs'
experiments with prose ranged from his drug writings, esoterica
about ancient Egypt, and discussions with extraterrestrials. If
there is a subculture *beneath* the Counterculture, Burroughs is its
chief representative.

——————— ✦ ———————

Paris, 1963

> *Hadn't seen Burroughs since that night with Beckett. So went to
> signing Rue de Seine. English Book Store. Home away from home
> for beats, et al. This time came to work, notebook and all. Burroughs
> signing* The Ticket That Exploded, *Olympia ("Lolita") Press.*

JOSEPH   You were born on Feb. 5, 1914, in St. Louis.
BARRY:

WILLIAM   Like T.S. Eliot, but I still have a Midwest accent.
BURROUGHS: [*Ghost of a smile or smile of a ghost.*] Eliot has
                lost his.

*Looks British anyway. Seedy British. Worn tweedy topcoat with
worn velvet collar. A slightly stooped 5-foot-11; thin; thin-faced
combo of Ralph Richardson and Buster Keaton. It's the poker face
that gives him the Keaton look—reserved as an old-fashioned Mississippi gambler. Ralph Richardson hat—curled brim.*

5   *When in Paris, lives at Beat Hotel, 9 rue Gît-le-Coeur, which
is about to be sold and character changed. Walk up to fifth floor,
room 30. Has two-burner gas stove on table in one corner. Wash-
stand in other. One window looks across narrow street to chim-
ney pots. Wardrobe with maybe one change of suit, maybe not.
Two chairs. A bed. Table with old Spanish portable. Sheet of paper in it with typing on it. Four wire file baskets hanging over
table on wall. "For mss in progress, material for fold-ins, proofs,
etc."*

*Would like whole wall of files for his work, and books, and two
tape-recorders. Has one now—out of order, boxes of used tapes
spilling out on shelf like* Krapp's Last Tape. *Room warm; not neat,
not disorderly. Just a room. One naked light bulb hanging over
table. None over bed.*

JB: Do you read a lot?

WB: No, I don't read much.

JB: Do you enjoy living in hotels?

WB: I would prefer my own apartment; one room strictly   10
for work, walls of books, files, tapes, etc. I live here
because it's cheap, $40 a month.

Has made average of $200 a month since Naked Lunch *was pub-
lished in Paris in 1959 by Olympia. Says he does have tiny income
from Grandpa Burroughs adding machine money. Went to school in
St. Louis and Los Alamos. Harvard, BA in English Lit, 1936. Did
grad work at Harvard in anthropology and archeology. Still interested
in latter. Tried to get into glider pilots during war; has pilot's license.*

BJ: Did you ever become a pilot?

WB: I was turned down for physical reasons.

*Was pvt. detective for three weeks—spotting embezzling
clerks—got sick of it; was bartender and exterminator—*

JB: How was that?   15

WB: Killing roaches and bed bugs, not a bad job, a day's
work in two hours.

*After war went down to Mexico and South America. Especially
Amazon region of Peru and Ecuador. As amateur anthropologist.
"Green hell country, really beautiful." Then went to Tangier for five,
six years. Met Paul Bowles, Brion Gysin. Got hooked on junk in
Tangier. Went to London for cure. Back to Tangier to write* Naked
Lunch. *Agent circulated mss among American publishers. No sale.
Then Girodias of Olympia Press saw it, published it. Became bible
of the beat. Finally published in U.S. last winter by Grove Press.*

*Living in Paris and London. Half and half. London hotel like
Paris hotel, near Earl's Court. About $3 a night. Loves fog, especially
big one this winter. Finds English food cheaper and better. Gets up
late in Paris. Has to get up early in London to get hotel breakfast.*

*Married twice. First wife was German Jewish refugee still living
in New York, working at travel agency. Second wife? Leads into*
Time *story on Burroughs and* Naked Lunch. *Discuss a paragraph
describing him as a former drug addict and jail-bird who mutilated
a finger joint when he was drafted.* Time *story also mentioned Burroughs' accidental shooting of wife in Mexico. No charges made.
Authorities decided killing due to negligence.*

20 JB: I heard you didn't like that story much.

WB: I'm considering suing *Time*. Ex-con is false; a con is a man convicted of a felony who has served time for it. I've been in jail for a day or two waiting trial on narcotics, generally charged with misdemeanor, then the case was either dismissed or nolle prosse. As for cutting off finger joint, that happened three years before America was in war.

JB: How did this finger-joint thing happen?

WB: Skip it.

JB: Back to *Naked Lunch* then. Were you on drugs at the time?

25 WB: I was not on drugs when I wrote it. It couldn't have been possible for me to write it on junk. Some can. I can't. Junk dims down the whole creative process physiologically. I've been off for six years.

JB: Does junk make one see more?

WB: You see less on junk, less of your physical surroundings than without it. However, the whole experience of addiction was useful. For me. Like a war experience. For a writer. I don't know if it's useful for anyone else. I've tried 10 cures, but none took. Then I went to London and saw Dr. Dent to try his apomorphine treatment. Now I just don't want junk.

JB: Does it take any will power?

WB: If you have to use will power, you're not free, because there is no such a thing as will power. But you should avoid alcohol. I've given that up since the night we were with Mr. Beckett.

30 JB: Why?

WB: I dislike feeling I don't remember anything, and I don't remember much of that evening. Drinking was heavy.

Recap evening for Burroughs.

JB: Beckett had had two objections to your fold-in method. He called it "plumbing" over and over again. "You're using other writers' work!" he cried, anguish in his Irish voice and eagle face. And he said you seemed to believe that writers you used for fold-ins had answers. "There are no answers!" Beckett shook and held his head. "Our

despair is total! Total! We can't even talk to each other.
That's what I felt in *Naked Lunch* and why I liked it."

WB: I don't remember that conversation. But I don't agree
with Mr. Beckett that there are no answers. There are.

JB: But that night when I asked Beckett why he wrote,   35
since he felt there was no communication between peo-
ple, you interrupted (gently): "A reporter's question, Mr.
Beckett," and Beckett just smiled and didn't answer.

"And why do you write, Bill?" I had asked.
"To survive," you said. "To make bread."

from *Scratching the Beat Surface*
Michael McClure

Michael McClure was present at the very beginnings of the Beat
movement, and took part in the famous 1955 "Six Gallery" reading with Gary Snyder, Philip Whalen, Philip Lamantia, and Allen
Ginsberg in New York City. Later, in San Francisco, he was part
of the North Beach poets and artists that centered around
Lawrence Ferlinghetti's City Lights bookstore. Unlike many of the
Beats, he centered his life around family and fatherhood. He has
continued as a poet and playwright through the years. His recent
books include *Touching the Edge* (1999), a collection of Zen
dharma poems, and *Huge Dreams* (2000), a retrospective of his
early Beat period. He continues to live in the Bay Area with his
wife, sculptor Amy Evans McClure.

———————— ✦ ————————

Three years before the peyote experience just described, I had
given my first poetry reading with Allen Ginsberg, the Zen poet
Philip Whalen, Gary Snyder, and the American surrealist poet
Philip Lamantia. The reading was in October 1955 at the Six
Gallery in San Francisco. The Six Gallery was a cooperative art
gallery run by young artists who centered around the San
Francisco Art Institute. They were fiery artists who had either
studied with Clyfford Still and Mark Rothko or with the newly
emerging figurative painters. Their works ranged from huge drip

and slash to minute precision smudges turning into faces. Earlier
in the year poet Robert Duncan had given a staged reading of his
play *Faust Foutu* (Faust Fucked) at the Six Gallery and, with the
audacious purity of an Anarchist poet, he had stripped off his
clothes at the end of the play.

On this night Kenneth Rexroth was master of ceremonies.
This was the first time that Allen Ginsberg read *Howl*. Though I
had known Allen for some months preceding, it was my first
meeting with Gary Snyder and Philip Whalen. Lamantia did not
read his poetry that night but instead recited works of the recently deceased John Hoffman—beautiful poems that left orange
stripes and colored visions in the air.

The world that we tremblingly stopped out into in that
decade was a bitter, gray one. But San Francisco was a special
place. Rexroth said it was to the arts what Barcelona was to Spanish Anarchism. Still, there was no way, even in San Francisco, to
escape the pressures of the war culture. We were locked in the
Cold War and the first Asian debacle—the Korean War. My self-
image in those years was of finding myself—young, high, a little
crazed, needing a haircut—in an elevator with burly, crew-cutted,
square-jawed eminences, staring at me like I was misplaced can-
non fodder. We hated the war and the inhumanity and the cold-
ness. The country had the feeling of martial law. An undeclared
military state had leapt out of Daddy Warbucks' tanks and
sprawled over the landscape. As artists we were oppressed and indeed the people of the nation were oppressed. There were certain
of us (whether we were fearful or brave) who could not help
speaking out—we had to speak. We knew we were poets and we
had to speak out as poets. We saw that the art of poetry was essentially dead—killed by war, by academies, by neglect, by lack of
love, and by disinterest. We knew we could bring it back to life.
We could see what Pound had done—and Whitman, and Artaud,
and D. H. Lawrence in his monumental poetry and prose.

The Six Gallery was a huge room that had been converted
from an automobile repair shop into an art gallery. Someone had
knocked together a little dais and was exhibiting sculptures by
Fred Martin at the back of it—pieces of orange crates that had
been swathed in muslin and dipped in plaster of paris to make
splintered, sweeping shapes like pieces of surrealist furniture. A
hundred and fifty enthusiastic people had come to hear us. Money
was collected and jugs of wine were brought back for the audience.
I hadn't seen Allen in a few weeks and I had not heard *Howl*—it

was new to me. Allen began in a small and intensely lucid voice. At some point Jack Kerouac began shouting "GO" in cadence as Allen read it. In all of our memories no one had been so outspoken in poetry before—we had gone beyond a point of no return—and we were ready for it, for a point of no return. None of us wanted to go back to the gray, chill, militaristic silence, to the intellective void—to the land without poetry—to the spiritual drabness. We wanted to make it new and we wanted to invent it and the process of it as we went into it. We wanted voice and we wanted vision.

Note on the Religious Tendencies
Gary Snyder

Gary Snyder is as popular a poet in the present day as he was in the Beat era. Immortalized as Japhy Ryder in Jack Kerouac's novel *Dharma Bums,* Snyder is best known for his interest in the environment and advocacy of community. His experiences as a logger and ranger in the Pacific Northwest influenced his first two collections of poetry, *Riprap* (1959) and *Myths and Texts* (1960). Currently a faculty member at the University of California at Davis, Snyder won the Pulitzer Prize for his collection *Turtle Island* (1975) and has continued writing and teaching poetry over the years.

──────────── ✦ ────────────

This religiosity is primarily one of practice and personal experience, rather than theory. The statement commonly heard in some circles, "All religions lead to the same goal," is the result of fantastically sloppy thinking and no practice. It is good to remember that all religions are nine-tenths fraud and are responsible for numerous social evils.

Within the Beat Generation you find three things going on:

1. *Vision and illumination-seeking.* This is most easily done by systematic experimentation with narcotics. Marijuana is a daily standby and peyote is the real eye-opener. These are sometimes supplemented by dips into yoga technique, alcohol, and Subud. Although a good deal of personal insight can be obtained by the intelligent use of drugs, being high all the time leads nowhere

because it lacks intellect, will, and compassion; and a personal drug kick is of no use to anyone else in the world.

2. *Love, respect for life, abandon, Whitman, pacifism, anarchism, etc.* This comes out of various traditions including Quakers, Shinshu Buddhism, Sufism. And from a loving and open heart. At its best this state of mind has led people to actively resist war, start communities, and try to love one another. It is also partly responsible for the mystique of "angels," the glorification of skidroad and hitch-hiking, and a kind of mindless enthusiasm. If it respects life, it fails to respect heartless wisdom and death; and this is a shortcoming.

5   3. *Discipline, aesthetics, and tradition.* This was going on well before the Beat Generation got into print. It differs from the "All is one" stance in that its practitioners settle on one traditional religion, try to absorb the feel of its art and history, and carry out whatever ascesis is required. One should become an Aimu bear-dancer or a Yurok shaman as well as a Trappist monk, if he put himself to it. What this bit often lacks is what 2 and 3 have, i.e. real commitment to the stewpot of the world and real insight into the vision-lands of the unconscious.

The unstartling conclusion is that if a person cannot comprehend all three of these aspects—contemplation (and not by use of drugs), morality (which usually means social protest to me), and wisdom—in his beat life, he just won't make it. But even so he may get pretty far out, and that's probably better than moping around classrooms or writing books on Buddhism and Happiness for the masses, as the squares (who will shortly have succeeded in putting us all down) do.

I Went into the Maverick Bar

GARY SNYDER

I went into the Maverick Bar
In Farmington, New Mexico
And drank double shots of bourbon
                    backed with beer.
My long hair was tucked up under a cap   5
I'd left the earring in the car.

Two cowboys did horseplay
                    by the pool tables,

A waitress asked us
            where are you from?   10
a country-and-western band began to play
"We don't smoke Marijuana in Muskokie"
And with the next song,
            a couple began to dance.

They held each other like in High School dances   15
            in the fifties;
I recalled when I worked in the woods
            and the bars of Madras, Oregon.
That short-haired joy and roughness—
            America—your stupidity.   20
I could almost love you again.

We left—onto the freeway shoulders—
            under the tough old stars—
In the shadow of bluffs
            I came back to myself,   25
To the real work, to
            "What is to be done."

Revolutionary Letter #1
DIANE DI PRIMA

One thing you will notice immediately in writings about the Beat
era—there are very few women featured. Women, in the writings
of Kerouac, were the love interests and sexual conquests of Neal
Cassady, they were not considered artists themselves. But as more
recent retrospectives have pointed out, women did participate in
the revolutions the Beats began, and they interpreted and tried to
live a bohemian lifestyle at a time when just being unmarried
marked a woman as the "other." Poet Diane di Prima raised her
five children from four different fathers in the midst of the sweeping revolutions of the Counterculture. (For an account by her
daughter Tara, see Daniel Pinchbeck's "Children of the Beats" in
Chapter 6.) Women did not enjoy the same freedoms of the male
Beats because they generally took on the child-rearing duties. The
"women's movement" for sexual equality and liberation occurred
much later. This poem from 1971 reveals di Prima's ferocious

anarchic individualism, demonstrating her uniqueness as both
Beat poet and woman.

———————— ✦ ————————

I have just realized that the stakes are myself
I have no other
ransom money, nothing to break or barter but my life
my spirit measured out, in bits, spread over
the roulette table, I recoup what I can   5
nothing else to shove under the nose of the *maître de jeu*
nothing to thrust out the window, no white flag
this flesh all I have to offer, to make the play with
this immediate head, what it comes up with, my move
as we slither over this go board, stepping always   10
(we hope) between the lines

from *Pictures of the Gone World #21*
[The world is a beautiful place]
LAWRENCE FERLINGHETTI

Still considered one of the most influential poets and publishers
of the Beat movement, Ferlinghetti's poems celebrate the nuances
of life as beatific, or beautiful, as this 1955 poem illustrates.
Although he was prosecuted on obscenity charges for publishing
Allen Ginsberg's poem "Howl," his own work is witty, political, but
not overtly sexual. He even urged Jack Kerouac to sober up. Born
in Yonkers, New York, in 1919, Ferlinghetti was raised by a female
relative in France after his mother was committed to an asylum
in the U.S. His doctoral dissertation at the Sorbonne, "The City as
Symbol in Modern Poetry: In Search of Metropolitan Tradition,"
links him to the *flaneur* nature of the city-strolling Beats, whose
legacies in coffee houses still linger. Arriving in San Francisco in
1951, two years later he founded the City Lights Bookstore (still a
thriving business and tourist attraction) with Peter Martin, the
publisher of *City Lights* magazine who returned to New York and
the "East Coast" Beat scene. The center of the Beats for the West
Coast (although the bohemian lifestyle required traveling across
America, Mexico, Europe, and Northern Africa), North Beach in

San Francisco retains its Counterculture air to this day, largely because of Ferlinghetti's corner location. Politically active throughout his long life, he attributes his pacificism to his arrival in Nagasaki, Japan, six weeks after the second nuclear bomb destroyed the city, ending World War II.

——————— ✦ ———————

The world is a beautiful place
                    to be born into
if you don't mind happiness
                    not always being
                            so very much fun   5
        if you don't mind a touch of hell
                            now and then
            just when everything is fine
                    because even in heaven
                they don't sing   10
                    all the time
    The world is a beautiful place
                    to be born into
    if you don't mind some people dying
                    all the time   15
                or maybe only starving
                        some of the time
            which isn't half so bad
                    if it isn't you
Oh the world is a beautiful place   20
                    to be born into
        if you don't much mind
                    a few dead minds
            in the higher places
                    or a bomb or two   25
                now and then
                    in your upturned faces
    or such other improprieties
                    as our Name Brand society   30
                is prey to
                    with its men of distinction
        and its men of extinction
                    and its priests
            and other patrolmen
                    and its various segregations 35

and congressional investigations
                              and other constipations
              that our fool flesh
                        is heir to
        Yes the world is the best place of all   40
                              for a lot of such things as
              making the fun scene
                        and making the love scene
        and making the sad scene
                    and singing low songs and having inspirations   45
              and walking around
                        looking at everything
                              and smelling flowers
              and goosing statues
                        and even thinking   50
                              and kissing people and
              making babies and wearing pants
                              and waving hats and
                        dancing
                              and going swimming in rivers   55
                    on picnics
                        in the middle of the summer
              and just generally
                        'living it up'
        Yes   60
              but then right in the middle of it
                              comes the smiling
                        mortician

My Generation

Frank Conroy

The Fifties was a time of progress for ordinary Americans: the population rose by 28 million and Americans were better fed and better housed than ever before. Yet the decade also saw an unprecedented arms race, and fear of the Bomb disturbed the normalcy symbolized by Ike's ear-to-ear grin. The startling contrast between daily life and Armageddon left the young with little to say, but one of their number, Frank Conroy, spoke up for the Silent Generation in the October 1968 issue . . . [of *Esquire*].

——————————— ✦ ———————————

I remember asking, as a very young child, what was in the newspapers when there wasn't a war going on. That was the Second World War, the war to eradicate evil from the face of the earth, the war in which all Americans believed. Victory gardens, V-Mail, Gold Star Mothers, ration books and air-raid drills were the order of the day. People talked lustfully of three-inch-thick steaks, automobile tires and real butter. My father carried in his vest pocket his own personal sugar dispenser for coffee and my mother could be reduced to tears by a run in her stockings. The rationing of food, the enemy without, common hardship, common purpose and the almost godlike presence of Franklin Delano Roosevelt served to unify the country as it had perhaps never been unified before. If the First World War, however bloody, had been a bit of a lark, the Second was quite clearly a war of survival. Americans did not expect to lose, yet they knew they'd have to fight like hell to win. The discovery of the death camps of Central Europe resolved all questions as to what the war had been about. The forces of light against the forces of darkness, that was what we believed, and no American thirty-two years old can be untouched by that memory.

We hated the evil Germans and the treacherous Japs, scorned the weak Italians, loved the stalwart Russians, the plucky English and the wise Chinese. The double-fuselage P-38 was the fastest plane we knew about, the B-25 our image of power. It was, to use Fitzgerald's phrase, "bracing to be an American." Then came the atomic bomb and it was no longer quite so bracing.

It goes without saying that the effects of the bomb on the American mind were profound. We who were children at the time, with our childlike sensitivity to mystery, magic, and the unknown, with our social antennae fully extended to pull in all sorts of information, regardless of its usefulness (the ravenous hunger of children's minds, storing everything away undigested, stockpiling the recognizable, the unrecognizable and the ephemeral against a future time), were perhaps most deeply affected. We felt exhilaration at the indisputable proof that America was the strongest power on earth, apprehension because the power was mysterious, and most significantly we felt guilt, secret guilt that verged on the traitorous, guilt we could not possibly talk about. Our political apathy later, as college students in the Eisenhower years, seems to me to trace directly to our inability to reorganize those simple, propagandistic concepts of democracy and political morality which had been our wartime heritage, and which the bomb had rendered untenable.

The war ended, the United Nations was born at Dumbarton Oaks, and America moved into a new phase. We grew toward adolescence during the postwar boom, a period of expansion and prosperity unparalleled in the history of man, a time of busy optimism during which America seemed to concern herself entirely with adult matters. The kids, and there were not many of us in those days, were more or less left out of things. We inhabited a shadow area within the culture—nothing was important about us except the fact that eventually we'd grow up. We were embarrassed at our minority and most of us kept quiet, attempting not to call attention to ourselves.

5   We were the last generation to grow up without television. The radio was our thing—*The Lone Ranger, The Green Hornet, Mr. and Mrs. North,* etc. When television arrived we greeted it in a state of tremendous excitement. Movies at home! Free! It was too good to be true. And of course it was. It disappointed, was oddly dull after the initial novelty had worn off, unsettlingly hypnogenetic, vaguely inducive of claustrophobia. TV was technically crude in those days, inferior in every way to the marvelously cathartic medium of films, so we kept on paying quarters to get into the children's sections of our neighborhood theatres. And we got a lot for our money. The programs changed every three or four days, with newsreel, cartoon, short, trailers and a double feature. I used to go to Loew's Orpheum, see the show, and then sneak into the balcony to wait for vaudeville at eight o'clock. Movies were a way of life.

We became teen-agers when to be a teen-ager was nothing, the lowest of the low. Our heroes were not of our own age group. For the most part they were athletes—Jackie Robinson, Joe DiMaggio, Sugar Ray Robinson. Our music was Dixieland jazz (a revival was going on at the time), pop music, and, for some of us, bebop. (When I met my wife's aged grandmother years later she turned to me, fixed me with her steel-blue New England eyes and said: "Ah, Mr. Conroy, I understand you are interested in music. Please tell me about bobeep.") At the age of fifteen I saw Charlie Parker on the stage of Carnegie Hall. Our clothing, manners and life-styles were unoriginal—scaled-down versions of what we saw in the adults. We had no sense of group identity, perhaps not much less than the teen-age generations that had preceded us, but unquestionably less than the generation that was to follow ten years later. We were mysteriously disenfranchised—the best-looking girls at high school would ignore the boys of their own age and prefer to go out with older men.

In college we were named. The Silent Generation. The Apathetic Generation. There was no doubt about it. The sleepy Eisenhower years. America in a trance, drifting leisurely through a long golf game while the clouds gathered. Among students it was hard to find a rebel, virtually impossible to find a Marxist, a mystic, a reformer, or indeed, anyone who felt very strongly about anything. When my roommate and I discovered secret fraternities in our college, a college which advertised itself probably to be fraternity-free, and exposed them in the newspaper, there was a bit of talk but not much more. Most students thought it was a ploy from the psychology department. One can imagine what would happen now.

We believed in civil rights but did nothing active about it. Picketing was unheard of, protest vaguely uncool. It was enough to send a few bucks to the N.A.A.C.P., an organization we believed to be utterly safe, no more and perhaps even less militant than the Parent-Teachers Association. We were not afraid of Negroes and so made no attempt, as the students do today, to identify ourselves with their power.

Our sexual mores were conservative in the extreme. It was the time of going steady. Fiercely monogamous, we frowned on playing the field and lived as if we were already married. Virginity in girls was not expected, but faithfulness most certainly was. Promiscuity, which we interpreted as going out with more than one person at a time, was a grievous sin. Our key words were discretion, privacy and propriety. Needless to say, we lived and breathed hypocrisy.

No one knew anything about drugs in those days. Marijuana, 10 which was to sweep through all levels of American society during the next decade, was smoked, as far as I know, by only two students in my college of five hundred. Heroin and cocaine were thought to be extremely dangerous (as they doubtless are) and no one would have dreamed of experimenting with them. LSD, Methedrine, and amyl nitrite were unknown. Mind-expansion was not a meaningless term, however. We read Blake, Zen, science fiction, the Christian mystics, and various studies on E.S.P. and psychic phenomena. We blew our minds without drugs. I remember lying, at the age of nineteen, in the enclosed garden of the Bryn Mawr library, under the cherry tree, watching the stars for hour after hour, aware that light from unimaginable distances was collecting in my eye, getting high on the universe. College was a straight scene for us. We didn't come across pot until many years later.

Our literary heroes were more likely to be figures from the past than from our own time. Most of us felt closer to the sixteenth, eighteenth, and nineteenth centuries than to the seventeenth or the twentieth. James Joyce, whom rightly or wrongly we thought of as a nineteenth-century writer, the penultimate romantic, was a god. We took apart his difficult prose without the least sense of resentment, dissecting clues as eagerly as Talmudic scholars. *Portrait of the Artist* and *Ulysses* were books we knew well. The difficulties of *Finnegans Wake* were thought by us to be the inevitable result of the depth of Joyce's art rather than any failure of Joyce's mind. It would have been sacrilegious to suggest psychosis, and we scorned Stanislaus for having done so. Beckett was respected as much for having been Joyce's secretary as for his writings.

Closer to our own time, we admired Faulkner, Hemingway, Fitzgerald, early Steinbeck, and hated Wolfe, Dos Passos, Sinclair Lewis and James T. Farrell. Among young writers we liked Mailer, Capote, Styron and Salinger (who turned out not to live up to our expectations). There was a flurry about Francoise Sagan, mainly because she was nineteen, but on the whole we recognized her as a creation of the advertising age. The Beats were just beginning, Kerouac, et al., and we greeted them with a certain amount of suspicion, convinced that art was not that easy. Our standards were rather high, I think. The New Critics had filled us with an almost religious awe of language. We read Leavis, Edmund Wilson and Eliot as well, taking it all very seriously, worrying over every little point as if Truth and Beauty hung in the balance. The conservatism that colored so much of our experience did not evaporate when we dealt with literature. We defended literary art as if it were a castle under seige, in imminent danger of being destroyed by the vulgarians. In every college or university I knew anything about the most hated course was Social Science, as much a result of the incredibly rotten prose of the texts as it was of our disinterest in things social. We winced at bad prose, all of us, even the mathematicians and physicists who were presumably more inter-ested in symbols than in language. We were neat, very neat, and sloppiness of any kind irritated us.

Fitzgerald calls a generation that reaction against the fathers which seems to occur about three times a century. There is the possibility that time has collapsed since he wrote those words, that life has accelerated to the point where changeovers occur much more rapidly, but nevertheless it is clear that those of us now in our early thirties were not a generation in any self-conscious sense. We had no leaders, no program, no sense of our own power, and no culture exclusively our own. Rather than say-ing, "Don't trust anyone over thirty," we would have been much more likely to say, "Don't trust anyone *under* thirty," or perhaps just, "Don't trust anyone." It is hard to believe that little more than ten years has gone by. Imagining, for the moment, American society as a huge mind, the students today can be thought of as representing the unconscious—they are pure emotion, they act first and figure it out later, they are the route through which revo-lutionary power is expressed—but most importantly they feel themselves to be a part of the social organism, they are the un-conscious sensing the dimensions of the whole mind and their role within it. We felt nothing remotely like that. We were much more suspicious of society, without faith in its ability to respond to our minority voice. We were filled with precocious cynicism. We were stoics in our youth.

Now, as we come into power, we are aware of the paucity of our history. We have generation envy. How colorless were our times! Fitzgerald's people believed in their world—it really mat-tered who won the Princeton-Harvard game, it really meant something to appear at the theatre or the opera—and because they believed in their world they owned it. Until the Depression destroyed them they must have had a marvelous time. Styron's people had the war, a real war, a long, elaborate educational event plunging them directly into life. They had to learn to swim after they were in the water and, however sad their time, it was not dull. Brackman's people have faith. In a nonreligious age they have rediscovered faith. They are experimenters, revolutionaries and freethinkers, possessed by their own creative force. They have their own particular kinds of sillinesses, of course, but they believe they can change the world, and recent evidence suggests they are correct in that assumption. It is no accident that they fol-low us, they are most immediately in revolt against the banality of those who immediately preceded them. We have already learned a great deal from them, and will learn more. We will never be like them, nor do we want to be, but we perhaps stand to gain more from their example than anyone else. We are still young, after all, relatively late bloomers, but still young. Our strength lies in our fluency in all languages now spoken in America, the old and the new. In tremendously exciting times, we stand at the exact center of American culture, ready for anything.

CHAPTER 2

Freaks and Hippies

The Literary Counterculture, Rock Music,
Communes, and Cults

The variety of readings in this chapter attest to the disparities that lay at the core of the Counterculture by the late 1960s. Themes that the Beats had introduced, and most of the Beat writers themselves, found a home with the disenfranchised youth culture that was developing. Allen Ginsberg, Michael McClure, Gary Snyder, and even William Burroughs (born in 1914) were popular with this new generation, and continued to make guest appearances in the countercultural spectacle. Alone among the Beat writers, Jack Kerouac wanted to distance himself completely from the Counterculture, even though he was now revered as the "founding father of the beats." Returning to his French-Canadian Catholic roots, he found the hippies, their appearance, sexual behavior, and political views ultimately disturbing.

Robert Pirsig's nonfiction memoir/hybrid *Zen and the Art of Motorcycle Maintenance* was devoured by readers who wanted testimonies and remedies for the alienation of their generation. Hippies became international, as Indian writer Tribhuwan Kapur observes American and European young people making pilgrimages to his country to "live poor," after the fashion of Allen Ginsberg, and the Beatles and the Rolling Stones. These journeys continue to this day as "hippie trails" can be found across landscapes as varied as Bali, Thailand, and Tibet.

Back on the west coast of the United States, the locus of the "scene" by about 1967 had moved from San Francisco's North Beach to the streets surrounding Haight-Ashbury and Golden Gate Park. Rock music, not the jazz of the Beats, became the universal language of the alienated, who sought solace in "happenings" such as the "human be-in," billed as "the gathering of the tribes" for peace, love, and music. Although some commentators on the rock concerts produced lyrical statements, White Panther leader John Sinclair provides a "manifesto" (always tongue-in-cheek, in Sinclair's case) for the dancers themselves. When a spectator was murdered during a Rolling Stones concert at Altamont Speedway in 1969, the word went around that the scene was over. The Diggers (see "The Digger Papers") took their name from a tiny band of sixteenth century proto-socialist rebels who wanted free land, and who offered free food, clothing, and shelter for a few of the millions of young people who had migrated west to San Francisco for the Summer of Love only two years before Altamont. Some of these youth stayed. Others found the urban scene, drugs, and poverty alarming and headed to places such as Taos, New Mexico, starting communes not entirely unlike the pioneer living their grandparents had experienced in the late nineteenth century. Author and actor Peter Coyote's memoir *Sleeping Where I Fall* reflects on the joys and pains of communal living. Selections from Iris Keltz's *Scrapbook of a Taos Hippie* give us a glimpse into their lives and those times. According to John Nichols, once and current resident of Taos and the author of the 1974 novel *The Milagro Beanfield War,* local residents were not amused by an influx of shaggy-haired hippies in busses. In *Dharma Bums,* Jack Kerouac's "vision of a great rucksack revolution, thousands or even millions of young Americans wandering around with rucksacks, going up to mountains to pray" had been largely realized by the Counterculture.

One of the darkest aspects of the communal living scene was the appearance of cults and their dangerous, charismatic leaders. Here were unscrupulous characters waiting to take advantage of the young drop-outs from the middle classes. Frightened suburban parents whose children started to look and act like these hippies became aware of various organizations using young people to sell products, religion (like the Hari Krishnas, with their orange robes and shaved heads), or themselves. But it was not until that day in 1969 when those parents opened their morning newspapers to read about "murders committed by a group of hippies" who lived in Southern California and a man named Charles Manson that the mainstream started a vehement backlash against the Counterculture that continues to this day. Gurus such as Timothy Leary were completely discredited by the emergence of cults that used and exploited young people, sometimes by giving them large doses of disorienting drugs. Parents paid "de-programmers" to get their children away from these cults. "Year of the Fork, Night of the Hunter" by David Felton and David Dalton, from their book *Mindfuckers* (1972), introduced readers to what they called "acid-fascism" and cults such as the Children of God, and the notorious Manson "family."

---

from *Zen and the Art of Motorcycle Maintenance*
An Inquiry into Values
ROBERT PIRSIG

Still a staple in many motorcycle shops, Pirsig's *Zen and the Art of Motorcycle Maintenance: An Inquiry into Values* (1974) was widely read by counterculturists who saw the author's vision as one with their own, although the author has serious problems with what he calls the "groovy dimension," and several sections of the book criticize the era's romanticism. Pirsig's description of a cross-country motorcycle trip rewrites Kerouac's *On the Road* (1955) for the philosopher and runs counter to the popular depictions of motorcycling as a sport for outlaws (as Hunter S. Thompson recalled in his *Hell's Angels*), unless one considers philosophers to be outlaws. The descriptions of the mythical character Phaedrus and his teaching of writing influenced a whole generation of college composition instructors to strive for "quality" in writing, and be less "uptight" in their teaching. This section provides a critique of what is wrong with the Counterculture's rejection of technology, and the difference between the "hip" and the "square," all from the seat of a motorcycle, a BMW.

◆

But many others are also following their natural feelings and not trying to imitate anyone and the natural feelings of very many people are similar on this matter; so that when you look at them collectively, as journalists do, you get the illusion of a mass movement, an antitechnological mass movement, an entire political antitechnological left emerging, looming up from apparently nowhere, saying, "Stop the technology. Have it somewhere else.

Don't have it here." It is still restrained by a thin web of logic that points out that without the factories there are no jobs or standard of living. But there are human forces stronger than logic. There always have been, and if they become strong enough in their hatred of technology that web can break.

Clichés and stereotypes such as "beatnik" or "hippie" have been invented for the antitechnologists, the antisystem people, and will continue to be. But one does not convert individuals into mass people with the simple coining of a mass term. John and Sylvia are not mass people and neither are most of the others going their way. It is against being a mass person that they seem to be revolting. And they feel that technology has got a lot to do with the forces that are trying to turn them into mass people and they don't like it. So far it's still mostly a passive resistance, flights into the rural areas when they are possible and things like that, but it doesn't always have to be this passive.

I disagree with them about cycle maintenance, but not because I am out of sympathy with their feelings about technology. I just think that their flight from and hatred of technology is self-defeating. The Buddha, the Godhead, resides quite as comfortably in the circuits of a digital computer or the gears of a cycle transmission as he does at the top of a mountain or in the petals of a flower. To think otherwise is to demean the Buddha—which is to demean oneself. This is what I want to talk about in this Chautauqua. . . .

I don't know if I've got any more Chautauqua left in me today. My head gets fuzzy about this time in the afternoon . . . maybe I can establish just one overview and let it go for today. . . .

5   Way back long ago when we first set out on this strange voyage I talked about how John and Sylvia seemed to be running from some mysterious death force that seemed to them to be embodied in technology, and that there were many others like them. I talked for a while about how some of the people involved in technology seemed to be avoiding it too. An underlying reason for this trouble was that they saw it from a kind of "groovy dimension" that was concerned with the immediate surface of things whereas I was concerned with the underlying form. I called John's style romantic, mine classic. His was, in the argot of the sixties, "hip," mine was "square." Then we started going into this square world to see what made it tick. Data, classifications, hierarchies, cause-and-effect and analysis were discussed, and somewhere along there was some talk about a handful of sand, the world of which

we're conscious, taken from the endless landscape of awareness around us. I said a process of discrimination goes to work on this handful of sand and divides it into parts. Classical, square understanding is concerned with the piles of sand and the nature of the grains and the basis for sorting and interrelating them.

Phaedrus' refusal to define Quality, in terms of this analogy, was an attempt to break the grip of the classical sand-sifting mode of understanding and find a point of common understanding between the classic and romantic worlds. Quality, the cleavage term between hip and square, seemed to be it. Both worlds used the term. Both knew what it was. It was just that the romantic left it alone and appreciated it for what it was and the classic tried to turn it into a set of intellectual building blocks for other purposes. Now, with the definition blocked, the classic mind was forced to view Quality as the romantic did, undistorted by thought structures.

I'm making a big thing out of all this, these classical-romantic differences, but Phaedrus didn't. He wasn't really interested in any kind of fusion of differences between those two worlds. He was after something else—his ghost. In the pursuit of this ghost he went on to wider meanings of Quality which drew him further and further to his end. I differ from him in that I've no intention of going on to that end. He just passed through this territory and opened it up. I intend to stay and cultivate it and see if I can get something to grow.

I think that the referent of a term that can split a world into hip and square, classic and romantic, technological and humanistic, is an entity that can unite a world already split along these lines into one. A real understanding of Quality doesn't just serve the System, or even beat it or even escape it. A real understanding of Quality *captures* the System, tames it, and puts it to work for one's own personal use, while leaving one completely free to fulfill his inner destiny.

Now that we're up high on one side of the canyon we can see back and down and across to the other side. It's as steep there as it is here—a dark mat of greenish-black pines going up to a high ridge. We can measure our progress by sighting against it at what seems like a horizontal angle.

That's all the Quality talk for today, I guess, thank goodness. I 10 don't mind the Quality, it's just that all the classical talk about it *isn't* Quality. Quality is just the focal point around which a lot of intellectual furniture is getting rearranged.

The Digger Papers
The Diggers

The original Diggers were formed by Gerrard Winstanley and a group of Englishmen and women who, in 1649, wanted free land to farm, and the abolition of private property, buying and selling. By 1650, persecution and execution by landowners and the government ended their movement. During the peak of the Haight-Ashbury Counterculture in the 1960s, waves of hippies migrated to the San Francisco area. The Diggers were formed by Emmett Grogan and others as a combination of street theater and social service agency. They are best known for distributing free food and clothing and creating the Free City. Their website (www.diggers.org) claims they coined expressions such as "Do your own thing" and "Today is the first day of the rest of your life." This reading explains their primary ideas.

———————————— ✦ ————————————

Our state of awareness demands that we uplift our efforts from competitive game playing in the underground to the comparative roles *of free families* in *free cities.*

We must pool our resources and interact our energies to provide the freedom for our individual activities.

In each city of the world there is a loose competitive underground composed of groups whose aims overlap, conflict, and generally enervate the desired goal of autonomy. By now we all have guns, know how to use them, know our enemy, and are ready to defend. We know that we ain't gonna take no more shit. So it's about time we carried ourselves a little heavier and got down to the business of creating free cities within the urban environments of the western world.

Free Cities are composed of Free Families (e.g., in San Francisco: Diggers, Black Panthers, Provos, Mission Rebels and various revolutionist gangs and communes) who establish and maintain services that provide a base of freedom for autonomous groups to carry out their programs without having to hassle for food, printing facilities, transportation, mechanics, money, housing, working space, clothes, machinery, trucks, etc.

5   At this point in our revolution it is demanded that the families, communes, black organizations and gangs of every city in

America coordinate and develop Free Cities where everything that is necessary can be obtained for free by those involved in the various activities of the individual clans.

Every brother should have what he needs to do his thing.

FREE CITY

An outline . . . a beginning.

Each service should be performed by a tight gang of brothers whose commitment should enable them to handle an overload of work with ability and enthusiasm. "Tripsters" soon get bored, hopefully before they cause an economic strain.

FREE CITY SWITCHBOARD/INFORMATION CENTER

should coordinate all services, activities, and aid and direct assistance where it is most needed. Also provide a reference point for legal aid, housing, machinery, etc.; act as a mailing address for dislocated groups or individuals and guide random energies where they are most needed. (The work load usually prevents or should prevent the handling of messages from parents to their runaway children . . . that should be left up to the churches of the community.)

FREE FOOD STORAGE AND DISTRIBUTION CENTER

should hit every available source of free food—produce markets, farmers markets, meat packing plants, farms, dairies, sheep and cattle ranches, agricultural colleges, and giant institutions (for the uneaten vats of food)—and fill up their trucks with the surplus by begging, borrowing, stealing, forming liaisons and communications with delivery drivers for the left-overs from their routes . . . best method is to work in two shifts: morning group picks up the foodstuffs and the afternoon shift delivers it to the list of Free Families and the poor peoples of the ghettoes, everyday, hard work.

This gang should help people pool their welfare food stamps 10 and get their old ladies or a group to open a free restaurant for people on the move and those who live on the streets. Giant scores should be stored in a garage-type warehouse equipped with freezers and its whereabouts known only to the Free Food Gang. This group should also set up and provide help for canning, preserving, bread baking, and feasts and anything and everything else that has to do with food.

FREE CITY GARAGE AND MECHANICS

to repair and maintain all vehicles used in the various services, the responsibility for the necessary tools and parts needed in their work is entirely theirs and usually available by maintaining friendly relations with junkyards, giant automotive schools, and generally scrounging around those areas where auto equipment is easily obtained. The garage should be large enough and free of tripsters who only create more work for the earnest mechanics.

FREE CITY BANK AND TREASURY

this group should be responsible for raising money, making free money, paying rents, for gasoline, and any other necessary expenses of the Free City Families. They should also organize and create small rackets (cookie sales, etc.) for the poor kids of the ghettoes and aid in the repair and maintenence of the machinery required in the performance of the various services.

FREE CITY LEGAL ASSISTANCE

high style, hard nosed, top class lawyers who are willing to defend the rights of the Free City and its services. . .no honky, liberal bleeding heart, guilt-ridden advocates of justice, but first class case-winners . . . turn on the best lawyers who can set up air-tight receivership for free money and property, and beat down the police harassment and brutality of your areas.

FREE CITY HOUSING AND WORK SPACE

rent or work deals with the urban gov't to take over spaces that have been abandoned for use as carpentry shops, garages, theatres, etc., rent whole houses, but don't let them turn into crash pads. Set up hotels for new arrivals or transients by working out deals with small hotel owners for free rooms in exchange for light house-work, porter duties, etc. Big warehouses can be worked on by environmental artists and turned into giant free dance-fiesta-feast palaces.

A strong trio of serious business-oriented cats should develop   15 this liberation of space within the cities and be able to work with the lawyers to make deals and outmaneuver urban bureaucracies and slum landlords . . . one of the main targets for space are the churches who are the holders of most real-estate and they should be approached with no-bullshit hard-line.

FREE CITY STORES AND WORKSHOPS

nothing in these stores should be throwaway items . . . space should be available for chicks to sew dresses, make pants to order, re-cut garments to fit, etc. The management should all be life-actors capable of turning bullshitters into mud. Important that these places are first class environments with no trace of salvation army/st. vinnie de paul charity rot. Everything groovy. Everything with style . . . must be first class. *It's all free because it's yours!*

FREE MEDICAL THING

should be established in all poverty areas and run by private physicians and free from any bureaucratic support. The Free City Bank should try to cover the expenses, and pharmaceutical houses should be hit for medical supplies, etc. Important that the doctors are *brothers* and do not ask to be salaried or are not out to make careers for themselves (witness Dr. David Smith of the Hippie Free Clinic in San Francisco who is far from a brother . . . very far).

FREE CITY HOSPITAL

should be a house converted into bed space and preferably with a garden and used for convalescence and people whose funds have been blown or who have just been released from a state institution and who need the comfort and solace of their people rather than the cold alienated walls of an urban institution.

FREE CITY ENVIRONMENTAL AND DESIGN GANG

gangs of artists from universities and art institutes should be turned on and helped in attacking the dank squalor of the slums and most of the Free City Family dwellings . . . paint landscapes

on the sides of tenements . . . fiberglass stairwells . . . make crazy.
Tight groups of good painters, sculptors, designers who comfortably construct environments for the community. Materials and
equipment can be hustled from university projects and manufacturers, etc.

FREE CITY SCHOOLS

20   schools designed and run by different groups according to the
consciousness of their Free Families (e.g., Black Man's Free
School, Anarchist's Creative Arts School, etc.). The schools should
utilize the space liberated for them by the Free City Space Gang.

FREE CITY NEWS AND COMMUNICATION COMPANY

providers of a daily newspaper, monthly magazine, free Gestetner
and printing of notices for other groups and any special bulletins
and propaganda for the various families of the Free City. The machinery should be kept in top condition and supplied by any of
the various services. Paper can be scavenged at large mills and
cut down to proper working size.

FREE CITY EVENTS . . . FESTIVAL PLANNING COMMITTEES

usually involves several Families interacting to sponsor tours for
the kids . . . Balls, Happenings, Theatre, Dance, and spontaneous
experiments in joy . . . Park Events usually are best set up by hiring a 20-foot flat-bed truck for the rock band to use as a stage and
to transport their equipment; people should be advised by leaflets
to bring food to exchange with their neighbors; banners, props,
balloons, kites, etc. should be handled by a committee; an electrician should be around to run the generator and make sure that
the P.A. systems work; hard work made easy by giving responsible
people the tough jobs.

CO-OPERATIVE FARMS AND CAMPSITES

the farms should be run by experienced hands and the Free Land
settled on by cottage industrial people who will send their wares
into the Free City. The farms must produce vital food for the families . . . some free land that is no good for farming should be used as

campsites and/or cabin areas for citizens who are in need of country leisure, as well as kids who could use a summer in the woods.

SCAVENGER CORPS AND TRANSPORT GANG

is responsible for garbage collection and the picking up and delivery of items to the various services, as well as liberating anything they think useful for one project or an other. They are to be responsible for the truck fleet and especially aware of the economic strain if trucks are mis-used by tripsters.

FREE CITY TINKERS AND GUNSMITHS, ETC.

will repair and keep things going in the houses . . . experienced re-   25
pair men of all sorts, electricians, and carpenters. They should maintain a warehouse or working space for their outfit.

FREE CITY RADIO, TV AND COMPUTER STATIONS

demand Free time on radio and TV stations; demand a Free City frequency to set up your own stations; rent computers to call the punches for the revolution or use them in any constructive way possible.

FREE CITY MUSIC

Free Music
Where is the place that your music comes from
do you know
What determines the rest between phrases
The Interval that grows from the cluster   5
of sounds around it
Hanging behind the beat
Clipping the front of it
That's the gift
The thing that blows through a body responds to spirit
and a mind that doesn't lock itself   10
It's that thing
We're all made of, forget about, and then try to grab again

That thing that's all there and all free
The fretless infinite string banjo has invented new
means of music which it   15
must buy from itself to sing

from *Hippies: A Study of Their Drug Habits and Sexual Customs*

TRIBHUWAN KAPUR

Examining the pilgrimages Counterculture youth make to India, social anthropologist Tribhuwan Kapur chronicles the varieties of "hippie available in India, and those that have been here since 1969 or before." Published in India in 1981, *Hippies: A Study of Their Drug Habits and Sexual Customs* discusses characteristics hippies (American and Western European) might display, and gives a non-westerner's view of the Counterculture. Although *The Counterculture Reader* presents the American Counterculture, Europeans were experiencing revolutions of their own. Notice the socio-economic groups most hippies come from as they adopt a self-imposed poverty in India, where millions of people are involuntarily impoverished.

———————————— ◆ ————————————

It was felt, after much deliberation on the subject, that a hippie could best be described in a series of proposals which highlight aspects of the categories' various facets; it was felt that this would help present the necessary, though not always sufficient, properties of the hippie personality. Given below are various proposed-observable properties of such people; not all of them conform to all of the proposed properties but some of them are both necessary as well as sufficient to make a person a hippie. Our first list of the proposed personality traits of a hippie will comprise, simply, various multi-facets that one finds the category replete with. The second list will isolate those that are absolutely, inalienably their characteristics alone, and which help us move toward a definition of who or what a hippie is.

PERSONALITY TRAITS PROPOSED AS PROPERTIES OF THE HIPPIE

Given below, as propositions, are properties that hippies might, or might not, have but some of which, as mentioned earlier, are inalienable to them, and in extreme cases, are all found in a single person. It is proposed that a hippie is:

1. A person in rebellion against his own culture.
2. A person in rebellion against each and every culture.
3. A person who is, and has been, using certain drugs.
4. A person who is, and has been, using every available kind of drug.
5. A person who has sexual mores and norms overtly apart from the cultural idea of mores and norms regarding sexuality.
6. A person who has sexual mores and norms that would violate all ideas of 'normality' no matter what culture they belonged to.
7. A person who had a rich/very rich economic-cultural background, or at least a middle-class upbringing with little economic want.
8. A person, irrespective of background, who discovered within himself an apathy to or violent hatred of affluence.
9. A person who has negated, and is negating, every form of employment and is against the concept of a boss.
10. A person for whom a job is only a means to carry on with his 'real' life which is lodged in the propositions, 1 to 9.
11. A person who feels that itinerance is an essential part of life.
12. A person to whom itinerant travel is life itself, and who perceives that stabilization in terms of living in one place for a stretch of more than three to six months is 'stagnation'.
13. A person to whom 'freedom' is the essence of life and to whom all effort should be garnered around that concept.
14. A person who feels freedom is the hippie way of life, i.e., following properties given above is freedom itself.
15. A person who feels that religion needs to be reinterpreted to become truly religious.
16. A person who feels that to be free one must negate one's own religion especially if one feels that it is false, and carry on in one's quest for freedom with the help of another religion.
17. A person who perceives himself as being superior in every way to all human beings not following his way of life.

18. A person who feels he is *the* most superior being in the world and that all others are not as free as him or her; perceives himself or herself as being 'wholly enlightened', as being 'saved' while all the rest are 'doomed'.
19. A person who has acquired an indifference to his or her clothes, personal appearance, and physical cleanliness.
20. A person who sees in his indifference to the body signs of having transcended the flesh.
21. A person who is weak, malnourished and suffering from some chronic disease.
22. A person who sees in living with disease evidence of a total detachment from the problems of the physical world.

The above cover the basic propositions that comprise the basic personality traits commonly found among those that can be classified, hippie. However, as we have noted, not all those who can be so called have all these traits, but there do exist several of the propositions which are necessary, and in themselves sufficient, to categorize a certain type of person as a hippie. It is to these conditions that we turn before attempting a definition of the persons who might be termed as such.

PERSONALITY TRAITS NECESSARY AND SUFFICIENT FOR CLASSIFYING A PERSON AS A HIPPIE

These traits can themselves be forwarded as observable data; however, since these propositions are all to be found as the nucleus of the hippie personality, they will be put into a more positive form so as to indicate the definite presence of the same in the hippie.

Thus we might note that a hippie is a person who

1. Is presently using, and has been using, for more than three years at least, drugs synthetic and natural.
2. Has a drug-of-preference which he or she tends to use more frequently than any other(s).
3. Has sexual mores and norms overtly apart from the mainstream of society, as it envelops him or her.
4. Sees in sexual experimentation and diversification evidence of a superiority to the member-in-society.
5. Has not suffered economic deprivation, or has developed an apathy to it, and to all forms of work that bind one to a regular salary, promotions and similar bureaucratic procedures.

6. Is itinerant and feels that staying in one place more than three months leads to stagnation, spiritual, mental and physical.
7. Is obsessed with the concept of freedom and orders his or her life with it as a central focus of motivating action.
8. Has acquired an indifference to the body, which leads to chronic disease, torn clothes, and bodily dirt.
9. Who sees in religion a way of negating his or her own religion and transferring allegiance to another or insists on interpreting the world from an egocentric focus while simultaneously negating all other points of view.

These nine observations are both necessary as well as suffi-   5
cient to categorize any person who possesses them in combination, a hippie. It is not being questioned here whether the hippie is or is not conscious and aware of what he is verbalizing, or is physically. However, these properties are essential to the hippie view of the world, whether the hippie comes from the East or West. Also we shall later take up the point of whether the hippie's view of the world is valid, invalid, or part valid and part invalid. That is a matter for later discussion, the present point being used to present an adequate description of the elements of the hippie world-view.

ON DEFINING A HIPPIE

We have noted previously, various traits that would have to be present within a single human being before he or she could be categorized a hippie. However, very clearly, this is an academic approach to the field being studied. Hence, the definition that will be proposed is one that only someone studying a person through various sociological methodologies will be able to verify. This is so since amongst the propositions forwarded are those that are

1. Overt or Manifest, in that they can be verified at a glance, for instance the criteria of bodily dirt, lack of interest in clothes, often resulting in selling them and donning a torn kurta-pyjama.
2. Covert or Latent, in that they can only be verified by an in-depth study of the people concerned, so that who is and who is not a hippie can be easily confirmed or negated. Thus if a dirty, dishevelled, long-haired appearance leads one to suppose that a person is a hippie, this cannot be confirmed

unless the ethnographer has an opportunity to question the person about his life-style.

Given the above we might combine both aspects of the syndrome and define a hippie as a person who uses drugs of all kinds, but has a drug-of-preference which he uses more often and in choice over the others; has a sexual norm and practice based on a wider overt and covert code than the member-in-society; and finally has a view of the world in which the concept of freedom, of self-transcendence, and a reinterpretation of religion or its abandonment for another separate religion and culture, forms a fundamental tenet. That which runs as a thread through all this is the fact of economic sufficiency, and the habit of compulsive itinerance, which is held as indispensible to the hippie way of life-in-freedom.

The above definition distinguishes the true hippie from the common man in revolt for a brief period in college or after school in his or her adolescent years since, although they might be

1. using drugs and even having a drug-of-preference, they do not consider this more than a fling, certainly not a permanent way of being;
2. having sexual norms apart from the other members-in-society, this is not in any way part of a true world-view; rather it is another aspect of the fling which shall one day inevitably end in marriage, permanent jobs, promotions and so on, inducting them back into the common fold, so to speak;
3. talking about freedom and self-transcendence is one matter, a complete commitment to the same is another. Here again the dilettante is separated from the committed practitioner, since for one, talk about the same ends in what any hippie would consider 'slavery to the system', while for the true hippie it entails a great deal of hardship and toil in terms of the physical aspects of the same;
4. aping the hippie way of itinerance for a holiday, the adolescent might pick up his or her rucksack and wander from place to place, but he always has a permanent base on which to fall back; the true hippie has burnt his boats;
5. negating and reinterpreting religion is not possible for an adolescent in college for as will be indicated, the hippie world-view is not single or homogenous, but has often a remarkable degree of personal thought involved in it, based on the person's experiences in a framework very separate

from that of society at large, which he has rejected as false and hypocritical.

The above helps make clear that we are not considering would-be hippies, those who pretend they are in revolt for a holiday season, and who drop out from being dropouts as soon as the opportunity presents itself to them. We are considering the hard core of the initial vanguard who had a 'new' and 'radical' vision of the world and then had the courage to throw themselves whole-heartedly into it, and wend their way through all the difficulties it presented.

Rock and Roll Is a Weapon of Cultural Revolution

JOHN SINCLAIR

In their first American hit, in 1964, the Beatles had sung "I Want to Hold Your Hand." By 1970 The Jefferson Airplane chanted, "Got a Revolution, Got to Revolution!" In the years between, rock music became more than a form of popular culture. Individuals such as John Sinclair found in its very existence a central component of the cultural revolution. Sinclair, manager of the Detroit political rockers MC5, attempted to merge politics and music to a greater extent than most, as his 1968 article makes clear.

———————— ✦ ————————

The duty of the revolutionary is to make the revolution." The duty of the musician is to make the music. But there is an equation that must not be missed: MUSIC IS REVOLUTION. Rock and roll music is one of the most vital revolutionary forces in the West—it blows people all the way back to their senses and makes them feel good, like they're *alive* again in the middle of this monstrous funeral parlor of western civilization. And that's what the revolution is all about—we have to establish a situation on this planet where all people can feel good all the time. And we will not stop until that situation exists.

Rock and roll music is a weapon of cultural revolution. There are not enough musicians around today who are hip to this fact. Too many of your every-day pop stars feel that music is simply a means by which they can make a lot of money or gain a lot of cheap popularity or whatever—dollars and ego power; both of which are just a killer ruse, in fact I would have to say the killer ruse of all time. Money is the biggest trick of all, next to the so-called ego, which comes out of the same scene as money anyway. I mean the ego developed strictly as an economic function, when there got to be too many people on the planet for the planet's natural resources and there wasn't enough for everybody any more. Then people had to start separating themselves out from the tribe and see themselves as individuals, because if there ain't enough for everybody then everybody's got to try to make sure he or she has got enough, and there's always somebody else around who wants to take it away from you. . . .

Think about it. If all the kids in high schools who can't stand that shit would stop going—all of you—then where would the schools be? They have to have you there. If you aren't there they won't be able to eat—they won't have a job any more. Your parents will go crazy too. . . .

If you're living at home, start planning for what you'll be doing when you split. Get together with your people who are waiting to split and plan a scene for when you can be together. Start practicing now, on your parents' money and time. Save up your money if you get any so you can buy your supplies and equipment when you split.

5 Don't waste your time pissing and moaning about how shitty everything is. Start getting it together so you can change it. Everybody knows what a drag it is. You're not telling anybody anything they can use. Exchange information. Get down. And when you *have* split, get your thing together so you'll be able to have a better time than just sitting around smoking bogus dope, dropping bogus speed-filled acid, shooting smack, and listening to brainwash low-energy jams. Tripping out is a dead end and a drag. *You always come down.* If you engage yourself in a total revolutionary program of self-reliance and serving the people any way you can, you will have a guaranteed good time forever (except for when they lock you up from time to time) and will help other people get it together too.

It isn't enough just to drop out though—you have to create new forms which will enable you to sustain yourselves while you're doing your work. The commune is the life-form of the future, it is *the* revolutionary organizational life-form, and the communal relationship must be realized in everything you do. Rock and roll is the best example. That's why I said at the beginning of this rant, that MUSIC IS REVOLUTION, because it is immediate, total, fast-changing and on-going. Rock and roll not only is a weapon of cultural revolution, it is the *model* of the revolutionary future. At its best the music works to free people on all levels, and a rock and roll band is a working model of the post-revolutionary production unit. The members of a rock and roll family or tribe are totally interdependent and totally committed to the same end—they produce their music collectively, sharing both the responsibility and the benefits of their work equally. They work on the frontiers of modern technology to produce a new form which is strictly contemporary in all its implications. *There is no separation.* And that's what it's all about. . . .

Capitalism is obsolete—it is based on the two horrible notions of private property and competition, both of which have to go right now. And the point is, that it's time for them to go, because there's no more room for that old-time shit in the world today. People have got to get it together, not apart. People are now stuck in bullshit jobs, bullshit schools, bullshit houses, bullshit marriages, bullshit social and economic scenes, and there's no need for it anymore. Most of the jobs that presently exist are useless and anti-human, and they'll be done away with immediately once the people are in power and the machines are freed to do all the work.

Likewise most of the products of the present consumer economy—they're bullshit and will no longer exist. Eighty-seven different brands of toothpaste! Millions of junky automobiles! That's all they are—junk—that people have been hooked on by the junk pushers of capitalism. The whole thing is ridiculous! Everything has to be free or else!

It is extremely important for urban groups to organize themselves around some form of popular cultural activity like a rock and roll band, a community newspaper, guerrilla theatre groups, a health clinic, or whatever you can put together. The cultural forms will give you access to the mass media and to mass audiences of pre-revolutionary youth who are just sitting around waiting to get totally turned on. High school groups can organize around newspapers and posters and bands and present a united front in their dealings with administrators and other old creeps. . . .

It's time to turn on, tune in and *take over!* Up against the ceiling, motherfucker!

from *Sleeping Where I Fall*
PETER COYOTE

Actor, writer, and activist, Peter Coyote's manifestations are as varied as the legendary Indian trickster he adopted for his surname. Born Peter Cohen, he lived through many of the movements that define the Counterculture: from communes to social protests to his work with the San Francisco Mime Troupe, Coyote explores the "limitless invention" of the times and his own life with eloquence and candor. *Sleeping Where I Fall* (1998) is one of the best of the recent memoirs of those times. These excerpts, from the preface and the chapter "Free Fall," place Coyote in the context of the Counterculture and describe some of the pitfalls of experiments in communal living.

✦

PREFACE

During the period covered by this book, I was a member of an anarchic West Coast community that had taken as its collective task the rethinking and recreation of our national culture. Such intentions were not unique; my generation was struggling openly with problems of racism, grossly inequitable distribution of goods and services, dishonorable foreign policies, and the war in Vietnam. Many people, dissatisfied to the point of despair with the available options of being either a "consumer" or an "employee," were searching for new and more liberating social structures. My peers and I were calling in the nation's markers on promises of social justice, and change was in the air.

These stories focus on a West Coast subset of this critical generation—a group whose original nexus was the San Francisco Mime Troupe, a radical street-theater company, from which several members spun off and evolved into the Diggers. The Diggers, in turn, became the larger Free Family.

This book attempts to describe what the pursuit of absolute freedom felt like, what it taught me, and what it cost. It is neither an apologia for nor a romance of the sixties. Coming to understand the necessity and value of limits should not be construed as either a defense of the status quo or as the contrite repentance of someone who has flapped his wings a few times and decided that flight was impossible.

Every culture has its priests and devils, its intoxications and follies, and the counterculture we created was neither more nor less ethical, diverse, or contradictory than the majority culture. You can't grow tomatoes without shit, they say, and while we may have had much of the latter, we also had plentiful tomatoes. The ideas and moral positions that emerged during this period—the civil rights movement, the peace movement, the ecology movement, feminism, holistic medicine, organic farming, numerous alternative physical and spiritual therapies and disciplines, and perhaps most important, bioregional or watershed political organization—were abetted by agents like the people remembered here: flawed and imperfect people certainly, but genuinely dedicated to creating more enlightened options for themselves and others.

One side of the story should not be sacrificed to the other. We may not approve of the fact that Sigmund Freud was shooting cocaine and writing randy letters during his investigations of the psyche or that the Reverend Martin Luther King Jr. may have enjoyed sex outside of marriage, but these very combinations and conjunctions of aspiration and frailty reveal the complex humanity of such stellar people and allow us to believe that we too, flaws and all, can mature and contribute something of worth.

I apologize to the numerous friends who should have been included or more fully represented in these pages. Such failures are due solely to the thrust of the narrative and the vagaries of memory, which could not always retrieve the appropriate story that included a valued friend. To those who may feel that I have misrepresented them, I can only say that this is how I perceived things: This is my own truth.

CHAPTER 17: FREE FALL

By now Sam had had our baby, Ariel, and moved back to Olema, asserting her right to be there by pointing out, "It's free, isn't it?" Because of its isolation, the ranch was a perfect laboratory for the exploration of absolute freedom, and before long was overflowing with eager pilgrims who devised ways to forge small niches for themselves in the already overpopulated environment. I nicknamed Olema "the Fool's School" (including myself as enrolled) because by and large, most who came up the road knew less about group life, hygiene, and labor than I did. However, since I had been blundering around there longer than they had, my stature was automatically elevated to the formless and far from invested role of patriarch. Among my self-appointed responsibilities was the struggle to instill a rudimentary sense of responsibility into each new arrival.

Some Pearls of Wisdom from the Leader

- If you let the baby shit on the floor and then eat it, you'll have a sick baby *and* a shitty floor.
- Free food doesn't mean that I cook and you eat all the time, asshole.
- It's fine if you want to take speed, just don't talk to *me!* I don't actually care that the insects are communicating with you.
- I *know* the Indians used moss for tampons, but you're picking poison oak.

People usually stayed long enough to get their acts together before leaving to present themselves as seasoned communards elsewhere. Despite the turnover, lack of hierarchical leadership, and aggressive libertarian values, we did learn a great deal about living together. Large meals were prepared more or less on a schedule; trucks were kept running; a garden was planted and harvested. There was pretty good music daily and usually an easy amicability reigned. This last was not inconsiderable when you consider that sometimes twenty people were living in and around the one-story ranch house with one bathroom and, until the gift from our dealer friend, a ten-gallon hot water heater.

10   Revolutionary experiments are fine in theory, but in practice they could frazzle the nerves of a mummy. My old Haight Street speed partner J. P. Pickens had moved his wife and three children into the barn. His methedrine-driven obsession with collecting had not abated; it now threatened to overwhelm the barn. He would disappear for days and return with his stake-sided pickup loaded to the top rail with impossible amounts of Industrial Age flotsam: ring-and-pinion gears, dental equipment cabinets, plastic tubing, soggy cardboard boxes filled with pipe fittings, and random Formica samples—all of it, by his estimation, invaluable and "too great a score to leave, man!" Trying to deter him was like trying to arrest a force of nature. One bizarre midnight, I heard an unusual low rumble outside. I calmed Sam, rolled out of bed, and looked out my window to discover next to the barn a full-sized tractor-trailer truck, idling

and rattling like a ball-bearing factory in an earthquake. J. P. was standing on the running board urging the driver in a hoarse whisper, "Be *quiet,* man! These people are a little uptight about my stuff." Something snapped and I ran outside stark naked, screaming at J. P. and the driver to get the fuck out. J. P. threw the man a look begging him to understand, as if he had brought a friend home for dinner only to find his wife having a tantrum. The truck executed a noisy, laborious three-point turn and shambled down the road. J. P. turned to me as if nothing had happened, grinned happily, and said, "You want some speed?"

J. P. had also colonized half of an old shed beside the kitchen. Bryden had claimed the other half. Bryden was working on a large painting of the *Four Horsemen of the Apocalypse,* a vivid and arresting canvas featuring four skeletons riding white horses and enjoying the hell out of themselves. Bryden's model was a human skull with a candle on the dome of its head, resting at eye level on a stepladder. Since Bryden's drug of choice was heroin, he would nod off occasionally, then glide back into the present moment with a little bob, and paint a bit more.

It might have been cozy except that Bryden and J. P. loathed each other. Bryden considered J. P. a noisy speed-freak dwarf and accused him of stealing (conveniently forgetting that Bryden himself had swindled some irate teenagers out of marijuana money, leaving them to await his nonexistent return in *my* house while I was on tour, which resulted in the theft of my guitar and guns). He would later gut my daughter's piggybank and leave an IOU.

J. P. thought Bryden was a "junkie fuck" (if I remember the exact phrase), and the misunderstandings between them eroded their mutual civility until they painted a white line down the center of the shed, and each commanded the other to stay on his respective side. One morning, carrying my first coffee of the day out of the kitchen door and into the anemic morning light, I observed J. P. tiptoeing around the corner of the shed, alert as a weasel, pistol in hand. He slipped stealthily along the wall and around the corner, nodding a greeting at me. No sooner had he disappeared than Bryden showed up, similarly armed, stalking J. P. It was a Keystone Kops routine with dangerous potential. Being a skillful leader, I intercepted the pending catastrophe by inserting myself between them, screaming "stupid motherfucking dirt-bag assholes" at the top of my terrified lungs and demanding their weapons, which, amazingly, they delivered.

Like it or not, I was considered a leader at Olema, or at least impartial enough to be called on to arbitrate disputes. I was painfully aware that I had little vision or wisdom to offer my "followers" and was, in fact, the victim of a dynamic I had unconsciously allowed to develop. As the "leader" I had permission to define the game, set the vocabulary, pontificate about it, and inspire others with fervid visions of what we were accomplishing collectively. "Followers," at least those who paid any attention to me at all, were more than willing to pitch in and bring these compelling visions to glorious fruition. The flaw in this system was that if the leader did not consistently supply visionary energy and inducement, the followers dropped everything for the predilections of the moment, and the brave new world faltered and then stopped dead. I had so appropriated the collective vision that I deprived others of the opportunity of developing their own; I had unwittingly assumed the full responsibility for actualizing Olema's potential. If that potential failed to materialize, Olema was little more than a grubby, overcrowded dirt farm with a large, licentious, dysfunctional family alternately groping for sanity and destroying itself in small increments. Since I refused to see myself and my efforts so minimalized, I was forced to keep everyone else on track with "the big picture."

15   Consequently I was already exhausted when J. P. pulled an ugly little nickled pistol on Dick the Burglar and demanded that he keep away from his family.

Dick was a handsome, muscular, Nordic type Bruce Weber would have loved to photograph. He had spent approximately nineteen of his twenty-six years in institutions and had been toughened to the core by it. What saved us all from being at his mercy, besides a certain innate sweetness, were his insecurity and difficulty with speech. When he did speak, which was a rare enough occasion, words tumbled out of his mouth and over one another with such intensity that they spent their energy in a formless avalanche. Also, since he had been raised under absolute authority his entire life, he overestimated mine and never challenged it.

Dick was with J. P.'s family because J. P. was not, and though his relationship with J. P.'s wife Maryanne was purely friendship based on a mutual need for kindness, J. P.'s speed-shredded nervous system read their camaraderie as a personal reproach. So one night, sweating and shaking, he pointed his pistol at Dick, screaming, "Stay the fuck away from my family," while Dick faced him down, chanting over and over again, "So who's got the gun? Who's the cop, J. P.? Who?" until I intervened, standing between the gun and Dick, hoping that J. P. would remember that we were friends. I had to mediate again when Dick, for unknown reasons, began head-butting Tattoo Larry around the living room, trying to provoke sweet, shambling Larry into throwing what would have been a decidedly ill-advised punch. I feigned indifference, stalling for time, while I tried to figure out how to rescue Larry without putting myself directly in the path of Dick's bad intentions. I did not want to lose whatever meager authority I possessed by being beaten to a pulp under Dick's hammer fists.

"Why don't you split his head open with the axe and save your own, Dick?" I asked casually. "Or better yet, if you've got all this energy, why don't we go haul some firewood?" This non sequitur derailed him long enough for Larry to disappear, and like a cat leaving a dead mouse, Dick turned his attention to something else.

Another explosive ingredient appeared one day in the form of a swarthy, handsome, and very streetwise troublemaker named Gregg. He had a practiced charm and soon inveigled a place for himself and his girlfriend among us. He set up a small camp under the trees in front of the house. He had a penchant for heroin, so occasionally we would get high together, and during these hiatuses he revealed his personal history: a long stint in reform school and a hustler's life on the streets.

Gregg was definitely not a follower. He soon developed a very pronounced intention to inhabit my role as chief and proceeded to test me and the security of my perceived position. One day I noticed that a set of my axle stands—steel tripods that hold a truck securely aloft in order to provide space under it for work—had moved from inside to outside the barn where I'd stored them. I marked it in passing. A day later they had moved again. One now rested about ten feet away from Gregg's camp, and he was using the other under his truck.

"Stick 'em back inside when you're done with 'em," I said, a bit piqued that he had not asked permission to use them. Despite our intention to abolish private property, it was a generally respected principle that personal possessions and particularly tools were exempt from collective ownership.

"Sure thing," he answered noncommittally, and continued with his work. The next morning the axle stands had been joined by my four-ton hydraulic jack. All three were plainly visible but had been moved quite definitely within the invisible boundaries

20

of Gregg's camp. I couldn't accuse him of stealing because they were in plain sight, and I didn't have any use for them at that moment that would justify taking them back. . . .

from *Scrapbook of a Taos Hippie*
IRIS KELTZ

Iris Keltz tells her story and those of others who left the towns and cities of America to experiment with group living in what would be called "communes." Much like their frontier great-grandparents (as illustrated in the PBS series "Frontier House"), they found living off the land difficult, particularly the women who often bore the brunt of household and agricultural chores. Keltz's *Scrapbook of a Taos Hippie* (2000) is the personal chronicle of people whose lives were shaped by those times. As she relates, "over thirty years have passed since 'the summer of love'. My life's dream has always been to become a village elder telling stories to the next generation."

✦

Close Encounters with New Buffalo

It was one year before I returned to New Buffalo. By then I was free, single and twenty-something, accountable only to the demands of my personal whimsy.

"Casablanca" played on television my last night in New York. When Rick and Louie were toasting to a glorious future, I wept with empathy. The pain of leaving my marriage merged with a sense of limitless possibilities.

I'd lived in my fourth-floor tenement too long. Summer evenings found me on the rooftop, watching science-fiction colors spew forth through a smoggy sunset while I herded my imaginary flock of sheep. Tribal rhythms beat in the night from the bongo players in Tompkins Square Park, giving the illusion that we were a heartbeat away from an African village. Chimneys belching black smoke from spiraling skyscrapers became less real than my vision of life in a commune.

That winter Faisel and I had gotten a letter from Moe, the New Buffalo goat lady, offering us a room if we wanted to come back. In my buoyant optimism, it never dawned on me that a vacant room meant an indication of drastic change. I remembered the New Age-extended families, bands of naked roving kids, orgiastic nights of drumming and dancing around fires, sleeping under a canopy of stars in a tipi, getting stoned and meetings with remarkable people. I couldn't wait to return.

Faisal did not share my enthusiasm for fly-ridden outhouses, 5 kerosene lamps, the one group bathroom and no privacy. For me, the idea of going to graduate school or getting a permanent job at a moment when the world was in transformation felt like shackles on the heels of possibility. I was willing to embrace poverty if it meant building a new way of life. I was convinced we were fated to slay the dragon of American imperialism and greed.

I sang along with the Jefferson Airplane, *"We are all outlaws in the eyes of America."* Faisal and I spent hours discussing our ideological differences. I always got stuck defending Western civilization in general and hippies in particular. Faisal called America decadent, confusing, and wished he could return to Jerusalem.

"You're lucky to have a place on earth to love. Look at me, I'm from Queens, New York. If someone told me I could never go back there, I wouldn't give a damn." Faisal said he loved Queens with its quiet neighborhoods and would be happy to live near my mother in Middle Village. The differences tore us asunder.

I asked for our tent, my sleeping bag and a brass candelabra that had been a wedding gift from my mother. It took a few minutes to divide everything we'd collected in our three-year non-materialistic marriage. I quit my teaching job, fixed up the '56 Chevy wagon, loaded my possessions and left New York singing "Cast Your Fate to the Wind" along the Jersey Turnpike, cruising along Route 66 into Albuquerque, never doubting my date with destiny.

A shock greater than the ruts in the driveway met me that blustery day in March. Most of my friends from last summer had left the commune. My optimism gave way to confusion as thick as the snow clouds enshrouding the mountain peaks. Only English Jane and redheaded Richard still lived here and they were anxious to rent their own house. They'd just had a baby and kept to themselves. Why did the people who built this place with the sweat from their dreams leave so suddenly?

Reggie the Hermit remembered me. I had barely noticed him 10 last summer since he tended to become invisible in groups. Susan from the corner room still lived here and asked about Faisal—she had just ended a long-term relationship with her old man and was eager to have someone to talk to.

"We split up in New York and I'm traveling alone. Where's Moe?" I asked. "She wrote us a letter inviting us to come back with the promise of a room."

"A few weeks ago Moe and Ira rented a house twenty miles north of here, near Questa." After giving directions, she added, "And you're welcome to share my room." I thanked her for the offer.

A very pregnant Moe quietly greeted me at the door. Her effusive joy was subdued. She no longer walked around half naked, flashing a wicked grin, saying "far out" and "dynamite."

"Remember that cute guy I liked last summer? Well, we got together on Halloween. He works at the Moly Mine. Now we're havin' a baby." She never told me why they left New Buffalo but her energies were clearly focused on her family and their newfound religion. Taking out a handmade cedar box, she showed me her sacred hawk and eagle feathers. Her days were filled with rubbing cocoa butter on her belly to prevent stretch marks and beading fans for the feathers. In hushed tones she intimated the great power and mystery of the Peyote Church.

"You're welcome to spend the night," she said, clearly defining her boundaries. We had a great visit. In the morning I drove to New Buffalo and never saw her again. With deflated expectations, I moved onto the commune anyway but gone was the sense of collective purpose. Carloads of people came and went all spring and summer. The ballast and vision had left with the founding families.

Susan informed me when the sun moved into Leo and then Virgo or when the moon was conjunct with some celestial body. Otherwise the days rolled uneventfully off the calendar. Susan volunteered to work at DaNahazli, the local hippie school in Taos. Her corner room at New Buffalo was lighter than most because it had two windows, one facing the east and the other looking onto the courtyard. Two single beds lined the walls separated by a pot-bellied stove in the corner. Kerosene lamps stood on the handmade wood shelves that held all her books and clothing.

In the morning, one of us would sprinkle water and rake the dirt floor to keep the dust down. In the evenings, we'd stoke up the wood stove to warm the room and make a pot of tea. Reggie the Hermit sometimes joined us for a cup of Mu tea, salad and a Milky Way. His blue eyes hiding behind wire-rimmed spectacles were usually focused on some invisible horizon or buried in a book. A scant beard covered his pointy chin. I'd heard from someone he was a draft dodger, but he never talked about it. His room was like an animal's lair. Old turds were thrown in the fireplace and an army blanket hung over the only window, leaving the space in perpetual twilight. He was a pack rat and piles of old newspapers and books lined his walls.

Susan and Reggie had lived here through the hey-day of the commune, when the original settlers were still here. Now they were disillusioned burned-out hippies who didn't know what to do next. Although people still ate in the communal kitchen, neither of them did. They had little interest in farming, gardening or in caring for the animals, but no one asked them to leave. If I was ever to meet the other people living here, I would have to get away from them.

There was less partner swapping and sexual promiscuity than the outside world imagined. No one seemed anxious to get attached or make a personal commitment, but even if you were single you never had to be lonely. Being one of the oldest women living there—23—and owning a running vehicle gave me instant respectability. On Susan's food-stamp day, we'd go to Safeway. I chipped in for groceries, which we kept in our room, not in the communal kitchen. The commune had become a group of individual hoarders.

Soon other women asked me for rides to the laundromat or 20 to carry groceries on food-stamp days. Thus began new friendships. Kathleen, sinewy and graceful, looked like Diana the Huntress galloping across the mesa on her white horse naked from the waist up. Returning to the pueblo with rabbits and prairie dogs slung over her strong shoulders, she skinned rabbits near the woodpile, in full sight of everyone, flashing her emerald eyes and her knife. Her nakedness was untamed. She was haughty towards the men except for Taylor, her hunting and fishing mentor. If he wasn't hunting, he was in his room near the kitchen sharpening his knives or tying fish flies. Kathleen's love for Taylor was unrequited. He told everyone there was a woman waiting for him in California.

Kathleen had taken over Moe's job as the goat lady. She loved the animals and made sure they had food. I helped her by hauling sacks of grain from the Feed Bin or transporting Mama Goat when she needed to get pregnant. Kathleen encouraged me to eat some meals in the communal kitchen. Soon after, I volunteered to cook dinner there a few nights a week.

Elaine the Lovely was Kathleen's closest friend. Her perfectly shaped breasts were brown from her sitting in the sun while weaving belts on a Navajo handloom—wearing only a cotton drawstring skirt. Her waist and her age were 19. Everything about her was sensual and soft, like someone's dream of the perfect valentine. When Kathleen went hunting, Elaine and I would lean against an adobe wall in the courtyard and weave silences around our talk. The loudest noise in the world was the buzzing of flies. We discovered we were both from Queens and became instant sisters-in-exile. Carlos, her lover, was a handsome Chicano from California with a deadly weakness for cheap wine. He was a gifted writer and a voracious reader, consuming books in the commune's library. Sometimes their screams of joy filled the courtyard, but at other times the courtyard echoed with sobbing, angry shouts, and broken bottles. Elaine the Lovely eventually found the strength to kick Carlos the hell out of her room.

Elaine, Kathleen and I were concerned about Sadira who was seven months pregnant and lived alone in a room on the western wing of the pueblo. Sadira's head was crowned with curly red hair and her face and body were covered with freckles. Her voice and mannerisms reminded me of my Aunt Betty from the Bronx. She sat naked on her wooden bed folding hand-me-down baby clothes. Wooden shelves strung from the vigas were already filled with baby stuff. An empty cradle sat next to her bed. She never spoke of the father but rumors floated that she'd gotten pregnant while visiting an ashram in Hawaii, which was believable since she meditated twice a day and smiled a lot in the midst of chaos. She planned on delivering the baby in her room with the help of a midwife. Kathleen and I placed our hands on her undulating belly to feel the unborn life. When Jamil was born, he looked like a little Buddha who told the world of a copper-colored daddy with dark almond-shaped eyes. I was disappointed that I was gone when she gave birth.

One evening in late spring, the weather turned cold again. Susan came home from town early and stoked up the wood stove. Reggie the Hermit wandered in; so did Elaine the Lovely. Snow whipped around the courtyard and thick clouds hung low over the mountains. Susan got to telling stories about the early days of the commune.

25   "Whatever happened to Buffalo Bob, the Philosopher King of the New Buffalo kitchen?" I asked.

"He died of TB last winter. One week he started coughing up blood. I don't think anyone knew what was wrong with him.

Someone took him to Holy Cross Hospital, where he died after twelve hours. It was George who went to claim his body even though they'd fought constantly when Bob was alive. Bob was buried on the edge of an arroyo, overlooking the commune. A pile of stones marks the grave. His last request to his friends was to prohibit any bullshit ritual at his funeral. Over 200 people showed up. Everyone was high. Four friends carried his wasted body and put him into the grave. Someone covered his face with dirt before shovels all around started filling in the hole." I remembered his haunted eyes and hoped he was in the white light he talked so much about.

When spring broke through again, I went to visit Joyce who lived at the other end of the Hondo Valley with her family. I remembered her as the Arabian princess who'd danced around the fire last summer. It was about a three-mile walk along the river, past the post office, Selso's Bar and across the highway. Joyce was diapering her baby when I got there. With safety pins in her mouth, she smiled and gestured me to come in. I walked past the laundry flapping in the breeze. Her long hair was cut short. After admiring the baby—her fourth—and drinking a cup of coffee, I asked why she'd left New Buffalo, hoping she'd tell me it was a terrible mistake. Her energy and vision had helped start the commune. George, her husband, had laid the adobes for the pueblo and plowed the land. Now they rented a small adobe house with minimal comforts. It had a cold-water tap in the kitchen and an outhouse in the back yard. Humor mixed with rancor when she spoke.

"Someday we're going to take that place back." From whom, I wondered? It had been their choice to move away and they were free to move back if they wanted. We sat at her kitchen table while she cut meat off an enormous bone.

"Chile stew for dinner. Want to stay?" She was calm and centered in her home.

"Can't. Promised to cook at Buffalo tonight."   30

Her family were no longer rice-and-beans hippies. Eating meat was daring at a time when people believed that vegetarians ascended more easily into the spiritual realms of universal peace and love. Everyone knew that meat eaters were more exploitive to the environment, more aggressive with their fellow humans and definitely not as healthy. Closer to the truth was the fact that unless someone went hunting or slaughtered an animal it was expensive to buy meat at the supermarket for a large group. Like Moe, Joyce's family went to Peyote Church meetings that gave everyone a sense of spiritual community without having to live communally.

Joyce gave me baby blankets and clothes to take back for Sadira. When I went to her room, Cave Dave was doing a silent vigil over the sleeping mother and baby. In his chaste way, Cave Dave was devoted to Sadira and Jamil. Before moving to New Buffalo he'd taken a vow of silence while living in a cave for three months. He carried around a little chalkboard to write cryptic messages on. He lived in the greenhouse because of his need to be in constant touch with the plants. He was into "vibrational biology." I'd talk to Cave Dave instead of writing in my journal and my words bounced back to me across the silence.

The first time I heard him speak was at a peyote meeting. It blasted his image of deep, centered and wise. He confessed in front of everyone to having lustful thoughts about another man's wife. If only he'd lusted after Sadira who needed a father for her baby, but he thought of her like the Virgin Mother.

One day, we heard gunshots in the courtyard and hoped it wasn't Toby run amuck. Toby was a casualty from Vietnam who'd left an essential part of himself there. No one knew the extent of his delusions that became violent when he got angry. Maybe he was still fighting the Viet Cong in his mind. Guns were kept away from him because he was capable of shooting himself or someone else. Certain women, like Sadira the Virgin Mother or Elaine the Lovely, invoked the gentle side of this man, who treated them with southern civility saying "yes ma'am" or "no ma'am" to their requests. He had the confused look of a person whose main victim is himself. When I opened the door to the courtyard, Elaine was scolding Toby as if he were a naughty kid and Taylor had already gotten his hunting gun back.

35   When Jamil was one month old, Elaine and I went with Sadira to Black Rock Hot Springs for the baby's baptism. We followed the Hondo River two miles into the Rio Grande gorge where swallows' nests and stubborn weeds clung to slate grey volcanic cliffs. When we got to the John Dunn Bridge, there was only one car parked at the top of the hill where the narrow footpath to the river started. That meant the hot springs wouldn't be too crowded. We passed the cave where Dave once lived. Down at the river, a circle of black rocks held water flowing from the bowels of the earth. Baby Jamil floated contentedly between us as we passed around a joint and talked about nothing in particular. The day was cloudless. After a while, I jumped into the icy river and

swam across the current to the other bank. People from all over the world somehow found this pool. When someone washed dirty socks and underwear in the hot springs, I lost hope for the peace and harmony promised by the Aquarian Age. Towards the end of my stay at New Buffalo, the fire rarely burned in the circle room. Communal meals and prayer circles were occasional. One day some visitors showed up from California and gave everyone a hit of mescaline. That night the fire in the drumming room burned until dawn. People came out of their rooms and shared food and played music. We wandered down to the hot springs and made love under the full moon. The founding families were gone but on nights like this I dreamed that one day new people would drive up—wisdom disguised as gypsy-clad hippies—and revive the vision. When the drug wore off and the sun came up, the temporary unity crumbled like dry sod.

New Buffalo nurtured me and became my home in spite of the disappointments. One day I heard of a dream fomenting on the other side of the valley—a dream of an experimental high school—a school of life—and I followed the sound of the piper across the valley and left.

from *Scrapbook of a Taos Hippie*
The Founding of Morningstar Commune
TOLD BY DAVID LEE PRATT TO IRIS KELTZ

How did I end up at Morningstar Commune in New Mexico?" David Pratt mused over a cup of hot coffee. "I don't know where to start because it's a complex case of cause and effect, all tied in with many different things happening around the world.

"It starts off in New York City where I'd been living as an artist. It was a creative time for me. I met my wife the first time I ate peyote. I was in a bar and it was the day Kennedy was shot.

"In retrospect, I see Vietnam as the catalyst. None of the rebellious hippie movement would have happened without it. It was the straw that broke the camel's back. Something in society broke apart and we were the reaction.

"A year or two before the hippie thing exploded, I moved to California. When I got there, I couldn't believe how different it was from New York City. Californians are laid back and always tripping on the cosmic ethers. The environment is much softer there—it's easier to survive. I was an old-time hipster or beatnik and never comfortably fit with the hippies, but that's what was happening so I followed the movement.

5   "The hippie-phenomenon was created for the most part by middle class kids who became disillusioned with the American dream. The kids from ethnic and lower socio-economic backgrounds tended to be less crazed. It's hard to reject what you've never had. They were fighting to get into the system.

"My wife and I were desperately poor. We used to go to Golden Gate Park on Sunday and watch the Diggers feed all these people. I admired them very much. They fit into my political, philosophical and religious thinking. If all these people had their basic needs taken care of, they would have more time and energy to explore the things people usually don't have time for.

"People are after two things: security or adventure. I always believed in adventure and admired the daring of the Diggers. They tended to be older. Many of them were transplanted New Yorkers. One day I saw a poster in the street inviting people to go and live on Morningstar Ranch in Sonoma County. I was desperate as usual, and tired of living off my friends, so my wife and I went to check it out.

"Lou Gottlieb, an ex-Limelighter—the number two folk group of that era—owned a ranch. It was 30 acres of land filled with apple trees. Gottlieb retired to devote himself to classical music, and wrote reviews for a San Francisco newspaper on the side.

"The ranch was named by the previous owner, a mystical Christian, who called it Morningstar after references from the Bible. The last words of Christ in Revelation had to do with the morning star. Christ said, 'I, Jesus, have sent My angel to testify to you these things in the churches. I am the Root and the Offspring of David, the Bright and Morning Star.' (Revelation 22.16 NKJ)

10   "There are references to the morning star in all the world's great religions and mythologies. Quetzalcoatl, from Aztec mythology, taught a doctrine of peace and love, very similiar to Jesus. He told the people to stop the human sacrifices and love one another. One day he told the people he was going to leave, but to take this as a symbol. 'I am the eastern morning star and one day I am coming back.' Cortez arrived on the day it was prophesied Quetzalcoatl would return. The people mistook Cortez for Quetzalcoatl and gave him everything. That's how the western hemisphere was conquered.

"Somehow the Diggers got wind of Gottlieb's ranch and posted a sign in the streets of the Haight Ashbury inviting hippies to move there. The summer of love in 1967 saw thousands of hippies pass through Morningstar in California. Some stayed and some didn't. I built a tree house there and always had apples to eat. The local people had never seen anything like this before. The health conditions were terrible and they tried to close the place down.

"Lou Gottlieb decided to deed his land to God. He ended up in court because they said he couldn't do that. The court said that land must be privately owned. He responded by saying, 'We belong to the earth, not the earth to us. Who can own the earth? If someone comes on my land I don't have to kick them off. It's my right.'

"The judges answered by saying, 'We have this regulation. Hippies carry diseases and we don't want them around.' The pressure got great. They kept throwing us in jail and fining Lou. As far as I know, we still do not have the legal right to deed land to God.

"One day I went to a party down in Sonoma Country with the rich hippies who always had lots of acid and other drugs. They had this mansion with a swimming pool. Owsley was there passing out acid. The Grateful Dead were playing music. I was real high on acid in this large group of people and things started to feel weird. People were breaking into small groups and hanging out in the shadows. There was a feeling of separateness. Suddenly I felt there wasn't much future in what was going on.

"My friend, a Digger who had just come from New Mexico, told me, 'New Mexico is where it's at.' I had nothing to lose—no money, no nothing—so I said, 'Okay, let's hitchhike to New Mexico tomorrow.'

"There were already a few people from Morningstar, California living in this ghost town four miles north of La Madera, New Mexico. We had problems with the local people. There were incidences of rape and violence against the hippies. The locals wanted middle-class life badly and there we were—a bunch of white kids from middle-class America flaunting those values. They thought we were the devil incarnate. In reality, we were a bunch of young kids trying to live right, the way we saw it. But we showed no respect for local culture.

"I had moved to an old adobe house in Truchas with my wife when my California friends started showing up. They'd found me through this incredible underground network. Some of the women were pregnant so I couldn't just throw them out. The local people started freaking out and attacking us. It was a violent place. Gunfights were not uncommon Saturday night events.

"We stuck out like a sore thumb. By now we were about 15 people living in this small adobe in Truchas. We bought wheat in the 100-pound bags used to feed cattle. It was difficult to go to the store and get food because every time we went out we were in danger of being shot. It became a life-threatening situation. We had to leave town or get killed. It was the only time in my life that I wanted to see a cop, maybe even be in jail. At that point we couldn't do anything but survive.

"One night some locals started burning the buildings. A kid who'd grown up in Truchas showed up and led us out of town through a secret route that he knew. We took refuge in someone's house on the north side of town. The next day I went down to the state government offices and said, 'You've got to help us or someone's gonna get killed.' There was so much violence against the hippies in this state at that time that the government had appointed a special liaison, Van Arsdale, who told us, 'I'll drive you around to a few places where rich hippies have already bought and settled on some land.' The group chose Larry Stein and me for this exploratory trip.

20   "We ended up at Michael Duncan's place. He'd just bought 800 acres on the mesa in Arroyo Hondo. It turned out that Michael Duncan and Larry Stein were old friends from many years ago. They were involved with Timothy Leary and the LSD scene together. Larry says to Michael, 'You've got to help us out. We're in a desperate situation. We've got children and pregnant women.' Michael said, 'Sure, come on over.' However, he wasn't really prepared for us. We weren't just wanting to come for a week or two. We were looking for a long-term thing. We borrowed a truck from someone and loaded fifty pounds of rice, an old rusty hammer and all the people and moved to the mesa owned by Michael Duncan.

"Reality Construction Company was already making their adobes when we arrived with nothing. Max Finstein, a visionary Jewish beatnick poet from New York, started Reality. He had helped to start New Buffalo, but the reality of it did not meet his dreams, so he started another commune that consisted of militant blacks, Chicanos and politically radical whites. They were bitter—their ethic derived from the have-nots. They had a strong political and self-sacrificing aspect.

"Reality had some sort of understanding with Michael Duncan. At best Michael tolerated us, at worst he tried to kick us off the land. Reality Construction Company was busy trying to set up systems while we were bent on breaking them down.

"We had no money and no experience with adobe. All we had were people and the will to survive. We observed how the Indians were building an adobe house for Michael. We watched the guys from Reality make adobe bricks and we started putting it together. We held meetings, nothing regular. There were no leaders. It was an anarchist expression. People would gather and talk. Since we all needed food and shelter, we talked about that.

"One night I went outside and lined up a dagger with the shadow of the full moon. We planned three rectangles lined up with the North Star. There would be three living quarters in each section and a communal space in between with a courtyard in the middle.

"We planted our first crops that spring and had a birth in a   25 lean-to before we had permanent shelter. We didn't even have tipis. Sometimes there was an attending midwife, sometimes not, but we never lost a baby or a mother. We were so poor the hippies from New Buffalo looked down on us and sent us their rejects, derelicts, psychopaths and winos. We should have been paid by the government to take care of these people who normally would have been institutionalized. We took them in and taught them how to grow food and build shelters. Some of them became whole again and were able to return to mainstream life. Some did not.

"Morningstar was a quest for freedom, a pure creative anarchy—hippie dippy, but live and let live. We were formless, which allowed anything to exist. The total freedom gave a person the chance to create new forms. Anything could happen and usually did. I used to think that—since we all have similar needs—if given the freedom to choose what to do with our lives, we would choose to take care of the earth and each other. That's not true. Lots of people just wanted to get drunk and stoned all the time, but that eventually plays itself out.

"Morningstar was a truly revolutionary experience. Without any money, the dregs, dropouts and rejects of society were able to build solid structures, feed lots of people and create a community. We made mistakes because we were naive and idealistic, but we were in the forefront of what was happening. In the Bible it says, 'The last shall be first.' And I believe it."

Update: *After living at Morningstar, David Lee Pratt whirred through life like a drunken wildfire. He spawned two boys both with angel hair of spun gold. Eventually he stumbled into Austin, Texas,*

*where he frolics with a mermaid in a magic trailer, works as a secu-
rity guard, helps run Alternate Current Productions, makes strange
art that few people ever get to see and acts in the movies whenever
they let him. He still walks the line between innocence and experience, art and life, reality and illusion, time and space, light and
shadow, life and death and he often wonders—what's next?*

Year of the Fork,
Night of the Hunter

DAVID FELTON AND DAVID DALTON

As associate editor and freelance writer for *Rolling Stone*, respec-
tively, Felton and Dalton were witnesses to the excesses and
tabloid publicity that accompanied what many viewed as the "end
of the Counterculture." The media played upon parents' fears that
their long-haired, rock-music-listening kids would turn into "hippies" and wind up victims of cults and drugs. Felton and Dalton's
aptly named collaborative book *Mindfuckers: A Sourcebook on the
Rise of Acid Fascism in America* (1972) came after Altamont, at the
end of the U.S. involvement of Vietnam, and chronicled various
cults that exploited idealistic young people searching for an alternative lifestyle. Many of these began as ostensible communes (as
described by Iris Keltz and David Lee Pratt in the previous readings), but were run by charismatic, authoritarian leaders (as Peter
Coyote points out in the excerpt "Free Fall" from *Sleeping Where I
Fall*). Using LSD and other drugs, and brainwashing their subjects, some of these, such as the Lyman "family," are not remembered anymore. Jim Jones' "People's Temple" and the Manson
"family," because they resulted in mass suicide and several murders, were. Part One of "Year of the Fork, Night of the Hunter,"
chronicles probably the single most notorious of these, the
Manson "family," in this excerpt from *Mindfuckers*.

————————— ✦ —————————

Three young girls dance down the hallway of the Superior Court
Building in Los Angeles, holding hands and singing one of
Charlie's songs. They might be on their way to a birthday party in

their short, crisp cotton dresses, but actually they are attending a preliminary hearing to a murder trial.

A middle-aged lady in Bel Air wants to "mother" Charlie, and two little girls send a letter to him in jail:

"At first we thought you were guilty. But then we read in the papers about these kids who were stabbed to death in the same way as the Sharon Tate murders. We knew you hadn't done it because you were in jail at the time. We knew you hadn't done it anyway when we saw your face in the newspaper . . . Love. . . ."

Charlie gets letters from little girls every day. They come from New Hampshire, Minnesota, Los Angeles. A convicted bank robber who met Charlie in jail writes "The Gospel According to Pawnee Fred, the Thief on the Other Cross," in which he asks:

"Is Manson Son of Man?"   5

Thirty miles northwest of the courthouse, seven miles due north of Leonard Nimoy's Pet Pad in Chatsworth (Supplies— Fish—Domestics—Exotics), a circle of rustic women at the Spahn Movie Ranch weave their own hair into an elaborate rainbow vest for Charlie.

Most of them are early members of Charlie's three-year-old family. There's Lynne Fromme—they call her Squeaky—Sandra Good, Gypsy, Brenda, Sue, Cappy, Jeany.

"We've been working on this vest for two years," says Sandra, "adding things, sewing on patches. It's for Charlie to wear in court." And Squeaky adds, "Wouldn't it be beautiful to have a photograph of Charlie wearing it? And all of us standing around close to him, hugging him like we used to?"

Wouldn't it be beautiful to have the others standing around too, the rest of the family, the others imprisoned? Tex Watson and Patty Krenwinkel and Linda Kasabian and, oh yeah, the snitch, Sadie Glutz. Her real name is Susan Atkins, but the family calls her Sadie Glutz because that's what Charlie named her.

Meanwhile Charlie sits blissfully in his cell at the Los Angeles   10 County Jail, composing songs, converting fellow inmates to his gospel of love and Christian submission, and occasionally entertaining a disturbing thought: Why haven't they gotten in touch? A simple phone call would do it. Surely they've received the telegrams, the letters. Surely they realize that he knows, he *understands* their glorious revelation; that he understands the whole double album.

Everywhere there's lots of piggies
Living piggy lives
You can see them out for dinner
With their piggy wives
Clutching forks and knives to eat their bacon.

Ten blocks from the new County Jail stands the old County
Hall of Justice, a grotesque, brown brick fortress that for decades
has guarded the Los Angeles Civic Center from aesthetic inroads.
The entire sixth floor belongs to the District Attorney and his
staff, a member of which, now alone on his lunch hour, unlocks a
file cabinet and withdraws several neatly bound, family-type
photo albums. Slowly he turns each page, studies each snapshot,
each personality:

Sharon Tate, considered one of Hollywood's prettier, more
popular promising young stars, wife of genius film sorcerer Roman Polanski. After her biggest film, *Valley of the Dolls*, she retreated to private life to enjoy her first pregnancy. The photographs show her in her eighth month.

Jay Sebring, the handsome young hair stylist who revolu-
tionized the fashion industry by introducing hair styling to men,
convincing them—despite early masculine scoffs—there was
something better looking than a 15-minute union trim even if you
had to pay ten times the price. He once was Miss Tate's fiance.

Wocjech Frykowski, Polanski's boyhood pal who came to
Hollywood with hopes of directing films himself. His luck at this
was dismal, and even Polanski later admitted he had little talent.
Instead, he began directing home movies inside his head, invest-
ing heavily in many forms of exotic dope.

15   **Abigail Folger,** heiress to the Folger's Coffee millions, an attractive Radcliffe girl considered by neighbors to be the most
charming of the Polanskis' house guests. She met Frykowski in
New York and became his lover.

Steven Parent, an 18-year-old from the Los Angeles suburb
of El Monte, a friend of Polanski's caretaker, unknown to the others, a nobody like the rest of us.

Leno La Bianca, owner of a grocery store chain, and his
wife, Rosemary, an ordinary couple of the upper middle class,
fond of such quiet pleasures as boating, water skiing and watching late night television in their pajamas. They knew nothing of
Sharon Tate and her friends, living miles away in different neighborhoods and different worlds.

Gary Hinman, music teacher, bagpipe player, and onetime friend of Charlie Manson's. He once, in fact, gave the Manson family his Toyota, although the circumstances surrounding that gift have since come into question.

The snapshots are homey little numbers, color polaroids taken by staff photographers from the County Coroner's office and the Los Angeles Police Department. They show all the wounds, the nakedness, the blood. Sometimes the exposure is a little off, but the relevant details are there—shots of the rooms, the bullet holes, the blood on the furniture and floors, the bizarre blood writing on the walls, words like RISE and HELTER SKELTER and PIGGIES.

And shots of the weapons found at the scene—ropes, pillow-   20
cases, forks and knives.

After replacing the albums, the D.A. investigator continues eating his lunch and now starts perusing an official looking 34-page document. It is an interview with Mary Brunner, a former member of Manson's family, conducted by detectives last December:

Q. Mary, did you ever see Charlie Manson or Bruce Davis hit Gary Hinman?

A. No.

Q. Do you know how he got the slash on the side of his face that severed his ear?

A. He got it from one of those two, he had to.   25

Q. Now, after everybody left on Sunday, did anybody ever go back to the house?

A. Yes.

Q. Who?

A. Bobby.

Q. Was anybody with Bobby?   30

A. Not that I know of. He told me about it and he talked like he was alone.

Q. What did Bobby tell you he went back to the house for?

A. He tried to erase that paw print on the wall.

Q. And how many days later did he go back to the house?

A. Two or three days after Sunday, Tuesday or Wednesday.   35

Q. All right. Did he describe to you what the house looked like or smelled like or anything like that?

A. He told me it smelled terrible. He could hear the maggots.

Q.   Hear the maggots? What?

A.   In Gary, eating Gary.

40   **Q.**   Is there anything else you would like to add about this that we haven't covered?

A.   There isn't anything else to it.

Los Angeles is the third largest city in America, according to population, but easily the largest according to raw real estate. It is bounded by the Pacific Ocean to the south and southwest, by Ventura County to the west, by the San Gabriel Mountains and fire-prone Angeles National Forest to the north and by scores of cruddy, smoggy little towns and cities to the east.

Its shape resembles some discarded prehistoric prototype for a central nervous system, the brain including the entire San Fernando Valley, the San Gabriel foothills, West Los Angeles, Venice, portions of the Santa Monica Mountains, Hollywood, Hollywood Hills and Highland Park—actually hundreds and hundreds of square miles—with a weird, narrow spinal chord extending from the Civic Center, through the country's largest black ghetto, to San Pedro Harbor 25 miles away.

Charles Manson knew his city well. Like many Los Angeles residents he learned to drive long distances regularly without a second thought. During his two years as a free man in Southern California he frequently "made the rounds," visiting friends, keeping business appointments, preaching to small groups, giving and taking material possessions.

45   For some reason, perhaps for no reason, many of the spots where he stopped or stayed are located on the extreme periphery of the brain of Los Angeles. Which at least makes it an easy, scenic drive—Sunday afternoon with the wife and kids. Who knows? Ten years from now these spots may be official points of interest, stations of the cross as it were. Save these handy directions for your personal map to the homes of the stars.

Starting at the Spahn Movie Ranch in the extreme northwestern corner of Los Angeles, drive two miles east on Santa Susana Pass Road to Topanga Canyon Boulevard. Now turn directly south for 15 miles or so, crossing the floor of the San Fernando Valley and heading into the heart of Topanga Canyon itself.

It was here that Manson and his family first lived after arriving from the Haight-Ashbury in late 1967, and it was here that Manson first met Gary Hinman. Hinman's house is a little further down the road, almost where Topanga Canyon meets the beach at Pacific Coast Highway.

You can't see into the house now, of course, because the cops boarded it up last July after they found Hinman's body perforated with stab wounds. They say he was tortured for 48 hours. On a nearby wall they found the words POLITICAL PIGGIES and a neat little cat's paw print in blood. Bobby Beausoleil, an electric guitarist and member of Manson's family, has already been sentenced to death, and Manson and Susan Atkins are awaiting trial in the matter.

After driving on to Pacific Coast Highway, take a left, and after two miles, take another left. Now you're on Sunset Boulevard, winding through wealthy Pacific Palisades where, for a short time in early 1968, the Manson family lived with Beach Boy Dennis Wilson. Wilson doesn't live there anymore, however; he moved shortly after Manson allegedly threatened him with a bullet.

Keep driving east on Sunset for another eight or ten miles past Brentwood Heights, past Mandeville Canyon, over the San Diego Freeway, past UCLA and Bel Air and Beverly Glen. And when you reach the center of Beverly Hills, turn left on Canon and head north into Benedict Canyon. 50

Now here you may need a more detailed map because the streets get pretty tricky with all the turns and culs-de-sac. But up in Benedict Canyon there's this little dirt road, Cielo Drive, which dead ends at the old, rambling, hillside house where producer Terry Melcher, Doris Day's son, used to live. Manson paid several business calls on him there, but the business was never completed before Melcher moved out early last summer.

Neighbors hardly had had a chance to meet the new residents when, on the bright Saturday morning of last August 9th, Mrs. Winifred Chapman, a maid, ran screaming from the house, across the huge grounds and parking lot, through the iron gate and down the road:

"There's bodies and blood all over the place!"

Not a bad description. Police found Steven Parent just inside the gate, shot five times in his white Rambler, the wheels of the car already turned toward the road in a desperate attempt to escape. Wocjech Frykowski's body lay in front of the house, shot and stabbed and stabbed again and again. Twenty yards down the rolling lawn, underneath a fir tree, they found Abigail Folger dead and curled up in a bloody nightgown.

55   Inside the house Jay Sebring and Sharon Tate lay stabbed to death near the living room couch. They were connected by a single nylon cord wrapped around their necks and thrown over a rafter. Sebring was also shot and his head covered with a pillowcase. On the front door police found the word PIG written in blood with a towel.

If the gate's locked, you won't be able to see the house because it's set back some from the road. But anyway, that's where it is.

Now make a U and head back down to Sunset. Continue east for another 10 miles, along the famous and more and more plastic Sunset Strip, past the tall, swanky office monuments to Hollywood flackery, past the decaying radio empires of the Forties, clear to Western Avenue, where you take a left.

A mile north, Western turns right and becomes Los Feliz Boulevard, cutting east through the wealthy, residential Los Feliz District that skirts the foothills of Griffith Park. After about three miles, just before Los Feliz crosses the Golden State Freeway, drive into the winding, hillside streets to your right, where you'll find Waverly Drive.

In August, 1968, Manson and his family started visiting Harold True, a UCLA student who lived with some other guys on Waverly. They were all good friends, and the family just liked to go up there and hang around and smoke dope and sing and shoot the shit. True later moved to Van Nuys, where he presently lives with Phil Kaufman, a former member of the family who produced Manson's record.

60   True's neighbors, incidentally, were Leno and Rosemary La Bianca who, a year later on the morning of August 10th, were found stabbed—or rather carved—to death inside their home. The words DEATH TO PIGS, HELTER SKELTER and RISE were written, again in blood, on the kitchen walls. And someone had etched WAR on Leno La Bianca's stomach with a fork.

Anyway, those are just some of the spots Manson liked to visit on his frequent tours of the big city. Cut back to Los Feliz, head north on the Golden State Freeway for 18 miles, cut west across the north end of the Valley on Devonshire Street—another 10 miles—turn right on Topanga Canyon Boulevard, and you're practically back at the Spahn ranch.

The whole round trip is eighty miles or so. That may seem like a big distance, but actually the roads are good and it shouldn't take longer than two or three hours, especially if you take it on a Sunday afternoon or, say, late at night.

Perhaps no two recent events have so revealed the cut-rate value of public morality and private life as the killing of Sharon Tate and the arrest of Charles Manson. Many were quick to criticize *The Los Angeles Times* for publishing bright and early one Sunday morning the grisly (and since recanted) confession of Susan Atkins. Any doubts about Manson's power to cloud men's minds were buried that morning between Dick Tracy and one of the world's great real estate sections. Sexie Sadie laid it down for all to see.

Critics accused the *Times* of paying a healthy sum to promoter Larry Schiller, who had obtained the confession from Miss Atkins' attorneys in return for a cut of the profits. The *Times* responded publicly with silence, privately with a denial. No money was paid, said the editors. Schiller had sold the story to various European Sunday editions, they said, and an eight-hour time difference allowed the *Times* to pick it up from one of their European correspondents. In other words, "If we hadn't run it here, some other paper would have." (Some other paper, in fact many other papers, did run it, of course, with the excuse the *Times* had done it first.)

The *Times* response sounded like a hype from the start. For one thing their Sunday edition is put to bed, not a mere eight hours before Sunday morning, but late Friday night so their vast, hair-curlered, beer-bellied Supermarket weekend readership can get its comics and classified ads a day early. Also, why was Schiller himself seen hanging around the *Times'* offices as the edition rolled off the presses?

Rolling Stone has since learned that the *Times* explanation was at least partly correct. No money was paid, that's true, or at least not much. Because, dig, the *Times* people didn't buy the confession, they *wrote* it. Word for word. Not only the confession but the book that followed, *The Killing of Sharon Tate*, with "eight pages of photographs," published by New American Library, a Times-Mirror subsidiary.

In the volume, Schiller gratefully acknowledges "the invaluable aid of two journalists who worked with the author in preparing this book and the original interviews with Susan Atkins."

Those two journalists, it turns out, were Jerry Cohen and Dial Torgerson, both veteran members of the *Times* rewrite crew. Torgerson wrote the first chapter to the book, and Cohen, an old friend of Schiller's, wrote the confession and the rest of the book. Both subsequently have reported much of the news related to the case, and Cohen has been assigned to cover Charlie's trial.

65

According to a freelance *Life* contributor in the area and since confirmed by several *Times* staffers, Miss Atkins' attorneys gave Schiller tapes of her confession on the condition that he sell the story to foreign papers only and split the money. But Schiller is a promoter, not a writer, and he needed someone to put the thing together fast.

70 After conferences with Cohen and various *Times* editors, it was decided Cohen and Torgerson would write a story and a book, both under Schiller's name. In return, New American would have exclusive rights to the book and the Times would publish the confession simultaneously with the foreign press.

All this was to be top secret, of course, But Schiller got careless. Not only did he awkwardly appear in the *Times* city room to see his freshly printed byline, he invited people like our *Life* correspondent over to his house the week before while Cohen was in the next room hacking away.

What possible justification could the *Times* editors have had in running the confessions? Where were their heads? Can an individual's right to a fair trial, free of damaging pretrial publicity, be so relative? Can it be compromised so easily by the dubious right of the public to be entertained?

The *Times* would argue that Susan Atkins' testimony to the County Grand Jury, later made public, had essentially the same impact as her confession. If so, why did the *Times* print both? Besides, there surely are many readers who trust in the *Times* who rightfully suspect the Grand Jury, realizing it consists mainly of retired old men and white, upper-middle-class housewives handpicked by the District Attorney.

If Miss Atkins' confession does not constitute damaging pretrial publicity, what does? What does the phrase mean?

75 Clearly Charles Manson already stands as the villain of our time, the symbol of animalism and evil. Lee Harvey Oswald? Sirhan Sirhan? Adolph Eichmann? Misguided souls, sure, but as far as we know they never took LSD or fucked more than one woman at a time.

Manson is already so hated by the public that all attempts so far to exploit his reputation have failed miserably. Of the 2,000 albums of his music that were pressed, less than 300 have sold.

A skin flick based weakly on popular assumptions about Manson and his family, *Love in the Commune*, closed after two days in San Francisco, only mustered two old men on a Saturday night in Los Angeles. Normally, one wouldn't expect skin flick buffs to be that discriminating, although certainly the few scenes in the film of a Manson-type balling a headless chicken probably had little mass prurient appeal.

Even Cohen and Torgerson's book is reportedly in financial trouble, although profits to the Times-Mirror Syndicate from sales to other American papers have already been counted.

Are there 12 people in the country, let alone Los Angeles, who can honestly say they have no opinions about Charles Manson? Mention of his name in polite conversation provokes, not words or heated argument, but noises, guttural sound effects, gasps, shrieks, violent physical gestures of repulsion. He is more than a villain, he is a leper.

Shortly after Manson's arrest, the president of the musicians' local in Los Angeles wrote the *Times* and said flatly that he had checked his union's records and that Manson definitely was not a musician. So there'd be no confusion, he added that most musicians were good clean fellows who believe in hard work and the American way of life.

Members of the Los Angeles Criminal Bar Association reduced Manson to the butt of a sick song-and-dance spoof during their 17th Annual Installation Banquet. Entitled "One Manson's Family—the family that slays together, stays together," the amateurish skit was performed before most of the city's criminal court judges, including Superior Judge William B. Keene, the man scheduled to preside at Manson's trial. According to the *Times*, Judge Keene "appeared to enjoy the skit."

But all this is really beside the point. Even if the *Times* could somehow prove that its confession did Manson absolutely no harm, what right did they have to take the risk? The moral decision must be made before, not after, the fact if a man's right to an impartial trial is to be taken seriously.

On the other hand, the most blatant—if less damaging—assault on the concept of pretrial impartiality comes not from the Establishment or the Far Right, but the Far Left, the Weatherman faction of the SDS.

According to an item from the Liberation News Service, the Weathermen have made Manson a revolutionary hero on the assumption that he is guilty. Praising him for having offed some "rich honky pigs," they offer us a prize example of bumper sticker mentality:

"MANSON POWER—THE YEAR OF THE FORK!"

The underground press in general has assumed kind of a paranoid-schizo attitude toward Manson, undoubtedly hypersensitive to the relentless gloating of the cops who, after a five-year-search, finally found a longhaired devil you could love to hate.

Starting in mid-January, the *Los Angeles Free Press* banner headlined Manson stories for three weeks in a row: "MANSON CAN GO FREE!" "M.D. ON MANSON'S SEX LIFE!" "MANSON INTERVIEW! EXCLUSIVE! EXCLUSIVE!"

The interview, by the way, ran for two more weeks, consisted mainly of attorney/author Michael Hannon talking to himself. Later, the *Free Press* began a weekly column by Manson written from jail.

About the same time, a rival underground paper, *Tuesday's Child*, ran Manson's picture across the entire front page with the headline "MAN OF THE YEAR: CHARLES MANSON." In case you missed the point, in their next issue they covered the front page with a cartoon of Manson on the cross. The plaque nailed above his head read simply "HIPPIE."

90   When the Manson record was released, both papers agreed to run free ads for it, but the chain of Free Press bookstores, owned by *Free Press* publisher Art Kunkin, refused to sell it, arguing it was an attempt to make profit of tragedy.

Of course, not all the stories in the *Free Press* and *Tuesday's Child* were pro-Manson. Some were very lukewarm, others were simply anti-cop. The question that seemed to split underground editorial minds more than any other was simply: Is Manson a hippie or isn't he?

It's hard to imagine a better setting for Manson's vision of the Apocalypse, his black revolution, than Los Angeles, a city so large and cumbersome it defies the common senses, deifies the absurd. For thousands of amateur prophets it provides a virtual Easter egg hunt of spooky truths.

Its climate and latitude are identical to Jerusalem. It easily leads the country in our race toward ecological doom. It has no sense of the past; the San Andreas Fault separates it from the rest of the continent by a million years.

If Manson's racial views seem incredibly naive, which they are (after preaching against the Black Panthers for two years, he recently asked who Huey Newton was), they are similar to views held by hundreds of thousands of others in that city and that city's Mayor. Citizens there last year returned to office Mayor Sam Yorty whose administration was riddled with conflicts of interest and bribery convictions, rather than elect a thoughtful, soft-spoken, middle-of-the-road ex-cop who happened to be black.

Full-page newspaper ads, sponsored by a police organization, pictured the man as a wild African savage and asked voters, "Will Your Home be Safe with Bradley as Mayor?"

The question to ask, therefore, maybe not now but five or ten   95
years from now, is this: Who would the voters prefer, Bradley or Manson? Would Your Home be Safe with Manson as Mayor?

"I am just a mirror," Manson says over and over. "Anything you see in me is you." He says it so often it becomes an evasive action. I'm rubber and you're glue. But there's a truth there nonetheless.

The society may be disgusted and horrified by Charles Manson, but it is the society's perverted system of penal "rehabilitation," its lusts for vengeance and cruelty, that created him.

The Spahn Movie Ranch may seem a miserable place for kids to live, with its filthy, broken-down shacks and stagnant streams filled daily with shoveled horseshit. Life there may seem degenerate, a dozen or more people eating garbage, sleeping, balling and raising babies in a 20-foot trailer.

But for more than two years most of those kids have preferred that way of life—life with Charlie—than living in the homes of their parents.

The press likes to put the Manson family in quotation   100
marks—"family." But it's a real family, with real feelings of devotion, loyalty and disappointment. For Manson and all the others it's the only family they've ever had.

Is Manson a hippie? One is tempted to say that Manson spent 22 of his 35 years in prison, that he is more a product of the penal system than the Haight-Ashbury.

But it cannot be dismissed that easily. Charles Manson raises some very serious questions about our culture, whether he is entirely part of it or not.

For actually we are not yet a culture at all, but a sort of pre-culture, a gathering of disenchanted seekers, an ovum unfertilized. There is no new morality, as *Time* and *Life* would have us believe, but a growing awareness that the old morality has not been practiced for some time.

The right to smoke dope, to pursue different goals, to be free of social and economic oppression, the right to live in peace and equity with our brothers—this is Founding Fathers stuff.

In the meantime we must suffer the void, waiting for the sub-   105
versives in power to die, waiting for the old, dead, amoral culture to be buried. For many, particularly the younger among us, the wait—the weight—is extremely frustrating, even unbearable. Life

becomes absurd beyond enjoyment. Real doubts grow daily whether any of the tools we have to change power still work. Into this void, this seemingly endless river of shit, on top of it, if you will, rode Charlie Manson in the fall of 1967, full of charm and truth and gentle goodness, like Robert Mitchum's psychopathic preacher in *Night of the Hunter* with LOVE and HATE inscribed on opposing hands. (A friend of Manson's said recently, "You almost could see the devil and angel in him fighting it out, and I guess the devil finally won.")

This smiling, dancing music man offered a refreshing short cut, a genuine and revolutionary new morality that redefines or rather eliminates the historic boundaries between life and death.

Behind Manson's attitude toward death is the ancient mystical belief that we are all part of one body—an integral tenet of Hinduism, Buddhism and Christianity as expressed by St. Paul in 1 Corinthians: "For as the body is one and hath many members, and all the members of that one body, being many, are one body; so also is Christ."

But Manson adds a new twist; he wants us to take the idea literally, temporally. He believes that he—and all human beings— are God and the Devil at the same time, that all human beings are part of each other, that human life has no individual value. If you kill a human being, you're just killing part of yourself; it has no meaning. "Death is psychosomatic," says Manson.

110   Thus the foundation of all historic moral concepts is nearly discarded. Manson's is a morality of amorality. "If God is One, what is bad?" he asks. Manson represents a frightening new phenomenon, the acid-ripped street fighter, erasing the barrier between the two outlaw cultures—the head and the hood— described by Tom Wolfe in *The Electric Kool-Aid Acid Test:*

> "The Angels were too freaking real. Outlaws? They were outlaws by choice, from the word go, all the way out in Edge City. Further! The hip world, the vast majority of acid heads, were still playing the eternal charade of the middle class intellectuals— Behold my wings! Freedom! Flight!—but you don't actually expect me to jump off that cliff, do you?"

Perhaps it was inevitable for someone like Manson to come along who *would* jump off that cliff; that a number of lost children seem willing to believe him is indeed a disturbing sign of the times.

"Little children," wrote St. John in a prophetic letter, "it is the last time: and as ye have heard that antichrists shall come, even now are there many antichrists; whereby we know it is the last time."

CHAPTER 3

Drugs and Bombs

LSD is air . . . Now that this breakthrough of consciousness has occurred, a new level of harmony and love is available. I must bring my family, my friends to this new universe.

TIMOTHY LEARY, "LSD IS AIR"

They build the Bank of America, kids burn it down. They outlaw grass, we build a culture of life and music. The time is now. Political power grows out of a gun, a Molotov, a riot, a commune . . . and from the soul of the people.

WEATHERMAN, *BERKELEY TRIBE*, JULY 31, 1970

Perhaps no countercultural issues are more hotly debated than the introduction of psychedelic drugs (among others) and violence on college campuses and the streets of America. Both the drugs and the protests against the Vietnam War and the Establishment garnered enormous media attention—largely negative. Most of the covers of books on the 1960s feature riot police choke-holding some long-haired protesters. (Popular posters of the times showed armed militants and captured the "Bring the War Home" armed-survivalist-mentality of some counterculturists after Nixon's victory in the 1968 election.) Those who look back with the benefit of hindsight are divided about many legacies of those times—the Vietnam War, sexual liberation, women's issues, gay rights, environmental issues—but few will defend the outrageous nature of former Harvard professor Timothy Leary's message to the young to "turn on, tune in, and drop out" through the use of LSD. Fewer still (especially after September 11th) would condone using guns and bombs for terrorist actions against the United States, as the Weather Underground advocated. The Weathermen (there were women, too) were a small group glamorized by revolutionary legend for white radicals the way the Black Panther Party (see Eldridge Cleaver's piece in Chapter Four) became icons for some African-Americans. Both groups wore black leather jackets and brandished guns. Both were radical offshoots from larger organizations—Students for a Democratic Society (SDS) in the case of the Weathermen, and Students Non-Violent Coordinating Committee (SNCC) for the Panthers. When legitimate political action and non-violent protest in the fashion of Henry Thoreau and Mahatma Gandhi's civil disobedience worked too slowly, some young people saw violence as the only way to draw attention to their causes. Very few people were actually members of these radical movements, but they splintered the Left by all the negative press and further police actions increasingly aimed at the entire Counterculture. "Communique #2 From the Weatherman Underground" gives a taste of the rhetoric of the manifesto employed by these radicals that circulated in the underground presses and posted in public places. Interestingly, in recent years, domestic terrorism has come more often from the Far Right, whose own manifestoes about the U.S. Government and "New World Order" sound quite similar those once used by the Left.

Throughout time and across cultures, various substances have been used (usually in religious ceremonies but also recreationally) to alter the mind. Plants were fermented to make various kinds of alcohols from the Old World to the New. Native Americans were aware of psychoactive substances and reserved them for ceremonies. Alcohol, hashish, and opium narratives can be found by English and French writers of the nineteenth century and remain a favorite subject of cultural historians. Americans at the turn of the nineteenth century were habitually using opiates in their cough medicines, and morphine addiction in Europe and America through the nineteenth and early twentieth centuries was rampant (*In the Arms of Morpheus*, Barbara Hodgson, 2001). Heroin was invented in 1898 and used to treat respiratory disorders and alleviate pain (although it quickly made its way to the street as "junk," as William Burroughs documented in his famous underground novels *Junky* and *Naked Lunch*). Cannabis, marijuana or "reefer," was outlawed in the United States the 1930s but is now accessible—although still illegal—in a more potent form. Marijuana continues to reappear on local ballots to be considered for medical purposes or decriminalization, and drug education programs attempt to prevent young people from trying it in the first place.

In the opinion of the Counterculture, the real "drug culture" began for Americans in the 1950s when more and more people were being prescribed powerful *legal* drugs in the form of stimulants (diet or "pep" pills), sedatives, anti-depressants, and drugs to alleviate anxiety. Those involved in the alternative or underground culture found doctors for the legal drugs and street dealers for the illegal ones. Most of our drug laws today derive from this era, and two government agencies, the Drug Enforcement Agency and the Food and Drug Administration, control their legitimate use (i.e., medicine and research). Drug trafficking became big business by the 1960s, due in large part to the Counterculture's pursuit of pleasure and "altered consciousness." "The War on Drugs" began in earnest when LSD was made illegal in 1966. (Before then, LSD was legally distributed by groups such as Ken Kesey's Merry Pranksters, subjects of Tom Wolfe's *Electric Acid Kool-Aid Test*, excerpted in this chapter.) The U.S. Government spends billions of dollars a year addressing illegal drugs, and debates about how best to combat them range from following the Netherlands policy of decriminalization of marijuana to increased education in schools, more law enforcement, and harsher penalties. Psychoactive drugs have perceptible effects on consciousness, and include narcotics (opium, heroin, and barbiturates), stimulants (amphetamines, "speed," cocaine, and caffeine), and psychedelics (LSD, mescaline, and psilocybin). The Beats preferred speed or pep pills, marijuana, and alcohol, but the hippies are known primarily for their use of LSD.

The readings in this chapter represent a range of drug literature and writings about violence in the 1960s. Hunter S. Thompson's "gonzo journalism" (*Fear and Loathing in Las Vegas*) is a classic work of satire about drugs. The excerpt from Cheryl Pellerin's *Trips* discusses politics and research science behind psychedelic drugs. The making of *Easy Rider* (1969)—the quintessential drug and biker movie—is documented here in screenwriter L. M. Kit Carson's interview with actor and director, and countercultural hero, Dennis Hopper. The theater of the absurd mentality that marked the era at the 1968 Democratic Convention in Chicago is prevalent in underground French writer Jean Genet's "The Members of the Assembly," which compares the American political process to the "Terror" of the French Revolution.

Turning on the World

TIMOTHY LEARY

The Psychedelic Era manifested in the rainbow paintings of Peter Max and in songs like "Lucy in the Sky with Diamonds" was inextricably caught up in the use of drugs. Dr. Timothy Leary, a lecturer at Harvard, became famous when he advocated the widespread use of LSD, a synthetic drug with mind-expanding capabilities, in his crusade for a more peaceful world. Leary wrote widely of the psychedelic experience and included this piece, published in July 1968, in his book High Priest.

———————— ✦ ————————

By the Fall of 1960 there was in existence an informal international network of scientists and scholars who had taken the psychedelic trip and who foresaw the powerful effect that the new alkaloids would have on human culture. The members of this group differed in age and temperament, and had varying ideas about tactics, but the basic vision was common to all—we believed these wondrous plants and drugs could free man's consciousness and bring about a new conception of man, his psychology and philosophy.

There was Albert Hofmann, who had invented LSD, who dreamed the utopian dream, but who was limited by the cautious politics of Sandoz Pharmaceuticals. What a frustrating web his genius had woven for Sandoz. How could a medical-drug house make a profit on a revelation pill?

Sandoz knew they had patented the most powerful mind-changing substance known to man. They expected to make millions when the psychiatric profession learned how to use LSD, and they were continually disappointed to discover that human society didn't want to have its mind changed, didn't want to touch a love-ecstasy potion.

In 1960 a top executive of Sandoz leaned across the conference table and said jokingly to me, LSD isn't a drug at all. It's a food. Let's bottle it in Coca-Cola and let the world have it. And his legal counsel frowned and said that foods still come under the jurisdiction of the Food and Drug Administration.

5   By 1966, when LSD was crowding Vietnam for the headlines, officials of Sandoz Pharmaceuticals were groaning, We wish we had never heard of LSD.

*I do really wish to destroy it! cried Frodo. Or well, to have it
destroyed. I am not made for perilous quests. I wish I had never seen
the Ring! Why did it come to me? Why was I chosen?*

—THE LORD OF THE RINGS

There were the detached philosophers—Aldous Huxley, Father Murray, Gerald Heard, Alan Watts, Harry Murray, Robert Gordon Wasson—who knew that the new drugs were reintroducing the platonic-gnostic vision. These men had read their theological history and understood both the glorious possibility and the angered reaction of the priestly establishment. They were not activists but sage observers.

Then there were the turned-on doctors—psychiatrists who had taken the trip, and came back hoping to fit the new potions into the medical game. Humphrey Osmond, witty, wise, cultured, had invented the name psychedelic and tolerantly wondered how to introduce a harmony-ecstasy drug into an aggressive-puritanical social order. Sidney Cohen, Keith Ditman, Jim Watt, Abram Hoffer and Nick Chewelos hoped to bring about a psychiatric renaissance and a new era of mental health with the new alchemicals.

And there was that strange, intriguing, delightful cosmic magician called Al Meyner, the rum-drinking, swashbuckling, Roman Catholic frontier salesman who promoted uranium ore during the Forties and who took the trip and recognized that LSD was the fissionable material of the mind and who turned on Osmond and Hoffer to the religious mystical meaning of their psychotomimetic drug. Al Meyner set out to turn on the world and flew from country to country with his leather bag full of drugs, claiming to have turned on bishops and obtained *nihil obstat* from Pope John. When the medical society complained that only doctors could give drugs, Meyner bought himself a doctor's degree from a Kentucky diploma mill and swept through northern California turning on scientists and professors and God seekers.

Right from the beginning this dedicated group of ring bearers was rent with a basic disagreement. There were those who said work within the system. Society has assigned the administration of drugs to the medical profession. Any non-doctor who gives or takes drugs is a dope fiend. Play ball with the system. Medicine must be the vanguard of the psychedelic movement. Any non-medical use of psychedelic drugs would create a new marijuana mess and set back research into the new utopia.

The medical point of view made little sense to religious philosophers. Aldous Huxley called the psychedelic experience a gratuitous   10 grace. His vibrant flame-colored wife, Laura, agreed. So, in gentle tones, did Huston Smith and Alan Watts and Gerald Heard.

And so did Allen Ginsberg, who had discovered the Buddha nature of drugs along with other writers.

I had been visited by most of the psychedelic eminences by this time and was under steady pressure to make the Harvard psychedelic research a kosher-medically-approved project. Everyone was aware of the potency of Harvard's name. Timothy, you are the key figure, said Dr. Al Meyner; I'm just old deputy-dog Al at your service. But the message was clear: Keep it respectable and medical.

And now here was Allen Ginsberg, the secretary-general of the world's poets, beatniks, anarchists, socialists, free-sex/love cultists.

November 26, 1960, the sunny Sunday afternoon that we gave Allen Ginsberg the mushrooms, started slowly. First in the cycle of breakfasts at noon were my son Jack Leary and his friend Bobbie, who had spent the night. Bobbie went off to Mass. When I came down I found Donald, an uninvited raccoon hipster-painter from New York, solemnly squatting at the table gnawing at toast and bacon. Frank Barron, who was visiting, and the poets, Allen Ginsberg and Peter and Lafcadio Orlovsky, remained upstairs and we moved around the kitchen with that Sunday-morning hush, not wanting to wake the sleepers. Lafcadio, Peter's brother, was on leave from a hospital.

15   About twelve-thirty the quiet exploded into family noise. Bobbie was back from church where he had excitedly told his father about the party we had given the night before for the Harvard football team and how I had given the boys, Bobbie and Jack, a dollar each for being bartenders.

I toted up the political profit and loss from this development. The Harvard football team rang up a sale. But the boys bartending? Bobbie's father is Irish so that's all right, All okay.

Then wham, the door opened and in flooded Susan Leary, my daughter, with three teen-age girls, through the kitchen, upstairs to get clothes, down to make a picnic lunch, up again for records, out, and then back for the ginger ale.

By now the noise had filtered upstairs and we could hear the late sleepers moving around and the bathroom waters running, and down came Frank Barron, half-awake, to fry codfish cakes for his breakfast. And then, Allen Ginsberg and Peter. Allen hopped around the room with nearsighted crow motions cooking eggs, and Peter sat silent, watching.

Afterward the poets fell to reading The *Times* and Frank
moved upstairs to Susan's room to watch a pro football game on
TV. I told Allen to make himself at home and got beers and went
up to join Frank. Donald the painter had been padding softly
around the house watching with his big, soft creature eyes and
sniffing in corners and at the bookcase and the record cabinets.
He had asked to take mushrooms in the evening and was looking
for records of Indian peyote drum music.

At dusk, Allen Ginsberg, hunched over a teacup, peering out   20
through his black-rimmed glasses, the left lens bisected by a
break, started telling of his experiences with ayahuasco, the fabled visionary vine of the Peruvian jungles. He had followed the
quest of Bill Burroughs, sailing south for new realms of consciousness, looking for the elixir of wisdom. Sitting, sweating
with heat, lonely in a cheap hotel in Lima, holding a wad of ether-
soaked cotton to his nose with his left hand and getting high and
making poetry with his right hand, and then traveling by second-
class bus with Indians up through the Cordillera de los Andes and
then more buses and hitchhiking into the Montaña jungles and
shining rivers, wandering through steaming equatorial forests.
Then the village Pucallpa, and the negotiations to find the
curandero [guide], paying him with *aguardiente*, and the ritual itself, swallowing the bitter stuff, and the nausea and the colors
and the drums beating and sinking down into thingless void, into
the great eye that brings it all together, and the terror of the great
snake coming. The old *curandero*, wrinkled face bending over
him and Allen telling him, *culebra*, and the *curandero* nodding
clinically and blowing a puff of smoke to make the great snake
disappear and it did.

> *The fate of fire depends on wood; as long as there is wood below, the
> fire burns above. It is the same in human life; there is in man like-
> wise a fate that lends power to his life.*
>
> —I CHING

I kept asking Allen questions about the *curandero*. I wanted
to learn the rituals, to find out how other cultures (older and
wiser than ours) had handled the visionary business. I was fasci-
nated by the ritual thing. Ritual is to the science of consciousness what experiment is to external science. I was convinced
that none of our American rituals fit the mushroom experience.
Not the cocktail party. Not the psychiatrist. Not the teacher-

minister role. I was impressed by what Allen said about his own fear and sickness whenever he took drugs and about the solace and comforting strength of the *curandero*, about how good it was to have someone there who knew, who had been to those far regions of the mind and could tell you by a look, by a touch, by a puff of smoke that it was all right, go ahead, explore the strange world, it's all right, you'll come back, it's all right, I'm here back on familiar old human earth when you need me, to bring you back.

Allen was going to take the mushrooms later that night and he was shaping me up to help him. Allen was weaving a word spell, dark eyes gleaming through the glasses, chain-smoking, moving his hands, intense, chanting trance poetry. Frank Barron was in the study now, and with him Lafcadio Orlovsky.

A car came up the driveway and in a minute the door opened, and Donald, furry and moist, ambled in. He had brought his friend, an anthropology student from Harvard, to be with him when he tripped. Donald asked if his friend could be there during the mushroom session. I liked the idea of having a friend present for the mushrooms, someone to whom you could turn at those moments when you needed support, so I said, Sure, but he couldn't take the pills because he was a university student. Everyone was warning us to keep our research away from Harvard to avoid complications with the university health bureau and to avoid the rumors. He wasn't hungry so I mixed him a drink and then I got the little round bottle and pulled out the cotton topping and gave Donald 30 mg. and Allen Ginsberg 36.

Allen started bustling around getting his cave ready. I brought Susan's record player up to his room and he took some Beethoven and Wagner from the study and he turned out the lights so that there was just a glow in the room. I told him we'd be checking back every fifteen minutes and he should tell me if he wanted anything.

By the time I got downstairs Donald was already high, strolling around the house on dainty raccoon feet with his hands clasped behind his back, thinking and digging deep things. I stayed in the study writing letters, reading The *Times*. I had forgotten about the anthropology student. He was waiting in the kitchen.

After about thirty minutes I found Donald in the hallway. He called me over earnestly and began talking about the artificiality of civilization. He was thinking hard about basic issues and it was obvious what was going on with him—clearing his mind of abstractions, trying to get back behind the words and concepts.

*And if he succeeds in assigning the right place to life and to fate,
thus bringing the two into harmony, he puts his fate on a firm footing. These words contain hints about the fostering of life as handed
on by oral tradition in the secret teachings of Chinese yoga.*

—I Cʜɪɴɢ

The anthropology student was standing by, watching curiously, and Donald asked if he minded leaving so that he could talk
to me privately. Anthro went back to the kitchen and Donald continued talking about the falseness of houses and machines and
deploring the way man cut himself off from the vital stuff with his
engines and structures. I was trying to be polite and be a good
curandero and support him and tell him, great boy, stay with it
and work it out.

Susan came back from her friends' about this time and went
upstairs to her homework, and I followed her up to check on
Allen. He was lying on top of the blanket. His glasses were off and
his black eyes, pupils completely dilated, looked up at me. Looking down into them they seemed like two deep, black, wet wells
and you could look down them way through the man Ginsberg to
something human beyond. The eye is such a defenseless, naïve,
trusting thing. Pʀᴏғᴇssᴏʀ Lᴇᴀʀʏ ᴄᴀᴍᴇ ɪɴᴛᴏ ᴍʏ ʀᴏᴏᴍ, ʟᴏᴏᴋᴇᴅ ɪɴ ᴍʏ ᴇʏᴇs,
ᴀɴᴅ sᴀɪᴅ I ᴡᴀs ᴀ ɢʀᴇᴀᴛ ᴍᴀɴ. Tʜᴀᴛ ᴅᴇᴛᴇʀᴍɪɴᴇᴅ ᴍᴇ ᴛᴏ ᴍᴀᴋᴇ ᴀɴ ᴇғғᴏʀᴛ ᴛᴏ ʟɪᴠᴇ
ʜᴇʀᴇ ᴀɴᴅ ɴᴏᴡ. —Allen Ginsberg

Allen was scared and unhappy and sick. And still he was lying
there voluntarily, patiently searching, pushing himself into panics
and fears, into nausea, trying to learn something, trying to find
meaning. Shamelessly weak and shamelessly human and greatly
classic. Peter was lying next to him, eyes closed, sleeping or listening to the record. I ɢᴏᴛ ɴᴀᴜsᴇᴏᴜs sᴏᴏɴ ᴀғᴛᴇʀ—sᴀᴛ ᴜᴘ ɪɴ ʙᴇᴅ ɴᴀᴋᴇᴅ
ᴀɴᴅ sᴡᴀʟʟᴏᴡᴇᴅ ᴅᴏᴡɴ ᴛʜᴇ ᴠᴏᴍɪᴛ ᴛʜᴀᴛ ʙᴇsɪᴇɢᴇᴅ ғʀᴏᴍ ᴍʏ sᴛᴏᴍᴀᴄʜ ᴀs ɪғ ᴀɴ ɪɴ-
ᴅᴇᴘᴇɴᴅᴇɴᴛ ʙᴇɪɴɢ ᴅᴏᴡɴ ᴛʜᴇʀᴇ ᴡᴀs ʀᴇʙᴇʟʟɪɴɢ ᴀᴛ ʙᴇɪɴɢ ᴅʀᴀɢɢᴇᴅ ɪɴᴛᴏ ᴇxɪs-
ᴛᴇɴᴄᴇ.

On the way downstairs I checked Susan's room. She was   30
curled up on the carpet, with her books scattered around her and
reading in the shadows. I scolded her about ruining her eyes and
flicked on the two wall bulbs. Downstairs Frank was still at the
study desk. Anthro was wandering in the living room and told me
that Donald had gone outside. The rule we had set up was that no
one would leave the house and the idea of Donald padding down
Beacon Street in a mystic state chilled me. Out on the front porch I
turned on the two rows of spotlights that flooded the long winding

stone stairs and started down, shielding my eyes and shouting Donald. Halfway down I heard him answering back and saw him standing under an oak tree on the lower lawn. I asked him how he was, but he didn't talk, just stood there looking wise and deep. He was barefoot and higher than Piccard's balloon. I want to talk to you, but first you must take off your shoes. Okay, why not? I sat down to unlace my shoes and he squatted alongside and told about how the machines complicate our lives and how cold and hot were abstractions and how we didn't really need houses and shoes and clothes because it was just our concepts that made us think we needed these things. I agreed with him and followed what his mind was doing, suspending for a moment the clutch of the abstract but at the same time shivering from the November wind and wanting to get back behind the warm glow of the windows.

The young anthropology student was standing in the hallway. I told him that Donald was doing fine, great mystical stuff, philosophizing without concepts. He looked puzzled. He didn't want a drink or food. I walked upstairs and found the door to Allen's room closed. I waited for a while, not knowing what to do and then knocked softly and said softly, Allen I'm here now and will be back in a few minutes. *Paradise Lost*, A BOOK I'D NEVER UNDERSTOOD BEFORE—WHY MILTON SIDED WITH LUCIFER THE REBEL IN HEAVEN.

I GOT UP OUT OF BED AND WALKED DOWNSTAIRS NAKED, ORLOVSKY FOLLOWING ME, CURIOUS WHAT I WOULD DO AND WILLING TO GO ALONG IN CASE I DID ANYTHING INTERESTINGLY EXTRAVAGANT. URGING ME ON IN FACT, THANK GOD.

Susan was sitting cross-legged on her bed brushing her hair when there came a patter of bare feet on the hallway carpet. I got to the door just in time to see naked buttocks disappearing down the stairway. It was Peter. I was grinning when I went back to see Susan. Peter is running around without any clothes on. Susan picked up her paraphernalia—curlers, brush, pins, and trotted up to the third floor. I headed downstairs.

When I got to the study Frank was leaning back in his chair behind the desk, grinning quizzically. In front of the desk looking like medieval hermits were Allen and Peter, both stark naked. I WENT IN AMONG THE PSYCHOLOGISTS IN STUDY AND SAW THEY TOO WERE WAITING FOR SOMETHING VAST TO HAPPEN ONLY IT REQUIRED SOMEONE AND THE MOMENT TO MAKE IT HAPPEN—ACTION, REVOLUTION. No, Allen had on his glasses and as I came in he peered out at me and raised his finger in the air. Hey, Allen, what goes on? Allen had a holy gleam in his eye and he waved his finger. I'm the Messiah. I've come down to preach love to the world. We're going to walk through the streets and teach people to stop hating. I DECIDED I MIGHT AS WELL BE THE ONE TO DO SO—PRO-NOUNCED MY NAKEDNESS AS THE FIRST ACT OF REVOLUTION AGAINST THE DESTROY-ERS OF THE HUMAN IMAGE.

Well, Allen, that sounds like a pretty good idea. Listen, said   35
Allen, do you believe that I'm the Messiah. THE NAKED BODY BEING THE HIDDEN SIGN. Look, I can prove it. I'm going to cure your hearing. Take off your hearing machine. Your ears are cured. Come on, take it off, you don't need it. AND GRABBED THE TELEPHONE TO COMMUNI-CATE MY DECISION—WANTED TO HOOK UP KHRUSHCHEV, KEROUAC, BURROUGHS, IKE, KENNEDY, MAO TSE-TUNG, MAILER, ETC.

Frank was still smiling. Peter was standing by, watching seri-ously. The hearing aid was dumped on the desk. That's right. And now your glasses, I'll heal your vision too. The glasses were laid on the desk too. ALL IN ONE TELEPHONE LINE AND GET THEM ALL TO COME IM-MEDIATELY TO HARVARD TO HAVE SPECTRAL CONFERENCE OVER THE FUTURE OF THE UNIVERSE.

Allen was peering around with approval at his healing. But Allen, one thing. What? Your glasses. You're still wearing them. Why don't you cure your own vision. Allen looked surprised. Yes, you're right. I will. He took off his glasses and laid them on the desk.

Now Allen was a blind Messiah squinting around to find his followers. Come on. We're going down to the city streets to tell the people about peace and love. And then we'll get lots of great people onto a big telephone network to settle all this warfare bit.

Fine, said Frank, but why not do the telephone bit first, right here in the house. Frank was heading off the pilgrimage down the avenue naked.

Who we gonna call, said Peter. Well, we'll call Kerouac on   40
Long Island, and Kennedy and Khrushchev and Bill Burroughs in Paris and Norman Mailer in the psycho ward in Bellevue. We'll get them all hooked up in a big cosmic electronic love talk. War is just a hang-up. We'll get the love-thing flowing on the electric Bell Telephone network. Who we gonna call first, said Peter. Let's start with Khrushchev, said Allen.

Look, why don't we start with Kerouac on Long Island. In the meantime, let's pull the curtains, said Frank. There's enough going on in here so I don't care about looking outside. Allen picked up the white telephone and dialed Operator. The two thin figures leaned forward wrapped up in a holy fervor trying to spread peace. The dear noble innocent helplessness of the naked body. They looked as though they had stepped out of a quattrocento canvas,

apostles, martyrs, dear fanatic holy men. Allen said, Hello, operator, this is God, I want to talk to Kerouac. To whom do I want to
talk? Kerouac. What's my name? This is God. G-O-D. Okay. We'll
try Capitol 7-0563. Where? Northport, Long Island. There was a
pause. We were all listening hard. Oh. Yes. That's right. That's the
number of the house where I was born. Look, operator, I'll have to
go upstairs to get the number. Then I'll call back.

Allen hung up the receiver. What was all that about, Allen?
Well, the operator asked me my name and I said I was God and I
wanted to speak to Kerouac and she said, I'll try to do my best, sir,
but you'll have to give me his number and then I gave her the
number of my mother's house. I've got Kerouac's number upstairs
in my book. Just a minute and I'll get it.

Back at the phone, Allen was shouting to Jack. He wanted Jack
to come up to Cambridge and then he wanted Jack's mother to
come too. Jack had a lot to say because Allen held the phone, listening for long spaces. Frank was still sitting behind the desk smiling.
Donald and the anthro student were standing in the hallway looking in curiously. I walked over to explain. Allen says he is the Messiah and he's calling Kerouac to start a peace and love movement.
Donald wasn't interested. He went on telling me about the foolish-
ness of believing in hot and cold. It occurred to me that Allen and
Peter were proving his point. The phone call continued and finally I
walked back in and said, Hey, Allen, for the cost of this phone call
we could pay his way up here by plane. Allen shot an apologetic
look and then I heard him telling Jack, Okay, Jack, I have to go now,
but you've got to take the mushrooms and let's settle this quarrel
between Kennedy and Khrushchev. BUT NEEDED MY GLASSES—THOUGH
HAD YELLED AT LEARY THAT HE DIDN'T NEED HIS EARPIECE TO HEAR THE REAL VI-
BRATIONS OF THE COSMOS. HE WENT ALONG WITH ME AGREEABLY.

Allen and Peter were sitting on the big couch in the living
room and Allen was telling us about his visions, cosmic electronic
networks, and how much it meant to him that I told him he was a
great man and how this mushroom episode had opened the door
to women and heterosexuality and how he could see new wom-
anly body visions and family life ahead. BUT THEN I BEGAN BREATHING
AND WANTING TO LIE DOWN AND REST. Peter's hand was moving back and
forth on Allen's shoulder. It was the first time that Allen had stood
up to Jack and he was sorry about the phone bill but wasn't it too
bad that Khrushchev and Kennedy couldn't have been on the line
and, hey, what about Norman Mailer in that psychiatric ward in
Bellevue shouldn't we call him.

I don't think they'd let a call go through to him, Allen. Well, it   45
all depends on how we come on. I don't think coming on as Allen
Ginsberg would help in that league. I don't think coming on as
the Messiah would either. Well, you could come on as big psychologists and make big demanding noises about the patient. It
was finally decided that it was too much trouble.

Still *curandero*, I asked if they wanted anything to eat or
drink. Well, how about some hot milk. IF I ATE OR SHIT AGAIN I WOULD
TURN BACK TO MERE NON-MESSIAH HUMAN. Allen and Peter went upstairs
to put on robes and I put some cold milk in a pan and turned on
the stove. Donald was still moving around softly with his hands
behind his back. Thinking. Watching. He was too deep and Buddha for us to swing with and I later realized that I hadn't been a
very attentive *curandero* for him and that there was a gulf between Allen and him never closed and that the geographic
arrangement was too scattered to make a close loving session. Of
course, both of them were old drug hands and ready to go off on
their own private journeys and both wanted to make something
deep and their own.

Anthro's role in all of this was never clear. He stood in the
hallway watching curiously but for the most part we ignored him,
treated him as an object just there but not involved and that, of
course, was a mistake. Any time you treat someone as an object
rest assured he'll do the same and that was the way that score was
going to be tallied.

We ended up with a great scene in the kitchen. I bustled
around pouring the hot milk into cups, and the poets sat around
the table looking like Giotto martyrs in checkered robes. Lafcadio
came down and we got him some food and he nodded yes when I
asked him about ice cream and Allen started to talk about his visions and about the drug scene in New York and, becoming eloquent, wound up preaching with passion about the junkies, help-
less, hooked, lost, thin, confused creatures, sick and the police
and the informers. I SAW THE BEST MINDS OF MY GENERATION DESTROYED BY
MADNESS, STARVING HYSTERICAL NAKED, DRAGGING THEMSELVES THROUGH THE
NEGRO STREETS AT DAWN LOOKING FOR AN ANGRY FIX. And then we started
planning the psychedelic revolution. Allen wanted everyone to
have the mushrooms. Who has the right to keep them from someone else? And there should be freedom for all sorts of rituals, too.
The doctors could have them and there should be *curanderos*, and
all sorts of good new holy rituals that could be developed and
ministers have to be involved. Although the church is naturally

and automatically opposed to mushroom visions, still the experience is basically religious and some ministers would see it and start using them. But with all these groups and organizations and new rituals, there still had to be room for the single, lone, unattached, non-groupy individual to take the mushrooms and go off and follow his own rituals—brood big cosmic thoughts by the sea or roam through the streets of New York, high and restless, thinking poetry, and writers and poets and artists to work out whatever they were working out.

Allen Ginsberg hunched over the kitchen table, shabby robe hiding his thin white nakedness, cosmic politician. Give them the mystic vision. They'll see it's good and honest and they'll say so publicly and then no one from the police or the narcotics bureau can put them down. And you're the perfect persons to do it. Big serious scientist professors from Harvard. That's right. I can't do it. I'm too easy to put down. Crazy beatnik poet. Let me get my address book. I've got lots of connections in New York and we'll go right down the list and turn them all on.

50   Now Allen Ginsberg, stooping over the kitchen table peering at his address book. There's Robert Lowell and Muriel Rukeyser, and LeRoi Jones. And Dizzy Gillespie. And the painters. And the publishers. He was chanting out names of the famous and the talented. He was completely serious, dedicated, wound up in the crusade. I'm NEARSIGHTED AND PSYCHOPATHIC ANYWAY. AMERICA, I'm PUTTING MY QUEER SHOULDER TO THE WHEEL.

And so Allen spun out the cosmic campaign. He was to line up influentials and each weekend I would come down to New York and we'd run mushroom sessions. This fit our Harvard research plans perfectly. Our aim there was to learn how people reacted, to test the limits of the drug, to get creative and thoughtful people to take them and tell us what they saw and what we should do with the mushrooms. Allen's political plan was appealing, too. I had seen enough and read enough in Spanish of the anti-vision crowd, the power-holders with guns, and the bigger and better men we got on our team the stronger our position. And then, too, the big-name bit was intriguing. Meeting and sharing visions with the famous.

It was around midnight. Donald still seemed high and would walk in and out of the room, silently, hands behind his back, Talmudic raccoon, studying the kitchen crowd seriously, and then padding out. The anthropology student had joined us around the table. We had given him something to drink and he was listening to the conversation and saying nothing. He made some comment about schedules back to Cambridge and it was time for him to make the last train, so I drove him down to the station. He asked some questions about the scientific meaning of the mushroom research and it was clear that he didn't understand what had happened and what we were doing. There wasn't time to explain and I felt badly that he had been dragged into a strange situation. We had made the rule that people could bring their friends when they took the mushrooms and this seemed like a good idea for the person taking the mushrooms but it was just beginning to dawn on me that the problem never was with the person taking the drug but rather the people who didn't. Like Brother Toriblo, the Spanish monk, who talked about cruelty and drunkenness caused by the Sacred Mushrooms. It's okay to bring a friend, but he should take the mushrooms with you. And poor Anthro, it turned out, wasn't even a friend of Donald's and as it turned out didn't like him and was clearly bewildered by and critical of what he had seen and heard and the nakedness of the poets. His train was about due and I was too preoccupied by what Allen had been saying to feel like explaining to Anthro. The uneasy feeling persisted and I suggested that he not tell people about the mystic visions and the naked crusaders because this might be misunderstood and he said he wouldn't talk about it and we shook hands and he left.

That was Sunday night. By Monday afternoon the rumors were spreading around Harvard Yard.

Beatniks. Orgies. Naked poets. Junkies. Homosexuality. Drug parties. Tried to lure a decent naïve graduate student into sin. Wild parties masquerading as research. Queers. Beards. Criminal types.

The chairman of my department called me. What the hell is   55 going on, Tim? Two graduate students have come to me indignant—demanding that your work be stopped.

I laughed. I'll send you the reports from the session as soon as they are typed. It was a good session. God would approve. We're learning a lot.

The disapproving gaze of the establishment was on us. You should
fear the wary eyes of the servants of Sauron were the words of
Elrond. I do not doubt that news . . . has already reached him, and
he will be filled with wrath.

—The Lord of The Rings

In the months that followed we began to see ourselves as unwitting agents of a social process that was far too powerful for us to control or more than dimly understand. A historical movement that would inevitably change man at the very center of his nature, his consciousness.

We did sense that we were not alone. The quest for internal freedom, for the elixir of life, for the draught of immortal revelation was not new. We were part of an ancient and honorable fellowship which had pursued this journey since the dawn of recorded history. We began to read the accounts of earlier trippers—Dante, Hesse, René Daumal, Tolkien, Homer, Blake, George Fox, Swedenborg, Bosch, and the explorers from the Orient—tantrics, Sufis, Bauls, Gnostics, hermetics, Sivaites, sadhus.

From this moment on my days as a respectable establishment scientist were numbered. I just couldn't see the new society given birth by medical hands, or psychedelic sacraments as psychiatric tools.

60   From this evening on my energies were offered to the ancient underground society of alchemists, artists, mystics, alienated visionaries, dropouts and the disenchanted young, the sons arising.

from *The Electric Kool-Aid Acid Test*
Tom Wolfe

"Contemporary novelists don't want to see the world, they want to suck their thumbs," so says Tom Wolfe, American satirist and author of *The Right Stuff* (about American astronauts), *Radical Chic and Mau-Mauing the Flak Catchers* (fashion), *The Kandy-Kolored Tangerine-Flake Streamline Baby* (custom cars), and *the* absolutely necessary, required reading for all "sixties" courses, *The Electric Kool-Aid Acid Test* (1968). His novels *In Our Time, Bonfire of the Vanities,* and others mix fiction with the kind of "new journalism" his non-fiction works pioneered, much to the consternation of Norman Mailer and other rivals in the literary world of the times. *The Electric Kool-Aid Acid Test,* from which this excerpt is taken, covers the misadventures novelist, family man, and countercultural *bon vivant* Ken Kesey and his group of Merry Pranksters encounter on their magic bus as they travel around following Timothy Leary's admonition to "turn [everyone they encounter] on" to LSD, free love, the nomadic lifestyle and communal bus living, among other great notions. Beat legend and Jack Kerouac's alter ego Neal Cassady is the bus driver. Need we say more?

——————————— ✦ ———————————

That's good thinking there, Cool Breeze. Cool Breeze is a kid with three or four days' beard sitting next to me on the stamped metal bottom of the open back part of a pickup truck. Bouncing along. Dipping and rising and rolling on these rotten springs like a boat. Out the back of the truck the city of San Francisco is bouncing down the hill, all those endless staggers of bay windows, slums with a view, bouncing and streaming down the hill. One after another, electric signs with neon martini glasses lit up on them, the San Francisco symbol of "bar"—thousands of neon-magenta martini glasses bouncing and streaming down the hill, and beneath them hundreds, thousands of people wheeling around to look at this freaking crazed truck we're in, their white faces erupting from their lapels like marshmallows—streaming and bouncing down the hill—and God knows they've got plenty to look at.

That's why it strikes me as funny when Cool Breeze says very seriously over the whole roar of the thing, "I don't know—when Kesey gets out I don't know if I can come around the Warehouse."

"Why not?"

"Well, like the cops are going to be coming around like all feisty, and I'm on probation, so I don't know."

Well, that's good thinking there, Cool Breeze. Don't rouse the   5
bastids. Lie low—like right now. Right now Cool Breeze is so terrified of the law he is sitting up in plain view of thousands of already startled citizens wearing some kind of Seven Dwarfs Black Forest gnome's hat covered in feathers and fluorescent colors. Kneeling in the truck, facing us, also in plain view, is a half-Ottawa Indian girl named Lois Jennings, with her head thrown back and a radiant look on her face. Also a blazing silver disk in the middle of her forehead alternately exploding with light when the sun hits it or sending off rainbows from the defraction lines in it. And, oh yeah, there's a long-barreled Colt .45 revolver in her hand, only nobody on the street can tell it's a cap pistol as she pegs away, kheeew, kheeew, at the erupting marshmallow faces like Debra Paget in . . . in. . . .

—Kesey's coming out of jail!

Two more things they are looking at out there are a sign on the rear bumper reading "Custer Died for Your Sins" and, at the wheel, Lois's enamorado Stewart Brand, a thin blond guy with a blazing disk on his forehead too, and a whole necktie made of Indian beads. No shirt, however, just an Indian bead necktie on bare skin and a white butcher's coat with medals from the King of Sweden on it. Here comes a beautiful one, attaché case and all, the day-is-done resentful look and the . . . shoes—how they shine!—and what the hell are these beatnik ninnies—and Lois plugs him in the old marshmallow and he goes streaming and bouncing down the hill. . . .

And the truck heaves and billows, blazing silver red and Day-Glo, and I doubt seriously, Cool Breeze, that there is a single cop in all of San Francisco today who does not know that this crazed vehicle is a guerrilla patrol from the dread LSD.

The cops now know the whole scene, even the costumes, the jesuschrist strung-out hair, Indian beads, Indian headbands, donkey beads, temple bells, amulets, mandalas, god's-eyes, fluorescent vests, unicorn horns, Errol Flynn dueling shirts—but they still don't know about the shoes. The heads have a thing about shoes. The worst are shiny black shoes with shoelaces in them. The hierarchy ascends from there, although practically all lowcut shoes are unhip, from there on up to the boots the heads like, light, fanciful boots, English boots of the mod variety, if that is all they can get, but better something like hand-tooled Mexican boots with Caliente Dude Triple A toes on them. So see the FBI—black—shiny—laced up—FBI shoes—when the FBI finally grabbed Kesey—

10   There is another girl in the back of the truck, a dark little girl with thick black hair, called Black Maria. She looks Mexican, but she says to me in straight soft Californian:

"When is your birthday?"

"March 2."

"Pisces," she says. And then: "I would never take you for a Pisces."

"Why?"

15   "You seem too . . . *solid* for a Pisces."

But I know she means stolid. I am beginning to feel stolid. Back in New York City, Black Maria, I tell you, I am even known as something of a dude. But somehow a blue silk blazer and a big tie with clowns on it and . . . a . . . pair of shiny lowcut black shoes don't set them all to doing the Varsity Rag in the head world in San Francisco. Lois picks off the marshmallows one by one; Cool Breeze ascends into the innards of his gnome's hat; Black Maria, a Scorpio herself, rummages through the Zodiac; Stewart Brand winds it through the streets; paillettes explode—and this is nothing special, just the usual, the usual in the head world of San Francisco, just a little routine messing up the minds of the citizenry en route, nothing more than psyche food for beautiful people, while giving some guy from New York a lift to the Warehouse to wait for the Chief, Ken Kesey, who is getting out of jail.

About all I knew about Kesey at that point was that he was a highly regarded 31-year-old novelist and in a lot of trouble over drugs. He wrote *One Flew Over the Cuckoo's Nest* (1962), which was made into a play in 1963, and *Sometimes a Great Notion* (1964). He was always included with Philip Roth and Joseph Heller and Bruce Jay Friedman and a couple of others as one of the young novelists who might go all the way. Then he was arrested twice for possession of marijuana, in April of 1965 and January of 1966, and fled to Mexico rather than risk a stiff sentence. It looked like as much as five years, as a second offender. One day I happened to get hold of some letters Kesey wrote from Mexico to his friend Larry McMurtry, who wrote *Horseman, Pass By*, from which the movie *Hud* was made. They were wild and ironic, written like a cross between William Burroughs and George Ade, telling of hideouts, disguises, paranoia, fleeing from cops, smoking joints and seeking satori in the Rat lands of Mexico. There was one passage written George Ade-fashion in the third person as a parody of what the straight world back there in the U.S.A. must think of him now:

"In short, this young, handsome, successful, happily-married-three-lovely-children father, was a fear-crazed dope fiend in flight to avoid prosecution on three felonies and god knows how many misdemeanors and seeking at the same time to sculpt a new satori from an old surf—in even shorter, mad as a hatter.

"Once an athlete so valued he had been given the job of calling signals from the line and risen into contention for the nationwide amateur wrestling crown, now he didn't know if he could do a dozen pushups. Once possessor of a phenomenal bank account and money waving from every hand, now it was all his poor wife could do to scrape together eight dollars to send as getaway money to Mexico. But a few years previous he had been listed in *Who's Who* and asked to speak at such auspicious gatherings as the Wellesley Club in Dah-la and now they wouldn't even allow him to speak at a VDC [Vietnam Day Committee] gathering. What was it that had brought a man so high of promise to so low a state in so short a time? Well, the answer can be found in just one short word, my friends, in just one all-well-used syllable:

"Dope!

"And while it may be claimed by some of the addled advocates of these chemicals that our hero is known to have indulged in drugs before his literary success, we must point out that there was evidence of his literary prowess well before the advent of the so-called psychedelic into his life but no evidence at all of any of the lunatic thinking that we find thereafter!"

20   To which he added:

> "(oh yeah, the wind hums
> time ago—time ago—
> the rafter drums and the walls see
> . . . and there's a door to that bird
> in the sa-a-a-apling sky
> time ago by—
> Oh yeah the surf giggles
> time ago time ago
> of under things killed when
> bad was banished and all the
> doors to the birds vanished
> time ago then.)"

I got the idea of going to Mexico and trying to find him and do a story on Young Novelist Real-Life Fugitive. I started asking around about where he might be in Mexico. Everybody on the hip circuit in New York knew for certain. It seemed to be the thing to know this summer. He is in Puerto Vallarta. He is in Ajijic. He is in Oaxaca. He is in San Miguel de Allende. He is in Paraguay. He just took a steamboat from Mexico to Canada. And everyone knew for certain.

I was still asking around when Kesey sneaked back into the U.S. in October and the FBI caught up with him on the Bayshore freeway south of San Francisco. An agent chased him down an embankment and caught him and Kesey was in jail. So I flew to San Francisco. I went straight to the San Mateo County jail in Redwood City and the scene in the waiting room there was more like the stage door at the Music Box Theatre. It was full of cheerful anticipation. There was a young psychologist there, Jim Fadiman—Clifton Fadiman's nephew, it turned out— and Jim and his wife Dorothy were happily stuffing three I Ching coins into the spine of some interminable dense volume of Oriental mysticism and they asked me to get word to Kesey that the coins were in there. There was also a little roundfaced brunette named Marilyn who told me she used to be a teenie grouper hanging out with a rock 'n' roll group called The Wild Flowers but now she was mainly with Bobby Petersen. Bobby Petersen was not a musician. He was a saint, as nearly as I could make out. He was in jail down in Santa Cruz trying to fight a marijuana charge on the grounds that marijuana was a religious sacrament for him. I didn't figure out exactly why she was up here in the San Mateo jail waiting room instead except that it was like a stage door, as I said, with Kesey as the star who was still inside.

There was a slight hassle with the jailers over whether I was to get into see him or not. The cops had nothing particularly to gain by letting me in. A reporter from New York—that just meant more publicity for this glorified beatnik. That was the line on Kesey. He was a glorified beatnik up on two dope charges, and why make a hero out of him. I must say that California has smooth cops. They all seem to be young, tall, crewcut, blond, with bleached blue eyes, like they just stepped out of a cigarette ad. Their jailhouses don't look like jailhouses, at least not the parts the public sees. They are all blond wood, fluorescent lights and filing-cabinet-tan metal, like the Civil Service exam room in a new Post Office building. The cops all speak soft Californian and are neat and correct as an ice cube. By the book; so they finally let me in to see Kesey during visiting hours. I had ten minutes. I waved goodbye to Marilyn and the Fadimans and the jolly scene downstairs and they took me up to the third floor in an elevator.

The elevator opened right onto a small visiting room. It was weird. Here was a lineup of four or five cubicles, like the isolation booths on the old TV quiz shows, each one with a thick plate-glass window and behind each window a prisoner in a prison blue workshirt. They were lined up like haddocks on ice. Outside each window ran a counter with a telephone on it. That's what you speak over in here. A couple of visitors are already hunched over the things. Then I pick out Kesey.

He is standing up with his arms folded over his chest and his   25
eyes focused in the distance, i.e., the wall. He has thick wrists and big forearms, and the way he has them folded makes them look gigantic. He looks taller than he really is, maybe because of his neck. He has a big neck with a pair of sternocleido-mastoid muscles that rise up out of the prison workshirt like a couple of dock ropes. His

jaw and chin are massive. He looks a little like Paul Newman, except that he is more muscular, has thicker skin, and he has tight blond curls boiling up around his head. His hair is almost gone on top, but somehow that goes all right with his big neck and general wrestler's build. Then he smiles slightly. It's curious, he doesn't have a line in his face. After all the chasing and hassling—he looks like the third week at the Sauna Spa; serene, as I say.

Then I pick up my telephone and he picks up his—and this is truly Modern Times. We are all of twenty-four inches apart, but there is a piece of plate glass as thick as a telephone directory between us. We might as well be in different continents, talking over Videophone. The telephones are very crackly and lo-fi, especially considering that they have a world of two feet to span. Naturally it was assumed that the police monitored every conversation. I wanted to ask him all about his fugitive days in Mexico. That was still the name of my story, Young Novelist Fugitive Eight Months in Mexico. But he could hardly go into that on this weird hookup, and besides, I had only ten minutes. I take out a notebook and start asking him—anything. There had been a piece in the paper about his saying it was time for the psychedelic movement to go "beyond acid," so I asked him about that. Then I started scribbling like mad, in shorthand, in the notebook. I could see his lips moving two feet away. His voice crackled over the telephone like it was coming from Brisbane. The whole thing was crazy. It seemed like calisthenics we were going through.

"It's my idea," he said, "that it's time to graduate from what has been going on, to something else. The psychedelic wave was happening six or eight months ago when I went to Mexico. It's been growing since then, but it hasn't been moving. I saw the same stuff when I got back as when I left. It was just bigger, that was all—" He talks in a soft voice with a country accent, almost a pure country accent, only crackling and rasping and cheese-grated over the two-foot hookup, talking about—

"—there's been no creativity," he is saying, "and I think my value has been to help create the next step. I don't think there will be any movement off the drug scene until there is something else to move to—"

—all in a plain country accent about something—well, to be frank, I didn't know what in the hell it was all about. Sometimes he spoke cryptically, in aphorisms. I told him I had heard he didn't intend to do any more writing. Why? I said.

30   "I'd rather be a lightning rod than a seismograph," he said.

He talked about something called the Acid Test and forms of expression in which there would be no separation between himself and the audience. It would be all one experience, with all the senses opened wide, words, music, lights, sounds, touch—*lightning*.

"You mean on the order of what Andy Warhol is doing?" I said.

. . . pause. "No offense," says Kesey, "but New York is about two years behind."

He said it very patiently, with a kind of country politeness, as if . . . I don't want to be rude to you fellows from the City, but there's been things going on out here that you would never guess in your wildest million years, old buddy. . . .

The ten minutes were up and I was out of there. I had gotten   35 nothing, except my first brush with a strange phenomenon, that strange up-country charisma, the Kesey presence. I had nothing to do but kill time and hope Kesey would get out on bail somehow and I could talk to him and get the details on Novelist Fugitive in Mexico. This seemed like a very long shot at this time, because Kesey had two marijuana charges against him and had already jumped the country once.

So I rented a car and started making the rounds in San Francisco. Somehow my strongest memories of San Francisco are of me in a terrific rented sedan roaring up hills or down hills, sliding on and off the cable-car tracks. Slipping and sliding down to North Beach, the fabled North Beach, the old fatherland bohemia of the West Coast, always full of Big Daddy So-and-so and Costee Plusee and long-haired little Wasp and Jewish buds balling spade cats—and now North Beach was dying. North Beach was nothing but tit shows. In the famous Beat Generation HQ, the City Lights bookstore, Shig Murao, the Nipponese panjandrum of the place, sat glowering with his beard hanging down like those strands of furze and fern in an architect's drawing, drooping over the volumes of Kahlil Gibran by the cash register while Professional Budget Finance Dentists here for the convention browsed in search of the beatniks between tit shows. Everything was The Topless on North Beach, strippers with their breasts enlarged with injections of silicone emulsion.

The action—meaning the hip cliques that set the original tone—the action was all over in Haight-Ashbury. Pretty soon all the bellwethers of a successful bohemia would be there, too, the ears going through, bumper to bumper, with everybody rubbernecking, the tour buses going through "and here. . . . Home of the

Hippies . . . there's one there," and the queers and spade hookers and bookstores and boutiques. Everything was Haight-Ashbury and the acid heads.

But it was not just North Beach that was dying. The whole old-style hip life—jazz, coffee houses, civil rights, invite a spade for dinner, Vietnam—it was all suddenly dying, I found out, even among the students at Berkeley, across the bay from San Francisco, which had been the heart of the "student-rebellion" and so forth. It had even gotten to the point that Negroes were no longer in the hip scene, not even as totem figures. It was unbelievable. *Spades*, the very soul figures of Hip, of jazz, of the hip vocabulary itself, man and like and dig and baby and scarf and split and later and so fine, of civil rights and graduating from Reed College and living on North Beach, down Mason, and balling spade cats—all that good elaborate petting and patting and pouring soul all over the spades—all over, finished, incredibly.

So I was starting to get the trend of all this heaving and convulsing in the bohemian world of San Francisco. Meantime, miraculously, Kesey's three young lawyers, Pat Hallinan, Brian Rohan, and Paul Robertson, were about to get Kesey out on bail. They assured the judges, in San Mateo and San Francisco, that Mr. Kesey had a very public-spirited project in mind. He had returned from exile for the express purpose of calling a huge meeting of heads and hippies at Winterland Arena in San Francisco in order to tell The Youth to stop taking LSD because it was dangerous and might french fry their brains, etc. It was going to be an "acid graduation" ceremony. They should go "beyond acid." That was what Kesey had been talking to me about, I guess. At the same time, six of Kesey's close friends in the Palo Alto area had put their homes up as security for a total of $35,000 bail with the San Mateo County court. I suppose the courts figured they had Kesey either way. If he jumped bail now, it would be such a dirty trick on his friends, costing them their homes, that Kesey would be discredited as a drug apostle or anything else. If he didn't, he would be obliged to give his talk to The Youth—and so much the better. In any case, Kesey was coming out.

40   This script was not very popular in Haight-Ashbury, however. I soon found out that the head life in San Francisco was already such a big thing that Kesey's return and his acid graduation plan were causing the heads' first big political crisis. All eyes were on Kesey and his group, known as the Merry Pranksters. Thousands of kids were moving into San Francisco for a life based on LSD

and the psychedelic thing. *Thing* was the major abstract word in Haight-Ashbury. It could mean *any*thing, isms, life styles, habits, leanings, causes, sexual organs; *thing* and *freak; freak* referred to styles and obsessions, as in "Stewart Brand is an Indian freak" or "the zodiac—that's her freak," or just to heads in costume. It wasn't a negative word. Anyway, just a couple of weeks before, the heads had held their first big "be-in" in Golden Gate Park, at the foot of the hill leading up into Haight-Ashbury, in mock observance of the day LSD became illegal in California. This was a gathering of all the tribes, all the communal groups. All the freaks came and did their thing. A head named Michael Bowen started it, and thousands of them piled in, in high costume, ringing bells, chanting, dancing ecstatically, blowing their minds one way and another and making their favorite satiric gestures to the cops, handing them flowers, burying the bastids in tender fruity petals of love. Oh christ, Tom, the thing was fantastic, a freaking mind-blower, thousands of high-loving heads out there messing up the minds of the cops and everybody else in a fiesta of love and euphoria. Even Kesey, who was still on the run then, had brazened on in and mingled with the crowd for a while, and they were all *one,* even Kesey—and now all of a sudden here he is, in the hands of the FBI and other supercops, the biggest name in The Life, Kesey, announcing that it is time to "graduate from acid." And what the hell is this, a copout or what? The *Stop Kesey* movement was beginning even within the hip world.

We pull up to the Warehouse in the crazed truck and—well, for a start, I begin to see that people like Lois and Stewart and Black Maria are the restrained, reflective wing of the Merry Pranksters. The Warehouse is on Harriet Street, between Howard and Folsom. Like most of San Francisco, Harriet Street is a lot of wooden buildings with bay windows all painted white. But Harriet Street is in San Francisco's Skid Row area, and despite all the paint, it looks like about forty winos crawled off in the shadows and died and turned black and bloated and exploded, sending forth a stream of spirochetes that got into every board, every strip, every crack, every splinter, every flecking flake of paint. The Warehouse actually turns out to be the ground-floor garage of an abandoned hotel. Its last commercial use was as a pie factory. We pull up to the garage and there is a panel truck parked just outside, painted in blue, yellow, orange, red Day-Glo, with the word BAM in huge letters on the hood. From out the black hole of the garage comes the sound of a record by Bob Dylan with his raunchy harmonica and Ernest Tubb voice raunching and rheuming in the old jack-legged chants—

Inside is a huge chaotic space with what looks at first in the gloom like ten or fifteen American flags walking around. This turns out to be a bunch of men and women, most of them in their twenties, in white coveralls of the sort airport workers wear, only with sections of American flags sewn all over, mostly the stars against fields of blue but some with red stripes running down the legs. Around the side is a lot of theater scaffolding with blankets strewn across like curtains and whole rows of uprooted theater seats piled up against the walls and big cubes of metal debris and ropes and girders.

One of the blanket curtains edges back and a little figure vaults down from a platform about nine feet up. It glows. It is a guy about five feet tall with some sort of World War I aviator's helmet on. . .glowing with curves and swirls of green and orange. His boots, too; he seems to be bouncing over on a pair of fluorescent globes. He stops. He has a small, fine, ascetic face with a big mustache and huge eyes. The eyes narrow and he breaks into a grin.

from *Fear and Loathing in Las Vegas*
HUNTER S. THOMPSON

"I don't like to write. I don't care what the fuck happens after I write. Once I've gotten the story in my mind, the rest is pain." Hunter S. Thompson's life and legend continue to make him one of the most popular writers about the Counterculture with his invention of "gonzo" journalism—a hybrid of new journalism mixed with sarcasm and colorful exaggeration, including wild hyperbole about his "wild times" on alcohol and drugs. *Fear and Loathing in Las Vegas* (1971), aptly subtitled *The Savage Journey to the Heart of the American Dream,* exemplifies the gonzo style, particularly in the excerpt here from Chapter 8, an elegy for the Counterculture.

———————— ◆ ————————

Genius 'round the world stands hand in hand, and one shock of recognition runs the whole circle 'round

—ART LINKLETTER

I live in a quiet place, where any sound at night means something is about to happen: You come awake fast—thinking, what does *that* mean?

Usually nothing. But sometimes . . . it's hard to adjust to a city gig where the night is full of sounds, all of them comfortably routine. Cars, horns, footsteps . . . no way to relax; so drown it all out with the fine white drone of a cross-eyed TV set. Jam the bugger between channels and doze off nicely. . . .

Ignore that nightmare in the bathroom. Just another ugly refugee from the Love Generation, some doom-struck gimp who couldn't handle the pressure. My attorney has never been able to accept the notion—often espoused by reformed drug abusers and especially popular among those on probation—that you can get a lot higher without drugs than with them.

And neither have I, for that matter. But I once lived down the hill from Dr. —— on —— Road,* a former acid guru who later claimed to have made that long jump from chemical frenzy to preternatural consciousness. One fine afternoon in the first rising curl of what would soon become the Great San Francisco Acid Wave I stopped by the Good Doctor's house with the idea of asking him (since he was even then a known drug authority) what sort of advice he might have for a neighbor with a healthy curiosity about LSD.

I parked on the road and lumbered up his gravel driveway, pausing enroute to wave pleasantly at his wife, who was working in the garden under the brim of a huge seeding hat . . . a good scene, I thought: The old man is inside brewing up one of his fantastic drug-stews, and here we see his woman out in the garden, pruning carrots, or whatever . . . humming while she works, some tune I failed to recognize.

Humming. Yes . . . but it would be nearly ten years before I would recognize that sound for what it was: Like Ginsberg far gone in the Om, —— was trying to *humm me off*. That was no old lady out there in that garden; it was the good doctor *himself*—and his humming was a frantic attempt to block me out of his higher consciousness.

I made several attempts to make myself clear: Just a neighbor come to call and ask the doctor's advice about gobbling some LSD

---

* Names deleted at insistence of publisher's lawyer.

in my shack just down the hill from his house. I did, after all, have weapons. And I liked to shoot them—especially at night, when the great blue flame would leap out, along with all that noise . . . and, yes, the bullets, too. We couldn't ignore that. Big balls of lead/alloy flying around the valley at speeds up to 3700 feet per second. . . .

But I always fired into the nearest hill or, failing that, into blackness. I meant no harm; I just liked the explosions. And I was careful never to kill more than I could eat.

"Kill?" I realized I could never properly explain that word to this creature toiling here in its garden. Had it ever eaten meat? Could it conjugate the verb "hunt?" Did it understand hunger? Or grasp the awful fact that my income averaged around $32 a week that year?

No . . . no hope of communication in this place. I recognized that—but not soon enough to keep the drug doctor from humming me all the way down his driveway and into my car and down the mountain road. Forget LSD, I thought. Look what it's done to *that* poor bastard.

So I stuck with hash and rum for another six months or so, until I moved into San Francisco and found myself one night in a place called "The Fillmore Auditorium." And that was that. One grey lump of sugar and BOOM. In my mind I was right back there in the doctor's garden. Not on the surface, but *underneath*—poking up through that finely cultivated earth like some kind of mutant mushroom. A victim of the Drug Explosion. A natural street freak, just eating whatever came by. I recall one night in the Matrix, when a road-person came in with a big pack on his back, shouting: "Anybody want some L . . . S . . . D . . . ? I got all the makin's right here. All I need is a place to cook."

The manager was on him at once, mumbling, "Cool it, cool it, come on back to the office." I never saw him after that night, but before he was taken away, the road-person distributed his samples. Huge white spansules. I went into the men's room to eat mine. But only *half* at first, I thought. Good thinking, but a hard thing to accomplish under the circumstances. I ate the first half, but spilled the rest on the sleeve of my red Pendleton shirt. . . . And then, wondering what to do with it, I saw one of the musicians come in. "What's the trouble," he said.

"Well," I said. "All this white stuff on my sleeve is LSD."

He said nothing: Merely grabbed my arm and began sucking on it. A very gross tableau. I wondered what would happen if some Kingston Trio/young stockbroker type might wander in and catch us in the act. Fuck him, I thought. With a bit of luck, it'll ruin his life—forever thinking that just behind some narrow door in all his favorite bars, men in red Pendleton shirts are getting incredible kicks from things he'll never know. Would he dare to suck a sleeve? Probably not. Play it safe. Pretend you never saw it. . . .

Strange memories on this nervous night in Las Vegas. Five 15 years later? Six? It seems like a lifetime, or at least a Main Era— the kind of peak that never comes again. San Francisco in the middle sixties was a very special time and place to be a part of. Maybe it *meant something*. Maybe not, in the long run . . . but no explanation, no mix of words or music or memories can touch that sense of knowing that you were there and alive in that corner of time and the world. Whatever it meant. . . .

History is hard to know, because of all the hired bullshit, but even without being sure of "history" it seems entirely reasonable to think that every now and then the energy of a whole generation comes to a head in a long fine flash, for reasons that nobody really understands at the time—and which never explain, in retrospect, what actually happened.

My central memory of that time seems to hang on one or five or maybe forty nights—or very early mornings—when I left the Fillmore half-crazy and, instead of going home, aimed the big 650 Lightning across the Bay Bridge at a hundred miles an hour wearing L. L. Bean shorts and a Butte sheepherder's jacket . . . booming through the Treasure Island tunnel at the lights of Oakland and Berkeley and Richmond, not quite sure which turn-off to take when I got to the other end (always stalling at the tollgate, too twisted to find neutral while I fumbled for change) . . . but being absolutely certain that no matter which way I went I would come to a place where people were just as high and wild as I was: No doubt at all about that. . . .

There was madness in any direction, at any hour. If not across the Bay, then up the Golden Gate or down 101 to Los Altos or La Honda. . . . You could strike sparks anywhere. There was a fantastic universal sense that whatever we were doing was *right*, that we were winning. . . .

And that, I think, was the handle—that sense of inevitable victory over the forces of Old and Evil. Not in any mean or military sense; we didn't need that. Our energy would simply *prevail*.

There was no point in fighting—on our side or theirs. We had all the momentum; we were riding the crest of a high and beautiful wave. . . .

20   So now, less than five years later, you can go up on a steep hill in Las Vegas and look West, and with the right kind of eyes you can almost *see* the high-water mark—that place where the wave finally broke and rolled back.

from *Trips*

CHERYL PELLERIN

An independent science writer for broadcast and print, Cheryl Pellerin's work appears regularly on the Discovery Channel and The Learning Channel. Her articles have appeared in *Environmental Health Perspectives, Industrial Robot, The Baltimore Sun,* and *The Washington Post.* Her book *Trips* (1998) presents the latest findings about hallucinogens, underground artists, regulators who control psychedelics, federal scientists who approve and fund research, and scientists who have spent careers studying them. Neuroscience for a general audience, *Trips* presents recent advances in molecular biology and non-invasive brain-imaging, but also discusses the Counterculture and its encounters with LSD.

———————— ✦ ————————

LSD studies began mainly with psychotherapy patients, and, in the 1950s and early '60s, researchers used hallucinogens to produce changes of perception, thought and mood that many psychiatrists thought looked a lot like schizophrenia.

Two decades later, in 1962, Congress enacted laws that said researchers had to prove a new drug's safety (it wouldn't kill anyone) and efficacy (it did exactly what they said it'd do) for the condition it was marketed to treat, before it went on the pharmacy shelf. The Food and Drug Administration (FDA) said LSD wasn't even close, and officially made LSD an experimental drug. That meant anyone who wanted to work with LSD had to get FDA permission. By officially making LSD an experimental drug, FDA was saying it could only be used for research and never in general psychiatric practice. Now it was impossible for psychiatrists to get legal psychedelics to use in therapy. Some of the best researchers said *Screw this* and walked away. At the same time, some federal officials suggested that doctors who practiced psychedelic therapy brought the LSD crack down on themselves.

"In a thinly veiled reference to [Timothy] Leary, Drs. Jonathan Cole and Robert Katz of NIMH expressed concern that some investigators 'may have been subject to the deleterious and seductive effects of these agents.'" American Medical Association (AMA) President Roy Grinkler said it was impossible to find investigators who'd work with LSD who weren't already addicts (even though the classic hallucinogens, including LSD, aren't addictive). Grinkler believed public health and safety depended on wiping out all hallucinogen research. Meanwhile, in California, on the East Coast and elsewhere, LSD and other hallucinogens were spreading faster than the Nairobi Ebola virus. Despite FDA limitations and AMA doubts, researchers got federal funds to test all kinds of hallucinogens on human volunteers, and more people were exposed to the drugs. Soon, the volunteers started having mighty raucous neighborhood parties. Add this to the growing numbers of private LSD sessions and you had first-round preliminaries to something called the '60s.

When drug abuse became a national pastime for a visible minority, the medical establishment had a really hard time understanding LSD. It wasn't medicine in the usual sense—it didn't relieve symptoms like coughing or headaches. As drugs not designed to treat specific problems, LSD and other psychedelics were "out of kilter with the basic assumptions of Western medicine."

June, July and August of 1967 was the Summer of Love. LSD, mescaline, MDA, PCP, peyote, DMT, psilocybin, Haight-Ashbury, hippies, headlines, head trips, hassles, heat. The same year, Congress modified the Drug Abuse Control Amendments to make selling LSD a felony and possession a misdemeanor, and shifted enforcement from FDA to the new Bureau of Narcotics and Dangerous Drugs (now DEA).

Federal officials were doing to hallucinogens what they'd done to every other drug the dominant culture had no use for—turning the freeway of sacred plants used throughout human history for their spiritual value into a narrow, twisted, badly marked off-ramp called psychedelic drugs. When they realized that compounds isolated from certain plants could change beliefs and behavior, even drive social movements, they panicked and groped for the tear gas and riot gear.

It didn't take them long (probably because they didn't waste time doing lots of pesky research) to announce that psychedelics were so toxic they could kill you and your whole future family. Or worse. And if the drugs didn't get you, the jail time would, because they'd made using, possessing or selling them a crime. Maybe they did it because they feared losing young people to an incomprehensible movement, losing future generations to suicide or insanity and—"maybe any government's worst nightmare—losing control."

In 1970, the Comprehensive Drug Abuse Prevention and Control Act dumped Public Law 639, the Harrison Narcotics Act of 1914, the Marijuana Tax Act of 1937 and every other major drug law passed since the turn of the century into one law commonly known as the Controlled Substances Act (CSA). The CSA cut research in experimental psychoses off at the knees and 'scheduled' all medications and drugs of abuse according to *medical utility*, *abuse potential* and *safety of use under medical conditions*. Schedule I was the most restrictive category, for drugs characterized as having no known medical use, high abuse potential and no demonstrated safety under medical supervision. The hallucinogens made Schedule I, but the classification was controversial because earlier studies clearly showed they were safe under medical supervision.

DEA Drug Control Schedule

SCHEDULE I-Drugs that have a high potential for abuse, no currently accepted medical use in U.S. treatment, and no accepted safety standards for use under medical supervision.

SCHEDULE II-Drugs that have a high potential for abuse and a currently accepted medical use in U.S. treatment, with or without severe restrictions. Drugs whose abuse might lead to severe psychological or physical dependence.

SCHEDULE III-Drugs that have less potential for abuse than drugs in Schedule I or II and have a currently accepted medical use in U.S. treatment. Drugs whose abuse might lead to moderate or low physical dependence or high psychological dependence.

SCHEDULE IV-Drugs that have a low abuse potential relative to Schedule III drugs and a currently accepted medical use in U.S. treatment. Drugs whose abuse might lead to limited physical or psychological dependence relative to Schedule III drugs.

SCHEDULE V-Drugs that have a low potential for abuse and a currently accepted medical use in U.S. treatment. Drugs whose abuse might lead to limited physical or psychological dependence relative to Schedule IV drugs.

Source: DEA

After that, U.S. researchers had a better chance of replicating Dr. 10
Frankenstein's last life-sciences experiment than of getting federal approval or funding to study hallucinogens in people. They
had to turn in their drug supplies. But animal research continued in the U.S. and some human studies continued in Europe.
Of course, *illegal* LSD field experiments didn't miss a beat.

Twenty years later, in 1990, the tectonic plates of federal drug
regulation shifted slightly, the earth rumbled and, for the first time
since 1970, FDA approved an application to study DMT in humans.
The same year, the National Institute on Drug Abuse agreed to fund
the research. Rick Strassman, a psychiatrist then working at the
University of New Mexico Medical School in Albuquerque, was the
first researcher in a generation to get federal approval and funding
to study psychedelics in human volunteers. In a November 1995
personal interview on Victoria on Vancouver Island, British Columbia, Canada, Strassman explained how it all happened.

After years of studying the pineal gland and melatonin, in
1988 he made the leap to hallucinogens by submitting a request to
FDA to study MDMA (the mild hallucinogen called ecstasy). This
was denied because animal tests showed that MDMA might be
neurotoxic, so he put psychedelic research aside and in 1987 sub-
mitted a complex melatonin proposal to NIMH. When this came
back with a low score, he took off for a month to reassess priori-
ties and on the trip spent time in California with colleagues who,
like Strassman, wanted to get clinical psychedelic therapy off the
black list. Together they realized that "11 million to 15 million people in the United States had taken a psychedelic compound at least
once," Strassman said. "Drugs affect the brain and people abuse
drugs and have bad trips. We ought to understand the effects and
mechanisms of these drugs in the brain. It was so obvious."

Easy Rider: A Very American Thing: An Interview with Dennis Hopper
L. M. KIT CARSON

Actor/writer L. M. Kit Carson's interview with actor/writer Dennis
Hopper brings together hippies, motorcycles, drugs, communes,
Mardi Gras, and filming across America in one of the quintessen-
tial Counterculture films of all time, *Easy Rider* (1969). It also her-

alded a new era in independent filmmaking. Hopper has been honored by the Taos Film Festival and others for his ground-breaking work.

————————— ✦ —————————

Q: *How did this film start? With what? With whom?*

A: It started with Peter [Fonda] calling me on the telephone, saying he had an idea for a movie about two guys who smuggle cocaine, sell it, go across the country for Mardi Gras and get killed by a couple of duck-hunters because they have long hair. "Do you think it can make a movie?" And I said, "Yeh. I think it can make a great movie."

Q: *At what point did Terry Southern come into it?*

A: Terry Southern was an old friend of mine. I asked if we could use his name to get money; then, would he help us with it. He said, "Sure, I like the idea." So we got some cameras and people together, ran down and shot Mardi Gras first; then began the rest of the movie a month later.

Q: *Why'd you shoot on a split and backwards schedule like*
5 *that?*

A: We wanted to use the real Mardi Gras and scheduled to shoot it. But Peter had gotten the wrong dates for Mardi Gras—we thought it was a month away. Suddenly we learned it was a week away. So we shot Mardi Gras without a script, without anything—with just what I had in my mind. I knew generally what I wanted the acid-trip to be, and what I wanted from Mardi Gras.

Q: *How many days did it take to shoot Mardi Gras?*

A: We had five days at Mardi Gras. The acid trip was shot on two different days—half of one day, the whole of another day. This was fast, but I'd learned to squeeze, learned to work fast from television—how to move quickly and utilize your time. . . .

Q: *You shot in Los Angeles first after New Orleans?*
10 **A:** We were in Los Angeles for three weeks. We shot the commune, which was the only set we built, up on Topango Canyon outside the city. Then shot the interior of the whorehouse—which is really the inside of a friend's

home. Then we shot four weeks cross-country. Whole movie: seven weeks including a week at Mardi Gras.

Q: *Elaborate on the way you handled the non-actors in the Southern café scene. It looked to me like the people in the booths had scriptcards on the table in front of them—they would refer to the cards, then look up and speak a line.*

A: Yeh, well, they weren't. They kept looking down because they were supposed to be playing dominoes. I never gave them the script. How I worked them? First of all, there was a man who preceded us into towns like that and got together people he thought would be right for the roles. I came into one village—Morganza, Louisiana—and looked at the people he'd chosen. I didn't care for them. And I saw a group of men standing over beside us doing the kind of joking that the guys in the café were to do. I said, "*Those* are the people I want." He said, "Well I don't know whether I can get them." And I said, "Those are the people I want." So he went over and asked them, and to his surprise they were more than happy to do it. Then I told these men that we had raped, killed a girl right outside of town; and there was nothing they could say about us in this scene that would be too nasty—I mean, they could say *anything* they wanted about us. (And they were pretty set in this frame of mind anyway.) All right. Then I gave them specific topics, things that were covered in the script: talk about long hair, is-it-a-boy-is-it-a-girl, the teeth I'm wearing around my neck, or Peter's black leather pants, or the sunglasses. Then I set up the camera in such a way that I could stop them: "Don't say that"; and isolate: "You say something about this." And the girls: I got them to flirting with one idea—they wanted a ride on the motorcycle. Because I wanted to get them outside. And because this flirting would aggravate the guys even more. So at first I just let them go at it, work their real feelings out. After watching a bit of this, I gave some definite lines: "Check the flag on that bike. Must be a bunch of Yankee queers." "You name it, I'll throw rocks at it." Those were lines from the script. But basically the scene, improvised and all, plays according to the *intention* of the café scene written in the script.

Q: *How long did this scene take to shoot?*

A: We shot it in half a day.

15 **Q:** *In regard to those cafe people: do you feel guilty of any indecency done to them?*

A: Do I feel that because of this film there's harm done to them personally?

Q: *Do you feel you violated them in any way?*

A: No, I don't believe that—well, you've got to understand that I believe that anything that is a creative act can be justified.

Q: *Murder included?*

20 **A:** Well, not quite that far, but almost. I don't know whether I violated them. But then we all violate. Still, there's an area in me where I hope I didn't hurt them because I happen to like those people. I didn't mean them any harm.

On the other hand, I know that if I'd come in there actually traveling across country alone, or if me, Peter, and Jack Nicholson had walked into that restaurant without a movie company behind us and those men had been sitting in there, we'd have been in a lot of trouble.

That's true—I know. I was in the Civil Rights March with King from Selma to Montgomery—it was crazy. There was one guy standing on the side of the road pissing on us. I mean, there he was with his cock in his hand pissing on nuns and priests, all over. And he was calling us white trash. Pissing on nuns and priests and rabbis and Protestants and all religious people in their uniforms, and on us—and calling us white trash. Crazy, you know: how can a man be pissing on people and calling *them* white trash? It doesn't make sense.

And I know that this time the only thing that stopped trouble was the fact that we were making a movie. And suddenly I could relate to these people as their director and they could relate to me.

Q: *Do you connect yourself to any actively political people today?*

25 **A:** I don't think anyone intelligent connects himself to anyone political today. The last time I mixed with politics was when I got kicked out of a SNCC meeting

in the South because they were going into black power, and all the whites had to get out. Which was all right; they were right. They were going to take care of their people, and we should take care of our people— because our people were in just as much a mess as their people. Unfortunately, it's harder to take care of whites because a great mass of them don't think we have any real problems. When SDS went out to Newark a couple of years ago to the poor whites, the people said: "What are you trying to help us for? We're cool." And at the moment I don't think there's going to be any serious change in this attitude—most of us think, "I'm cool. *He's* the trouble." Until we have some sort of war. It'll have to be some kind of war because a lot of things need changing.

I think the movie says this—I mean, it creates this dangerous atmosphere. I know when we were making the movie, we could feel this: the whole country seemed to be burning up—Negroes, hippies, students. The country was on fire. And I meant to work this feeling into the symbols in the movie, like Peter's bike— Captain America's Great Chrome Bike—that beautiful machine covered with stars and stripes is America. I'm not sure that people understand but that bike with all the money in the gas tank is America and we've got all our money in a gas tank—and that any moment we can be shot off it—BOOM—explosion—that's the end. We go up in flames. I mean, at the start of the movie, Peter and I do a very American thing—we commit a crime, we go for the easy money. We go for the easy money and then we're free. That's one of the big problems with the country right now: everybody's going for the easy money. I think Americans basically feel the criminal way is all right *if you don't get caught;* crime pays, *if* you get away with it. Not just obvious, simple crimes, but big corporations committing corporate crimes— swindling on their income tax, freezing funds abroad.

Q: *Are you saying that Peter in the movie represents America?*

A: Yeh. But more than that. Me and Peter are the Squire and his Knight, Sancho Panza and Don Quixote, also Billy the Kid and Wyatt Earp, *also* Captain America, the comic book hero, and his sidekick Bucky. I'm saying that Peter, as Captain America, is the Slightly Tarnished Lawman, is the sensitive, off-in-the-stars, the Great White Liberal who keeps saying, "Everything's going to work out," but doesn't do anything to help it work out. He goes to the commune, hears the people have been eating dead horses off the side of the road—does he break any of that fifty thousand out of his gas tank? What does he do? Nothing. "Hey, they're going to make it." Hey, the Negroes, the Indians, the Mexicans are going to make it. What does he do? He rides a couple of the girls over to another place because he's eating their food. *He does nothing.*

Finally he realizes this when he says, "We blew it." "We blew it" means to me that they could have spent that energy in something other than smuggling cocaine, could have done something other than help the society destroy itself.

30   **Q:**   *All right. But I wonder whether this disfavor you've just explained toward Captain America comes across in the movie. I've seen the movie four times, and only the last time did I begin to pick up some ambivalence toward Captain America in the commune sequence. I'm asking you as a filmmaker, could you have made it more clear how you wanted us to feel about Captain America—just done it in that one sequence which, I think, is very crucial? Because when Captain America says, "They're going to make it," a lot of people get confused: "Does Hopper really believe that? That's bullshit. But sounds like he believes it."*

   A: I don't think it comes through. I think Peter comes off as simply a Super Hero, or Super Anti-Hero. Bucky doesn't believe they're going to make it. Bucky says, "Hey man, they're not going to grow anything here. This is *sand.*"

   Q: *Right, but you give Captain America the last line: "They're going to make it."*

   A: Yeh. Doesn't Captain America always have the last line? "Go to Vietnam." I go to Vietnam. I don't question Captain America. I may be bitchy or carry on, but Captain America always has the last line. That's the way things are.

Q: *What do you think the moral effect of your film is going to be—for instance, what will happen when the scene in which Jack Nicholson smokes pot is shown at the Majestic Theatre in Dallas, Texas?*

A: I don't know. You do something and you do it for a lot 35
of different reasons. I look at that scene on several
levels. First, it's dishonest if those two guys on
motorcycles don't smoke grass. It's ridiculous,
unrealistic. You can't make a movie about these
characters in the late 1960s and not have them turn on.
And if they have a guy like Jack Nicholson around,
they're going to turn him on. That's all, it's that simple,
no propaganda intended. But the *main* reason I used
pot in that scene was to give me a humorous handle for
the Venusian speech—which I consider a very serious
piece of work, heavy propaganda.

Q: *It succeeds as both.*

A: What I'm saying is, without that device of humor,
people would get uptight, say, "Wh-what's he saying?"
And this way nobody says, "What's he saying?" I've
never had anybody say, "What are you saying in that
scene?" And what we're saying is either an incredible
lot of nonsense or an incredible lot of not-nonsense. So
we made it funny, as in the Victorian period or other
periods of oppression, when you wanted to say
something hard to take, you always dressed it up as a
folk ballad or a humorous little ditty that was sung in a
tavern somewhere.

    To get back to the moral effect of the scene—the
only time a reaction really hit me, really hurt me: in
Cannes, Omar Sharif's nineteen-year-old daughter came
up—she'd never turned on before—and said that after
the film she turned on. I said, "Oh, how'd you like it?"
She said, "It didn't do anything for me." I said, "It's
probably very difficult for anyone as frivolous as you to
feel anything anyway." Because it hurt me, man.
Because I didn't make that movie for her to use it as an
excuse to turn on—I don't want any nineteen-year-old
to go get high just because they see the movie. Look,
I've been smoking grass for seventeen years—there've
been bummers and good times. All in all, I'm glad I did

it because smoking gave me some insight, some
paranoia, some self-searching I wouldn't have had
otherwise. But not everybody can handle it. And I did
not make this movie to turn everybody in the country
on to grass. I already assumed everybody was turned
on or about to be turned on—without my movie.

Q: *You're prepared for some very righteous people to come
raging up and saying, "What the hell are you trying to do?"*

A: Yeh, well I've had that. Right. In Cannes, we held a
press conference after the film and UPI or one of those
news services got up and said, "Why are you making a
movie like this? Don't you realize how bad this is for
the country? We have enough problems without you
doing this terrible movie, etc." Then a young
communist said, "Why did you make a movie for three
hundred and seventy thousand dollars? Why didn't you
make a 16mm. or 8mm. movie and give that money to
the Cause? Why are you copping out, putting
commercial music to this movie? Blah-blah." And I
said, "You're only kidding yourself. If you make a
propaganda film, art film, any film you feel has
something to say—you *can* work small and show it to
people who think like you already, dress like you, wear
their hair like you, and you can all sit in a little room
somewhere and look at your movie over and over.
Great. But if you want to reach a large mass of people
at this point in history, you *have* to deal with the people
who are going to *release* your picture." And I also told
the kid, "Hey, all I know is how to make movies. I don't
know anything else. It took me fifteen years to raise
three hundred and seventy thousand dollars. I'm not
going to give it to the Cause—I am the Cause."...

Q: *The end shook me up quite a bit, probably because it
seems so accidental.*

A: Not so accidental really. I believe that if Billy hadn't
shot the finger to the guys in the truck, there wouldn't
have been that existential moment when the guy
decided to pull the trigger. It was action-reaction
operating when they killed me. They killed Peter
because they just didn't know what else to do—it was
too complicated for them to work it out any other way.

40

But I'm not denouncing the South in this ending: I say it was action provoking reaction. Businessmen have come up to me after the movie: "I like your movie, but I'm not the guys in the truck. You're saying I'm the guys in the truck." I'm not saying that. The guys in the truck and the guys on the motorcycles are both the same: criminals, victims of the climate of the country today.

Communique #2 From the Weatherman Underground
WEATHERMEN

The formation of Students for a Democratic Society (SDS) shocked members of mainstream society who were used to college students who got into little more trouble than cheering at football games and having frat parties. During the first half of 1968, nearly 40,000 students participated in major demonstrations at 101 colleges and universities. Although most protests were peaceful, invoking Mahatma Gandhi and Martin Luther King, Jr., some involved bombings, physical assaults on university officials, and confrontations between students and the police. The most dramatic of these was the wounding of 9 and killing of 4 students at Kent State University by National Guardsmen on May 4, 1970. Two students were killed and 12 were wounded at Jackson State College, Mississippi, on May 14 of that year. The U.S. Commission on Campus Unrest reported that the crisis on American college campuses could threaten "the very survival of the nation." Although the majority of students were continuing their studies and carrying on with their day-to-day lives, few were unaffected by these events. When the SDS was viewed as being too "soft" on the authorities, a splinter group, calling itself the Weather Underground, or Weathermen, was formed (from a line in Bob Dylan's "Subterranean Homesick Blues": "You don't need a weatherman to know which way the wind blows"). Their 16,000 page position paper claimed that it was the duty of white radicals to wage the anti-imperial fight through guerilla warfare and terrorist activities. This 1970 piece exemplifies the language and the literal violence they espoused. Although representing only a small fraction of the New Left, it shows how difficult it became for national leadership to maintain philosophical cohesiveness.

————————— ✦ —————————

SLIP NR 12/1909/JUNE9-70/POLICE HDQTRS/77
BOMBEXPLOSION - 240 CENTRE ST - POLICE HDQTRS - UNK
DAMAGE AND INJURIES AT THIS TIME - DETAILS LATER

Tonight, at 7 p.m., we blew up the N.Y.C. police headquarters. We called in a warning before the explosion.

The pigs in this country are our enemies. They have murdered Fred Hampton and tortured Joan Bird. They are responsible for 6 black deaths in Augusta, 4 murders in Kent State, the imprisonment of Los Siete de la Raza in San Francisco and the continual brutality against Latin and white youth on the Lower East Side.

Some are named Mitchell and Agnew. Others call themselves Leary and Hogan. The names are different but the crimes are the same.

The pigs try to look invulnerable, but we keep finding their weaknesses. Thousands of kids, from Berkeley to the UN Plaza, keep tearing up ROTC buildings.

5   Nixon invades Cambodia and hundreds of schools are shut down by strikes. Every time the pigs think they've stopped us, we come back a little stronger and a lot smarter. They guard their buildings and we walk right past their guards. They look for us— we get to them first.

They build the Bank of America, kids burn it down. They outlaw grass, we build a culture of life and music.

The time is now. Political power grows out of a gun, a Molotov, a riot, a commune . . . and from the soul of the people.

The Members of the Assembly*
JEAN GENET

French playwright and countercultural *provocateur* Jean Genet brings news from one of the central media events of the

———————

*Translated by Richard Seaver

Counterculture in the 1960s—the 1968 Democratic Convention in Chicago. Newsman Eric Sevareid called it "the most disgraceful spectacle in the history of American politics." Violence erupted when countercultural protesters under various banners, but usually identified as the National Mobilization Committee to End the War in Vietnam, were confronted by Mayor Daly's police force. One result of the convention's disruption by the protesters (Senator Eugene McCarthy was the lead candidate) was the victory of Republican candidate Richard Nixon who did eventually, in 1972, end U.S. involvement in Vietnam. Genet's ironic style, as translated from the French here by Richard Seaver, focuses on the spectacle of the hippies, Indians, political leftists, and the police, and includes such countercultural characters as Allen Ginsberg.

———————— ✦ ————————

Chicago reminds me of an animal which curiously is trying to climb on top of itself. Part of the city is transformed by the life—or the parade, in both senses of the term—of the hippies.

Saturday night, about ten o'clock, the young people in Lincoln Park have lighted a kind of bonfire. Close by, scarcely visible in the darkness, a good-sized crowd has formed beneath the trees to listen to a black band—flutes and bongo drums. An American Indian, carrying a furled green flag, explains to us that it will be taken tomorrow to the airport when Senator McCarthy is scheduled to arrive and speak. Unfurled, the flag bears upon its green background the painted image of a seventeen-year-old boy—some say he was Indian, others black—killed two days before by the Chicago police.

The cops arrive, in brief but still unangry waves, to put out the fire and disperse the demonstrators. One word about them: the demonstrators are young people of a gentleness almost too gentle, at least this evening. If couples are stretched out on the grass in the park, it seems to me it is for the purpose of angelic exchanges. Everything strikes me as being very chaste. The darkness of the park is not solely responsible for the fact that all I can see are shadows folded in each other's arms.

A group of demonstrators, which had at first dispersed, has re-formed and is singing a kind of two-syllable chant, not unlike a Gregorian chant, a funeral dirge to the memory of the dead boy. I can scarcely speak of the beauty of this plaintive wail, of the anger and the singing.

5   Around the park, which is almost totally dark, what I first see
is a proliferation of American cars, heavy with chrome, and beyond them the gigantic buildings of the city, each of whose floors
is lighted, why I don't know.

Are these four democratic days going to begin with a funeral
vigil in memory of a young Indian—or black—murdered by the
Chicago police?

If man is, or is searching to be, omnipotent, I am willing to
accept Chicago's gigantism; but I should like the opposite to be
accepted as well: a city which would fit in the hollow of one's
hand.

Sunday, Midway Airport, Chicago. McCarthy's arrival. Almost
no police, and the few who do check our press credentials are
extremely casual. Across from the press platform itself, actually
the empty back of a parked trailer truck, are three similar plat-
forms: one is occupied by a brass-dominated orchestra whose
members are men in their thirties and forties, another by a rock
group in its twenties. Between them is the platform reserved for
McCarthy and his staff. McCarthy's plane is a few minutes late;
the crowd massed behind the press platform consists of men and
women whose faces reflect that peculiar image which only profound honesty and hope can give.

McCarthy finally arrives; and the crowd comes dramatically
to life: every man, woman, and child, shouting "We Want Gene,"
brandishes signs devoid of the customary slogans but generously
bedecked with flowers drawn or painted each according to the
bearer's whim, and it is this flower-crowd that McCarthy is going
to address. He is extremely relaxed; he smiles; he is about to
speak, but the battery of microphones is dead. Sabotage? Smiling, he walks over and tries the mikes of the musical group in its
thirties and forties: dead. Still smiling, he tries the mikes of the
rock group in its twenties: dead! Finally, he makes his way back to
his platform and tries his own microphones, which in the interim
have been repaired, at least to some degree. He smiles. He is also
serious, and he declares that he will speak only if the men and
women the farthest away from the speaker's platform can hear
him. Finally, he does speak, and you have all heard what he said
on television.

10   As he leaves the speaker's platform, it seems that no one is
protecting him, save for the sea of flowers painted by the hope-
filled men and women.

A few hours later, at McCarthy's headquarters in the Hilton Hotel, there again appears to be almost no police security, or if there is any it is subtle, invisible. We are received with great courtesy.

This leads me to what, in my opinion, is one of the basic questions I ask myself: after eight months of campaigning, in order for this little-known Senator—or known all too well through a name steeped in shame—in order for McCarthy to arouse such enthusiasm, what concessions has he made? In what ways has his moral rectitude been weakened?

And yet the fact remains that all his speeches, all his statements, reveal intelligence and generosity. Is it a trick?

For a city with as large a black population as Chicago has, I note that there were very few blacks out to greet and acclaim him.

THE FIRST DAY: THE DAY OF THE THIGHS

The thighs are very beautiful beneath the blue cloth, thick and muscular. It all must be hard. This policeman is also a boxer, a wrestler. His legs are long, and perhaps, as you approach his member, you would find a furry nest of long, tight, curly hair. That is all I can see—and I must say it fascinates me—that and his boots, but I can guess that these superb thighs extend on up into an imposing member and a muscled torso, made even firmer every day by his police training in the cops' gymnasium. Higher up, into his arms and hands which must know how to put a black man or a thief out of action.

In the compass of his well-built thighs, I can see . . . but the thighs have moved, and I can see that they are splendid: America has a magnificent, divine, athletic police force, often photographed and seen in dirty books . . . but the thighs have parted slightly, ever so slightly, and through the crack which extends from the knees to the too-heavy member, I can see . . . why, it's the whole panorama of the Democratic Convention with its star-spangled banners, its star-spangled undress, its star-spangled songs, its star-spangled fields, its star-spangled candidates, in short the whole ostentatious parade, but the color has too many facets, as you have seen on your television sets.

What your television fails to bring you is the odor. No: the Odor, which may have a certain connection with order? The reason is that the Democratic Convention is being held right next to the stockyards, and I keep asking myself whether the air is being befouled by the decomposition of Eisenhower or by the decomposition of all America.

A few hours later, about midnight, I join Allen Ginsberg to take part in a demonstration of hippies and students in Lincoln Park: their determination to sleep in the park is their very gentle, as yet too gentle, but certainly poetic, response to the nauseating spectacle of the Convention. Suddenly the police begin their charge, with their grimacing masks intended to terrify: and, in fact, everyone turns and runs. But I am well aware that these brutes have other methods, and far more terrifying masks, when they go hunting for blacks in the ghettos, as they have done for the past hundred and fifty years. . . .

About ten o'clock this evening, part of America has detached itself from the American fatherland and remains suspended between earth and sky. The hippies have gathered in an enormous hall, as starkly bare as the Convention Hall is gaudy. Here all is joy, and in the enthusiasm several hippies burn their draft cards, holding them high for everyone to see: they will not be soldiers, but they may well be prisoners for five years. The hippies ask me to come up onto the stage and say a few words: this youth is beautiful and very gentle. It is celebrating the Un-Birthday of a certain Johnson who, it seems to me, hasn't yet been born. Allen Ginsberg is voiceless: he has chanted too loud and too long in Lincoln Park the night before.

20 Order, real order, is here: I recognize it. It is the freedom offered to everyone to discover and create himself.

About midnight, again in Lincoln Park, the clergy—also between earth and sky in order to escape from America—is conducting a religious service. I am subjected to another, but also very beautiful, kind of poetry. And what of the trees in the park? At night they bear strange fruit, clusters of young people suspended in their branches. I am as yet unfamiliar with this nocturnal variety: but that's the way it is in Chicago. The clergymen invite us to be seated: they are singing hymns in front of an enormous wooden cross. They joke too, and use slang. "Sit or split," says one of the bantering and slangy priests. "Sit or split." The cross, borne by several clergymen, moves away into the night, and this imitation of the Passion is very mov—I don't have time to finish the word: enormous projectors are turned on directly in front of us, and the police, throwing canisters of tear gas, rush at us. We have to run. Once again it is this police, azure but inexorable, who are pursuing us and pursuing the cross. Spellman-the-cop would have had a good laugh.

We take refuge in Ginsberg's hotel, across the street from the Park: my eyes are burning from the gas: a medic pours water into them, and the water spills over me down to my feet. In short, in their blundering clumsiness, the Americans have tried to burn me and a few minutes later to drown me.

We pause to collect ourselves in Allen Ginsberg's hotel room. And what of the convention? And democracy? The newspapers have kept you posted about them.

We leave the hotel: another azure policeman—or the beautiful girl in drag—holding his billy club in his hand the way, exactly the way, I hold a black American's member—escorts us to our car and opens the door for us: there can be no mistake about it: we are White. . . .

A few hours before going to the convention, where our free   25 and easy manner has petrified the police and made them suspicious, we have taken part in the Peace March organized by David Dellinger in Grant Park. Thousands of young people were there, peacefully listening to Phil Ochs sing and to others talk; we were covered with flowers. A symbolic march set off in the direction of the slaughterhouse. A first row of blacks, then behind them, in rows of eight abreast, anyone who cared to join the demonstration. No one got very far: more bellies charged, firing tear gas at the young people. Trucks filled with armed soldiers drove endlessly back and forth through the streets of Chicago.

TO THE HIPPIES

Hippies, young people of the demonstration, you no longer belong to America, which has moreover repudiated you. Hippies with long hair, you are making America's hair curl. But you, between earth and sky, are the beginning of a new continent, an Earth of Fire rising strangely above, or hollowed out below, what once was this sick country—an earth of fire first and, if you like, an earth of flowers. But you must begin, here and now, another continent.

FOURTH DAY: THE DAY OF THE REVOLVER

Is it necessary to write that everything is over? With Humphrey nominated, will Nixon be master of the world?

The Democratic Convention is closing its doors. The police, here as elsewhere, will be less brutal, if it can. And is the revolver, in turn, going to speak?

The Democratic Convention has made its choice, but where, in what drunken bar, did a handful of democrats make their decision?

30   Across from the Hotel Hilton, again in Grant Park, a sumptuous happening. The youth have scaled a bronze horse on which is seated a bronze rider. On the horse's mane—whose head is bowed as if in sleep—young blacks and whites are brandishing black flags and red flags. A burning youth, which I hope will burn all its bridges; it is listening, attentive and serious, to a Presidential candidate who was not invited to the convention: Dick Gregory. Gregory is inviting his friends—there are four or five thousand of them in the park—to come home with him. They won't let us march to the Amphitheater, he declares, but there's no law that says you can't come on down to my house for a party. But first, he says, the four or five policemen who have stupidly allowed themselves to be hemmed in by the crowd of demonstrators must be freed. With great wit and humor, Gregory explains how the demonstrators are to walk, no more than two or three abreast, keeping on the sidewalk and obeying all traffic lights. He says that the march may be long and difficult, for he lives in a house in the black ghetto of South Chicago. He invites the two or three beaten delegates (that is, McCarthy delegates) to head the march, for the police whose job it will be to stop the march may be less brutal with them.

We walk along a hedge of armed soldiers.

At long last America is moving because the hippies have shaken their shoulders.

The Democratic Convention is closing its doors.

A few random thoughts, as usual:

America is a heavy island, too heavy: it would be good, for America, and for the world, for it to be demolished, for it to be reduced to powder.

35   The danger for America is not Mao's *Thoughts:* it is the proliferation of cameras.

So far as I know, there were no scientists among the demonstrators: is intelligence stupid, or science too easy?

The policemen are made of rubber: their muscles are of hard rubber; the convention itself was pure rubber: Chicago is made of rubber that chews chewing gum; the policemen's thoughts are made out of soft rubber, Mayor Daley of wet rubber. . . .

As we are leaving the Democratic Convention, a young policeman looks at me. Our gazes are already a settling of scores: he has understood that I am the enemy, but not one of the policemen is aware of the natural but invisible road, like that of drugs, which has led me, underground or via the route of heaven, into the United States, although the State Department refused me a visa to enter the country.

Too many star-spangled flags: here, as in Switzerland, a flag in front of every house. America is Switzerland flattened out by a steamroller. Lots of young blacks: will the delegates' hot dogs or the revolver bullet murder the democrats before it is too late?

Fabulous happening. Hippies! Glorious hippies, I address my 40 final appeal to you: children, flower children in every country, in order to fuck all the old bastards who are giving you a hard time, unite, go underground if necessary in order to join the burned children of Vietnam.

CHAPTER 4

"Why the Counterculture Loves Indians, Black People, and Everybody"

AIM, Indian National Literature, and Black Power

To trace some of the willingness of people in the early part of the twenty-first century to take on and make their own the trappings of other cultures—what some would call the New Age and others old-fashioned hucksterism—we might think back thirty-five years or so. By paying attention to how Native American cultures and African-American music and social protest functioned as symbols of authenticity for the Counterculture, we can perhaps see how we got to where we are now, with movies, bookstores, and seminars full of "Indian" vision quests, peyote and Sun Dance ceremonies, Caucasian Rastafarians and the "Honky Shaman" *du jour*. When one of the most popular rap artists of the moment is a white person from Michigan who calls himself Eminem, it is almost impossible to look back now and imagine what the Counterculture supposed Native Americans and African Americans represented or, indeed, if they imagined anything. The concerns of the time for the most part had to do with political and social tensions within white society rather than with actual native people, as we have seen from the previous pieces in this reader. The images they mined for their countercultural costumes and poster art came directly from television and the movies— hardly sources outside the culture. Some of the young people involved in civil rights demonstrations had not had much contact with real "black people." And despite the revisionist movies of the early 1970s and the Blaxsploitation films that followed later, the commodified images they sought to affirm drew on and stayed in the same narrow range as those in traditional westerns, but the

127

roles of the good guys and the bad guys were reversed. On a lighter note, Al Calloway makes much fun of whites longing suddenly to be hip in his 1968 *Esquire* magazine article "An Introduction to Soul." Certainly, Black Panther leader Eldridge Cleaver sees the serious dichotomy in his mini-biography from prison, *Soul on Ice*, while Frances M. Beal, in "Double Jeopardy: To Be Black and Female," demonstrates that gender added another dimension to discussions of race. Many of the pieces you are reading changed traditional ideas from American history about who were the victims and villains. Of course, much of this derives from views about the Vietnam War. The colonialist assumptions that got America into Vietnam in the first place did cause people to look back into our own history of "settling the frontier." Those who sought deeply enough did not come back with many romantic images. Certainly those of us who have studied the U.S. Government's treatment of Native Americans, including the "Indian Wars," are not inclined to paint our faces, live in tepees, and wear warbonnets.

How was the Counterculture's ostensible rejection of the mainstream "white" world mirrored in popular images of Native Americans? Keep in mind that this was many years before there were ethnic studies programs on university campuses in America. In early films and literature, Native Americans appeared as "savages" that threatened the new civilizers of the frontier. As the 1960s approached, Native Americans began to appear as victims of an inevitable historical fate, executed and enforced by the Spanish, the Catholic Church, the U.S. Government, the Army, and swarms of settlers. It was the movies' subtext—that Native Americans are destined to vanish in the face of progress—that made indigenous people seem heroic to the hippies and made them want to wear long hair, headbands, and feathers as a way of showing solidarity and loathing for the "Imperialist" (their parents' or the Establishment) commodity culture.

Why would relatively privileged people, both in the countercultural "delirium" of the 1960s and the New Age of today, identify with people presented as victims? To paraphrase Native American poet John Trudell, one of the people who "occupied" Alcatraz Island as a symbol of protest—there is a difference between being oppressed and being powerless: Native people may have been oppressed, but their traditions have power. The Establishment may have been in charge, but the Counterculture lured many of their young people away, and they stayed away, or started new programs (for example, Native American Studies, African American Studies, Ethnic Studies, Women's Studies) until they were old enough to be in charge.

RED POWER, COMMUNES, AND PEYOTE

Fortunately, Native American writers were already identifying the extreme ironies in the Counterculture's quest for "Indianness." And thanks in part to the Counterculture, and media interest in Native Americans (not seen since Edward Curtiz's sepia-toned photographs of Native Americans from the early twentieth century), the publishing establishment began to make these writers known. Thus begins the Indian National Literature, which had a brief start in the 1920s and 1930s with Darcy McNickle and others but then died out after World War II. These days, this writing is among the most revered in American literature for both popular audiences and the academy. In Simon Ortiz's early 1970s story "The San Francisco Indians," a young hippie asks an aging Indian she meets at a shelter if he can get some peyote and perform a ceremony. Searching for his granddaughter whom he never finds, he reassures himself that she's okay, that "Indians are everywhere," even in big cities. But he cannot help the hippie; he doesn't know the rituals or the stories anymore. Some may claim that the Counterculture reminded the Native Americans about their own traditions, and members of the American Indian Movement (AIM) remember those times and places when "Indianness" become a potent political meeting ground. The "Red Power" movement borrowed from the white radicals, and Native American resistance appealed to all sorts of non-Indian sympathizers such as actor Marlon Brando. Brando sent Sasheen Little Feather to refuse his Academy Award in 1973 for *The Godfather* with a Red Power speech attacking the film industry's portrayals of Native people. Brando, she said, had been "a friend of the American Indian long before it was fashionable to pile on the turquoise and feathers." Eager non-Indians appeared at fishing protests in the same way they had for civil rights demonstrations in Selma, Alabama, nearly a decade earlier. They came with the Trail of Broken Treaties caravan to Washington, D.C., to Wounded Knee, and for the All Tribes' seizure and occupation of Alcatraz Island (in the San Francisco bay) in 1969. Red Power also drew ideological weight from the far more visible Black Power movement. This habit of yoking any number of themes with the word "power" points to the pastiche or collage nature, as well as the looseness of symbolic meaning, of Countercultural statements. Revolution, rebellion, and cultural gesture all work together. Marlon Brando's anti-hero character in the 1950s film *The Wild Ones* set up the Counterculture when he was asked, "What are you rebelling against?" and replied, "What have you got?"

Although the Native American grandfather in Ortiz's story could not get any peyote, poet Michael McClure, who transitioned smoothly from the Beat to hippie era, did. His description of the wonders of the sacred plant— "this is powerful knowledge/we smile with it"— brings instant transcendence (perhaps not exactly in the way Ralph Waldo Emerson had in mind); "And the Indian thing. It is true!/Here in my apartment I think tribal thoughts." Indeed. Those who found urban apartment life too constraining, even with access to peyote, went out to the country, as documented in excerpts from the "commune scene" in Chapter 2 of this reader.

Native Americans often think they have to turn themselves into some version of "Indian" because they cannot find a way to transform and comprehend their own traditions. That is the theme of much Native American literature. Leslie Marmon Silko, Wendy Rose, and many others belong to several traditions, from American to Native American, and different times, past, and present. The excerpts that follow in this chapter, such as Mary Crow Dog's struggles with being a modern Indian woman and a member of the political organization AIM, give a glimpse of those times. When the "love" of Native Americans professed by counterculturalists old and new has nothing to do with Native people nor with supporting such contemporary struggles as land and treaty rights, then it is not love at all but rather another instance of what Philip Deloria calls "playing Indian," something he accuses white Americans of doing since the Boston Tea Party in the eighteenth century. Current debates about removing affirmative action for certain ethnic groups (in place since the 1970s and arising out of Countercultural movements) are a reminder of how controversial these issues remain.

from *Lakota Woman*
Mary Crow Dog

Mary Brave Bird lived without a father in a one-room cabin, without running water or electricity, on a South Dakota reservation. As she grew up, she became enamored of the new movements of Indian pride in the sixties and seventies and eventually married Leonard Crow Dog, the chief medicine man for what would become the American Indian Movement (AIM). A poignant account of a mother who does not consider herself part of the Counterculture, this excerpt from *Lakota Woman* (1990) illustrates an encounter between hippies and "Indians" that would define its very existence.

——————————— ✦ ———————————

I knew when I brought my body here,
it might become food for the
worms and magpies.
I threw my body away before
I came here.

—Young man from Eagle Butte

I do not consider myself a radical or revolutionary. It is white people who put such labels on us. All we ever wanted was to be left alone, to live our lives as we see fit. To govern ourselves in reality and not just on paper. To have our rights respected. If that is revolutionary, then I sure fit that description. Actually, I have a great yearning to lead a normal, peaceful life—normal in the Sioux sense. I could have accepted our flimsy shack, our smelly outhouse, and our poverty—but only on my terms. Yes, I would have accepted poverty, dignified, uninterfered-with poverty, but not the drunken, degrading, and humiliating poverty we had to endure. But normality was a long time in coming. Even now I don't have the peace I crave.

When my husband was in a maximum-security prison in Lewisburg, Pennsylvania, I spent many months in New York with white friends in order to be near him. For the first time I lived a life which white Americans consider "normal." I have to admit that I developed a certain taste for it. It was a new, comfortable, exciting life for a young Indian hobo girl like me. I became quite a New Yorker. I took my little boy Pedro down to the Village to Pancho's, buying wonderful-tasting nachos for him and virgin coladas for myself. I liked to go window-shopping. Everything was so much cheaper than on the reservation where the trading posts have no competition and charge what they please. Everything is more expensive if you are poor. I went down to Greene's on 38th Street in the millinery district and bought beads at one-sixth the price Indian craftworkers are charged by the white dealer in Rosebud. They had many more beads to choose from, the kinds of beads I had not seen for years, indistinguishable from the old, nineteenth-century ones, like tiny, sweaty green and yellow beads, and cut-glass beads of the type Kiowas use in beading peyote staffs and gourds. I learned to like spicy Szechuan and Hunan food, learned to accept and talk with white friends, and lost some of my shyness to the extent of making public speeches on behalf of my imprisoned husband. I luxuriated in bathtubs with hot and cold running water and admitted that modern flush toilets were suiting me a lot better than our Leaning Tower of Pisa privies, even though they were products of white American technology which I usually condemned. Once, in a fit of total irresponsibility, I blew $99.99 on an imitation Persian rug on special sale at Macy's. I took this thing home and spread it on the floor of our shack, feeling smugly middle-class. The rug didn't last long, what with the dogs, the kids, and many people dropping in constantly with their problems. Once even a horse forced its way in through the unlocked door and relieved itself on this proud possession of mine. This rug was a symbol of the good little housewife I could have been. It is the government which made me into a militant. If you approach them hat in hand as a "responsible, respectable" apple, red outside, white inside, you get nowhere. If you approach them as a militant you get nowhere either, except giving them an excuse to waste you, but at least you don't feel so shitty. Wounded Knee was not the brainchild of wild, foaming-at-the-mouth militants, but of patient and totally unpolitical, traditional Sioux, mostly old Sioux ladies.

The trouble started with Dicky Wilson, or rather it started long ago with the Indian Reorganization Act of 1934. At that time a government lawyer decided to do something for "Lo, the poor Indian," and wrote a constitution for all the tribes. Indians were to have their own little governments patterned after that of the Great White Father in Washington. Every Indian nation

was to have an elected tribal president and council. Poor be-
nighted Mr. Lo was to have the blessings of democracy be-
stowed upon him by all-wise white benefactors. The people who
thought it all up probably really meant to do well by us. Sometimes I think that the do-gooders do us more harm than the
General Custer types. There were two things very wrong with
this sudden gift of democracy. The most important was that the
Reorganization Act destroyed the old, traditional form of Indian self-government. . . .

Leonard had a hard time keeping the dancers in line because
it was a near-killing situation. Among the dancers was a group of
young people calling themselves "Indians of All Tribes." They
came from San Francisco where they had taken part in the occupation of Alcatraz Island. They wanted to fight the police. It took
a great effort by Leonard and Uncle Bill to prevent bloodshed.
Everybody was hauled off to court and fined. After a few hours
the dancers were released but police occupied the dance ground
to make sure that the ceremony could not be continued.

The dancers asked Leonard, "What are we going to do now?"   5
One could not leave a Sun Dance half done. Not finishing it to the
point of piercing was unthinkable. Leonard said, "We have made
a vow to the Great Spirit and we must keep it." Somebody suggested continuing the dance at Rosebud, on Crow Dog's private
land, where nobody could interfere with it, and all agreed that
this was a good idea. But there was the problem of the tree. The
sacred Sun Dance pole standing at the center of the Sun Dance
circle is always a two-forked cottonwood tree. Men are sent out to
scout for the most perfect tree they can find. They count coup
upon it as in battle. A young maiden who has never been with a
man makes the first symbolic cut with the axe. The tree must not
touch the ground when falling but must be caught by the men
who will carry it to the dance ground.

Leonard was disturbed. The Crow Dog place was over eighty
miles distant. How could men carry the heavy tree that far? The
tree is sacred. At the height of the dance sick persons lie beneath
the tree to be cured. Looking at it, some dancers had already received visions. How could it be transported?

Just about that time a large truck with long-haired young
white people arrived. They had come all the way from the East
Coast to learn about Indian ways. One of them told Leonard, "We
overheard what you said. We'll put your tree on our truck and
drive it all the way to your place."

Leonard objected. The tree had to be carried on foot in a sacred manner. To put it on a truck would be very bad. But then Bill Eagle Feathers, twice as old as Leonard and a sun-dancer many times over, stepped in. He thanked all those, Indian and white, who were present. He pointed to the young, long-haired people. "Great Spirit, look at them. They are poor like us. Look at their clothes. Look at their shoes. They call me a lousy Indian. They call them lousy hippies. We travel the same road. Grandfather, Tunkashila will understand. The Sacred Tree will understand. What we are doing is good."

10   He smoked up the young hippies with cedar and sweetgrass. And then the Sun Dance pole was loaded on top of the truck with all the offerings still attached to it, the four direction flags streaming from it in the wind. The truck was followed by a whole caravan of decrepit Indian cars. For a few miles it was escorted by a tribal police car and in it the unhappy police chief was standing up, praying to the sacred tree with his pipe.

After arriving at Crow Dog's place the dancers planted the tree in a hole filled with buffalo fat. Henry made two figures of buffalo hide, one figure of a man and the other of a buffalo bull. They stood for the renewal of all life, human and animal, because that, too, is an aspect of the Sun Dance. In the old days these figures always had huge male organs symbolizing what the dance was about—more people and more buffalo to feed them.

Everybody pitched in to smooth down the dance circle, put up the shade cover of pine boughs, and make everything holy. It took them the whole day to get everything ready to continue the dance. The next morning, at sunrise, Bill Eagle Feathers raised his pipe and blew on his eagle-bone whistle, praying for an eagle to come in as a sign that the dance was blessed. Within minutes, an eagle flew in low over the hills from the east, circled slowly over the dance ground, then disappeared in the west. They then finished the dance among the grass and pines, without loudspeakers or electric floodlights, in the old, traditional way. At this dance Leonard for the first time revived the old custom of dragging buffalo skulls embedded in the flesh of his back. He told me, "I took five steps with those skulls and it felt as if my heart was being torn out through my back." From that day on, every summer there has always been a Sun Dance at Crow Dog's place, and always the person acting as intercessor prays for an eagle to come in to bless the dancers and always the eagle appears. I was only a teenager when that took place.

I have sun-danced myself. I did not pierce until the second year after I began living with Leonard. At first I did not understand the whole ritual, but I felt it deeply. I understood it with my heart even though not yet with my mind. I saw the tree, the people sitting under the shade, the dancers with their wreaths of sage, their red kilts, medicine bundles dangling on their chests. I heard the many eagle-bone whistles making the sound of a thousand birds. It made me feel good because I sensed the strong feeling between the different people and tribes. I looked at the men with their long, flowing black hair and at the women in their white, beaded buckskin dresses. It was so beautiful that it brought tears to my eyes. I wanted to be part of this, I wanted to feel it, spiritually and in my flesh. It was real compared to what I had known, not a hand-me-down belied but a personal reawakening which stirred a remembrance deep inside me. So I made a vow to sun-dance for four years, and the first time I found it hard to fulfill my commitment.

I began my dance by making a flesh offering. Leonard told me, "I'll cut the skin from your arm. That's a sacrifice. Your prayers go out for those suffering in jail, for friends who are sick. I will put the pieces from your arm into a square of red cloth, make a little bundle of it, and tie it to the sacred pipe That way you'll remember this always.". . .

For the White Poets Who Would Be Indian

WENDY ROSE

One of the many voices that came to be heard out of the Counterculture's interest in Native American literature, Rose has published more than a dozen books of poetry. *Hopi Roadrunner Dancing* (1973) came out just as the AIM was becoming visible. Wendy Rose "creates both delicate lyrics and harsh protest poems," A. LaVonne Brown Ruoff wrote in *American Indian Literatures* (1990). "For the White Poets Who Would be Indian" reflects the responses Native American writers would come to have for the white Counterculture who admired them.

✦

just once
just long enough
to snap up the words
fish-hooked
from our tongues.   5
You think of us now
when you kneel
on the earth,
turn holy
in a temporary tourism   10
of our souls.
With words
you paint your faces.
chew your doeskin,
touch breast to tree   15
as if sharing a mother
were all it takes,
could bring
instant and primal
of knowledge.   20
You think of us only
when your voice
wants for roots,
when you have sat back
on your heels   25
and become primitive.
You finish your poem
and go back.

from *Almanac of the Dead*

LESLIE MARMON SILKO

The acclaimed author of *Ceremony* (1977), *Storyteller* (1981),
Yellow Woman (1996), *Gardens in the Dunes* (1999), and numerous works of fiction took ten years to write the apocalyptic
Almanac of the Dead (1991). The "many-layered narrative of the
novel unfolds to tell the magnificent, tragic, and unforgettable
story of the clash of two civilizations," white and Native
American. In this excerpt from near the end of the novel, "The

International Holistic Healers Convention," Silko parodies the "Indian lovers" and counterculturalists of the New Age.

———————— ◆ ————————

Angelita looked around the ballroom of the Tucson resort carefully. She was alert for familiar faces from the Freedom School in Mexico City. If the Israelis or Chinese had sent spies to the International Holistic Healers Convention that meant they were on to the plan. She saw none of the familiar faces, but that did not mean there were no spies. She had left Wacah and El Feo in the mountains with the people. Hundreds of people kept coming to listen to Wacah talk about the ancient prophecies and explain the future. German and Dutch tourists had witnessed Wacah's sessions with the people, and soon a German television crew had trekked up the muddy paths with their equipment to record the odd new mystical movement among Indians in Mexico, who were growing their hair long and painting their faces again in imitation of the twin brothers, who served the macaw spirits, and who promised the people the ancient prophecies were about to be fulfilled.

The video cameras had recorded a slow but steady trickle of people, mostly Indian women and their children, trudging along muddy, steep paths and rutted, muddy roads. The people came from all directions, and many claimed they had been summoned in dreams. Wacah had proclaimed all human beings were welcome to live in harmony together. People from tribes farther south, peasants without land, *mestizos*, the homeless from the cities and even a busload of Europeans, had come to hear the spirit macaws speak through Wacah. The faithful waited quietly by their sleep shelters and belongings. After the German television report, the cash had started flowing in from "Indian lovers" in Belgium and Germany. They had received a large amount of cash from a Swiss collector of pre-Columbian pottery in Basel. A people's army as big as theirs would not need weapons. Their sheer numbers were weapons enough. A people's army needed food. Wacah said the people would eat as long as they were with him. All they had to do was walk north with him.

After the cable news report there had been trouble. Authorities heard rumors that the native religion and prophecies were a cover, and the true business of Wacah and his brother was to stir up the Indians, who were always grumbling about stolen land. The Mexican federal police had sent truckloads of armed agents to search the mountains for secret caves suspected to contain caches of weapons the Indians had allegedly received from the Cubans. But even the four-wheel-drive trucks the police drove could not cross the landslides which the mountains had shaken down in previous weeks. Straggling in to the villages on foot, the police had found nothing; all the able-bodied had followed the twins. Those too sick or weak to travel said the mountain spirits were shaking the earth and would not stop until the white man's cities were destroyed.

The cable television news crew had still been at Wacah's camp when the federal police arrived; the calm of the people and the frenzy of the police had been televised all over the world. But the police had soon realized they were greatly outnumbered and they had withdrawn. Wacah's invitation to address the world convention of holistic healers had arrived within days of the federal police raid. But the spirit macaws would not permit Wacah or El Feo to leave. They had to walk with the people. Wacah and El Feo must not ride in automobiles or helicopters. The spirits required that the people walk. Wacah and El Feo had sent Angelita to the healers convention to make apologies for them, and to invite all those gathered to join them. All were welcome. It was only necessary to walk with the people and let go of all the greed and the selfishness in one's heart. One must be able to let go of a great many comforts and all things European; but the reward would be peace and harmony with all living things. All they had to do was return to Mother Earth. No more blasting, digging, or burning.

5   Wacah's message to the holistic healers assembly was to be prepared for the changes, welcome the arrival of the people, and send any money they could. All money went for food; the people were protected by the spirits and needed no weapons. The changes might require another hundred years, until the Europeans had been outnumbered and the people retook the land peacefully. All that might be okay for Wacah and El Feo, but Angelita had plans of her own. What Wacah and El Feo didn't know, wouldn't hurt them. Angelita was in charge of "advance planning." From villagers in Sonora, Angelita had heard about certain people and families living in Tucson who might wish to help.

Wacah, El Feo, and the people with them believed the spirit voices; if the people kept walking, if the people carried no weapons, then the old prophecies would come to pass, and all the dispossessed and the homeless would have land; the tribes of the Americas would retake the continents from pole to pole. They did not fear U.S. soldiers or bullets when they reached the border to the north because they did not believe the U.S. government would bomb its own border just to stop unarmed religious pilgrims. But Angelita wasn't so sure. The U.S. Treasury might be nearly empty, and the United States might be caught in civil unrest and strikes—but the white men would spend their last dime to stop the people from the South. The U.S. government might have no money for the starving, but there was always government money for weapons and death. The Mexican Treasury had been bankrupt for months, but still the federal police got paid. The U.S. was no different. The people themselves might be finished with wars, but their generals and business tycoons were not.

El Feo and Wacah had to obey the spirit macaws. What they might personally think did not matter. Wacah believed the spirits would protect them, but personally El Feo had agreed with Angelita La Escapía, his comrade-in-arms: the U.S. government might not wait for the twin brothers and the people to reach the border. The unarmed people would most likely be shot down before they even reached the border, but still they must have faith that even the federal police and the soldiers would be caught up by the spirits and swept along by the thousands. How long could the soldiers and police keep pulling the triggers? They might fall by the hundreds but still the people would keep walking; not running or screaming or fighting, but always walking. Their faith lay in the spirits of the earth and the mountains that casually destroyed entire cities. Their faith lay in the spirits outraged by the Europeans who had burned alive the sacred macaws and parrots of Tenochtitlán; for these crimes and all the killing and destruction, now the Europeans would suffocate in their burning cities without rain or water any longer.

El Feo told Angelita she must do what she felt was best. What was coming could not be stopped; the people might join or not; the tribal people of North America could come to the aid of the twins and their followers or they could choose not to help. It made no difference because what was coming was relentless and inevitable; it might require five or ten years of great violence and conflict. It might require a hundred years of spirit voices and simple population growth, but the result would be the same: tribal people would retake the Americas; tribal people would retake ancestral land all over the world. This was what earth's spirits wanted: her indigenous children who loved her and did not harm her.

The followers of the spirit macaws believed they must not shed blood or the destruction would continue to accompany them. But Wacah did say the pilgrims would be protected by natural forces set loose, forces raised by the spirits. Among these forces there would be human beings, warriors to defend the religious pilgrims. These warriors were already waiting far to the north. Wacah believed that one night the people would all dream the same dream, a dream sent by the spirits of the continent. The dream could not be sent until the people were ready to awaken with new hearts.

10   Angelita did not see how any spiritual change could take place overnight, especially not in the United States where the people of whatever color had become desperate in the collapse of the economy. Angelita did not believe in leaving the people or the twin brothers defenseless, even if the spirit macaw had said the end of the Europeans in the Americas was inevitable.

Angelita did not care if El Feo teased her or called her by her war name La Escapía, all the time. She wasn't taking any chances. She had come to the healers convention in Tucson to make contacts with certain people, the people with the weapons she needed to protect the followers of the spirit macaws from air attacks. Those amazing shoulder-mounted missiles worked as simply as holiday skyrockets. Angelita had fired one herself and it hadn't been much different from holding a Roman candle. The missiles were purely defensive measures, of course, against government helicopters and Wacah and El Feo need never know. Angelita heard from spirits too—only her spirits were furious and they told her to defend the people from attack.

from *Soul on Ice*

ELDRIDGE CLEAVER

This firebrand leader of the Black Panther Party, radical writer, confessed rapist, and international fugitive gained worldwide fame with the publication of his prison essays in the book *Soul on Ice* (1968), excerpted here. The memoir became a bestseller and, for many in the Counterculture and beyond, expressed the rage and alienation the increasingly violent members of the Left felt they had in common with black people. Cleaver called for armed resistance to seize economic and political power and, as members of the Black Panther Party were either killed or jailed, Cleaver became a lead spokesman. In the late 1970s and 1980s, Cleaver professed to be a born-again Christian and Republican, writing about his religious conversion in *Soul on Fire* (1978), but it would never have the appeal of his earlier "black power" phase. Here, he analyzes the white Counterculture.

———————— ✦ ————————

But they consider it bad form to connect the problems of the youth with the central event of our era—the national liberation movements abroad and the Negro revolution at home. The foundations of authority have been blasted to bits in America because the whole society has been indicted, tried, and convicted of injustice. To the youth, the elders are Ugly Americans; to the elders, the youth have gone mad.

The rebellion of the white youth has gone through four broadly discernible stages. First there was an initial recoiling away, a rejection of the conformity which America expected, and had always received, sooner or later, from its youth. The disaffected youth were refusing to participate in the system, having discovered that America, far from helping the underdog, was up to its ears in the mud trying to hold the dog down. Because of the publicity and self-advertisements of the more vocal rebels, this period has come to be known as the beatnik era, although not all of the youth affected by these changes thought of themselves as beatniks. The howl of the beatniks and their scathing, outraged denunciation of the system—characterized by Ginsberg as Moloch, a bloodthirsty Semitic deity to which the ancient tribes sacrificed their firstborn children—was a serious, irrevocable declaration of war. It is revealing that the elders looked upon the beatniks as mere obscene misfits who were too lazy to take baths and too stingy to buy a haircut. The elders had eyes but couldn't see, ears but couldn't hear—not even when the message came through as clearly as in this remarkable passage from Jack Kerouac's *On the Road*:

> At lilac evening I walked with every muscle aching among the lights of 27th and Welton in the Denver colored section, wishing I were a Negro, feeling that the best the white world had offered was not enough ecstasy for me, not enough life, joy, kicks, darkness, music, not enough night. I wished I were a Denver Mexican, or even a poor overworked Jap, anything but what I so drearily was, a "white man" disillusioned. All my life I'd had white ambitions. . . . I passed the dark porches of Mexican and Negro homes;

soft voices were there, occasionally the dusky knee of some mysterious sensuous gal; the dark faces of the men behind rose arbors. Little children sat like sages in ancient rocking chairs.

The second stage arrived when these young people, having decided emphatically that the world, and particularly the U.S.A., was unacceptable to them in its present form, began an active search for roles they could play in changing the society. If many of these young people were content to lay up in their cool beat pads, smoking pot and listening to jazz in a perpetual orgy of esoteric bliss, there were others, less crushed by the system, who recognized the need for positive action. Moloch could not ask for anything more than to have its disaffected victims withdraw into safe, passive, apolitical little nonparticipatory islands, in an economy less and less able to provide jobs for the growing pool of unemployed. If all the unemployed had followed the lead of the beatniks, Moloch would gladly have legalized the use of euphoric drugs and marijuana, passed out free jazz albums and sleeping bags, to all those willing to sign affidavits promising to remain "beat." The non-beat disenchanted white youth were attracted magnetically to the Negro revolution, which had begun to take on a mass, insurrectionary tone. But they had difficulty understanding their relationship to the Negro, and what role "whites" could play in a "Negro revolution." For the time being they watched the Negro activists from afar.

Double Jeopardy: To Be Black and Female
FRANCES M. BEAL

A peace and justice activist as well as a writer, Beal has focused on Black women and African American political issues over the last three decades. She first became active in the 1950s, protesting Jim Crow laws, and in the early 1960s, while in France, was influenced by the Algerian people's struggle to free themselves from French rule. She later became involved in the Student Nonviolent Coordinating Committee (SNCC), where she worked on its international affairs commission and was a founding member of its

Black Women's Liberation Committee, which evolved into the Third World Women's Alliance. Beal was the editor of the Third World Women's Alliance newpaper, *Triple Jeopardy*, and helped to develop the view that the intersection of race, class, and gender is the theoretical foundation for analyzing the oppression of Black women. She has taught Black Studies and Women's Studies at Richmond College and City University of New York, and has continued to write on issues such as Black women, the anti-apartheid movement, and African American politics. Currently residing in San Francisco, she is a member of the National Writers Union and works with the ACLU and Black Radical Congress, and a columnist for the *San Francisco Bay View*.

———————— ✦ ————————

In attempting to analyze the situation of the black woman in America, one crashes abruptly into a solid wall of grave misconceptions, outright distortions of fact and defensive attitudes on the part of many. The system of capitalism (and its afterbirth, racism) under which we all live, has attempted by many devious ways and means to destroy the humanity of all people, and particularly the humanity of black people. This has meant an outrageous assault on every black man, woman and child who resides in the United States.

In keeping with its goal of destroying the black race's will to resist its subjugation, capitalism found it necessary to create a situation where the black man found it impossible to find meaningful or productive employment. More often than not, he couldn't find work of any kind. And the black woman likewise was manipulated by the system, economically exploited and physically assaulted. She could often find work in the white man's kitchen, however, and sometimes became the sole breadwinner of the family. This predicament has led to many psychological problems on the part of both man and woman and has contributed to the turmoil that we find in the black family structure.

Unfortunately, neither the black man nor the black woman understood the true nature of the forces working upon them. Many black women tended to accept the capitalist evaluation of manhood and womanhood and believed, in fact, that black men were shiftless and lazy, otherwise they would get a job and support their families as they ought to. Personal relationships between black men and women were thus torn asunder and one result has been the separation of man from wife, mother from child, etc.

America has defined the roles to which each individual should subscribe. It has defined "manhood" in terms of its own interests and "femininity" likewise. Therefore, an individual who has a good job, makes a lot of money and drives a Cadillac is a real "man" and conversely, an individual who is lacking in these "qualities" is less of a man. The advertising media in this country continuously informs the American male of his need for indispensable signs of his virility—the brand of cigarettes that cowboys prefer, the whiskey that has a masculine tang or the label of the jockstrap that athletes wear.

5   The ideal model that is projected for a woman is to be surrounded by hypocritical homage and estranged from all real work, spending idle hours primping and preening, obsessed with conspicuous consumption, and limiting life's functions to simply a sex role. We unqualitatively reject these respective models. A woman who stays at home, caring for children and the house, often leads an extremely sterile existence. She must lead her entire life as a satellite to her mate. He goes out into society and brings back a little piece of the world for her. His interests and his understanding of the world become her own and she cannot develop herself as an individual, having been reduced to only a biological function. This kind of woman leads a parasitic existence that can aptly be described as "legalized prostitution."

Furthermore, it is idle dreaming to think of black women simply caring for their homes and children like the middle-class white model. Most black women have to work to help house, feed and clothe their families. Black women make up a substantial percentage of the black working force and this is true for the poorest black family as well as the so-called middle-class family.

Black women were never afforded any such phony luxuries. Though we have been browbeaten with this white image, the reality of the degrading and dehumanizing jobs that were relegated to us quickly dissipated this mirage of womanhood. . . .

Unfortunately, there seems to be some confusion in the movement today as to who has been oppressing whom. Since the advent of black power, the black male has exerted a more prominent leadership role in our struggle for justice in this country. He sees the system for what it really is for the most part, but where he rejects its values and mores on many issues, when it comes to women, he seems to take his guidelines from the pages of the *Ladies' Home Journal.* Certain black men are maintaining that they have been castrated by society but that black women somehow escaped this persecution and even contributed to this emasculation.

Let me state here and now that the black woman in America can justly be described as a "slave of a slave." By reducing the black man in America to such abject oppression, the black woman had no protector and was used, and is still being used in some cases, as the scapegoat for the evils that this horrendous system has perpetrated on black men. Her physical image has been maliciously maligned; she has been sexually molested and abused by the white colonizer; she has suffered the worst kind of economic exploitation, having been forced to serve as the white woman's maid and wet nurse for white offspring while her own children were more often than not starving and neglected. It is the depth of degradation to be socially manipulated, physically raped, used to undermine your own household, and to be powerless to reverse this syndrome.

It is true that our husbands, fathers, brothers and sons have   10 been emasculated, lynched and brutalized. They have suffered from the cruellest assault on mankind that the world has ever known. However, it is a gross distortion of fact to state that black women have oppressed black men. The capitalist system found it expedient to enslave and oppress them and proceeded to do so without consultation or the signing of any agreements with black women.

It must also be pointed out at this time that black women are not resentful of the rise to power of black men. We welcome it. We see in it the eventual liberation of all black people from this corrupt system of capitalism. Nevertheless, this does not mean that you have to negate one for the other. This kind of thinking is a product of miseducation: that either it's X or it's Y. It is fallacious reasoning that in order for the black man to be strong, the black woman has to be weak.

Those who are exerting their "manhood" by telling black women to step back into a domestic, submissive role are assuming a counter-revolutionary position. Black women likewise have been abused by the system and we must begin talking about the elimination of all kinds of oppression. If we are talking about building a strong nation, capable of throwing off the yoke of capitalist oppression, then we are talking about the total involvement of every man, woman, and child, each with a highly developed political consciousness. We need our whole army out there dealing with the enemy and not half an army.

There are also some women who feel that there is no more productive role in life than having and raising children. This attitude often reflects the conditioning of the society in which we live and is adopted from a bourgeois white model. Some young sisters who have never had to maintain a household and accept the confining role which this entails, tend to romanticize (along with the help of a few brothers) this role of housewife and mother. Black women who have had to endure this kind of function are less apt to have these utopian visions.

Those who project in an intellectual manner how great and rewarding this role will be and who feel that the most important thing that they can contribute to the black nation is children, are doing themselves a great injustice. This line of reasoning completely negates the contributions that black women have historically made to our struggle for liberation. These black women include Sojourner Truth, Harriet Tubman, Mary McLeod Bethune and Fannie Lou Hamer, to name but a few.

15   We live in a highly industrialized society and every member of the black nation must be as academically and technologically developed as possible. To wage a revolution, we need competent teachers, doctors, nurses, electronics experts, chemists, biologists, physicists, political scientists, and so on and so forth. Black women sitting at home reading bedtime stories to their children are just not going to make it. . . .

Much has been written recently about the women's liberation movement in the United States and the question arises whether there are any parallels between this struggle and the movement on the part of black women for total emancipation. While there are certain comparisons that one can make, simply because we both live under the same exploitive system, there are certain differences, some of which are quite basic.

The white women's movement is far from being monolithic. Any white group that does not have an anti-imperialist and antiracist ideology has absolutely nothing in common with the black woman's struggle. In fact, some groups come to the incorrect conclusion that their oppression is due simply to male chauvinism. They therefore have an extremely antimale tone to their dissertations. Black people are engaged in a life and death struggle and the main emphasis of black women must be to combat the capitalist, racist exploitation of black people. While it is true that male chauvinism has become institutionalized in American society, one must always look for the main enemy—the fundamental cause of the female condition.

Another major differentiation is that the white women's liberation movement is basically middle class. Very few of these women suffer the extreme economic exploitation that most black women are subjected to day by day. This is the factor that is most crucial for us. It is not an intellectual persecution alone; it is not an intellectual outburst for us; it is quite real. We as black women have got to deal with the problems that the black masses deal with, for our problems in reality are one and the same.

If the white groups do not realize that they are in fact fighting capitalism and racism, we do not have common bonds. If they do not realize that the reasons for their condition lie in the system and not simply that men get a vicarious pleasure out of "consuming their bodies for exploitive reasons" (this kind of reasoning seems to be quite prevalent in certain white women's groups), then we cannot unite with them around common grievances or even discuss these groups in a serious manner because they're completely irrelevant to the black struggle.

The black community and black women especially must be-   20
gin raising questions about the kind of society we wish to see established. We must note the ways in which capitalism oppresses us and then move to create institutions that will eliminate these destructive influences.

The new world that we are attempting to create must destroy oppression of any type. The value of this new system will be determined by the status of the person who was low man on the totem pole. Unless women in any enslaved nation are completely liberated, the change cannot really be called a revolution. If the black woman has to retreat to the position she occupied before the armed struggle, the whole movement and the whole struggle will have retreated in terms of truly freeing the colonized population. . . .

An Introduction to Soul
AL CALLOWAY

While the black community was beginning to take pride in being black, white society as a whole was beginning to take greater notice of Afro-American civilization. Fads in everything from sneakers (Converse tennis shoes as streetwear) to hairstyles (the Afro) that started among black youth were soon copied by whites. In this piece, published in April 1968, Al Calloway, then publisher of an Afro-American magazine called *The Probe*, distilled the essence of Soul.

———————— ◆ ————————

Soul is sass, man. Soul is arrogance. Soul is walkin' down the street in a way that says, "This is me, muh-fuh!" Soul is that nigger whore comin' along . . . ja . . . ja . . . ja, and walkin' like she's sayin', "Here it is, baby. Come an' git it." Soul is bein' true to yourself, to what is you. Now, hold on: soul is . . . that . . . uninhibited . . . no, extremely uninhibited self . . . expression that goes into practically every Negro endeavor. That's soul. And there's swagger in it, man. It's exhibitionism, and it's effortless. Effortless. You don't need to put it on; it just comes out.

—Claude Brown

When I walk on Eighth Avenue, man, I see rhythms I don't see downtown. Polyrhythms. You look at one cat, he may be doin' bop, bop-bop bop, bop-bop, and another one goin' bop-de-bop, de-bop. Beautiful, man. Those are beautiful people. Yeah. But when I go downtown to Thirty-fourth Street, everybody's walkin' the same, you dig? They don't put themselves into it. Their walk tells you nothing about who they are. Polyrhythms. That's what it is. Like a flower garden in a breeze. The roses swing a little bit from side to side, kind of stiff, not too much. The lilacs swing wide, slow, lazy, not in a hurry. A blade of grass wiggles. It's 'cause they're all different and they're bein' themselves. Polyrhythms, like on Eighth Avenue. That's soul.

—Al Calloway

SOUL IS MOTION AND SOUND

It is stomping and clapping with the gospel music of the First Tabernacle of Deliverance (Spiritual), American Orthodox Catholic Church on Harlem's One Hundred Twenty-fifth Street, and boogalooing the Funky Broadway to the Memphis gospel soul blues of Otis Redding while walking down the street. Soul is "Doin' the Thing" with the church-oriented funky jazz of Horace Silver and just *moving* back down home with John Lee Hooker's gutbucket folk blues. Soul is being natural, telling it like it is. In the plantation fields and later the church, black people were allowed to keep *some* form of their self-expression going. The beautiful simple poetry of spiritual work songs like *Steal Away*—let's sneak back to the "Good Ship Jesus" and sail all the way home—is part of the blues of today, just as the spiritual ecstasy in a Yoruba Temple in West Africa is akin to what is felt in the soul-stirring Sanctified and Baptist churches of America's black ghettos. When Mahalia Jackson sings, the gospel and the blues of Bessie Smith become the *essence* of soul. Ray Charles throws his head back and shouts, "Oh, yeah!" and transmits an inner feeling of goodness. When you've heard it like that, you *know* you have been moved. Then he comes in with, "Don't it make you want to feel all right," and it's like everything has been unraveled and you just lay in there and groove. Ray Charles turns you on. So does Aretha Franklin and "Mister Soul" James Brown. On a warm day in Harlem one can see and feel an infinite variety of rhythms. People stand on tenement stoops and on the sidewalks and sway to juke-box music here, WLIB and WWRL radio there. Some get caught up in front of record shops and just soul dance like they want to. All around you, Watusi, Boston Monkey, Shing-a-ling, Karate, Boogaloo, The Pearl, the Funky Broadway. Storefront-church tambourines ring and two young men in red shirts walk down the street, one playing a sheepskin drum and the other a cowbell or a fife. A saxophone riffs, a trumpet wails, and then there's the shout. The black poet LeRoi Jones calls it "Ka'ba. . . . Our world is full of sound/our world is more lovely than anyone's. . . ."

SOUL HEROES

At Forty-third Street and Langley Avenue, on Chicago's South Side, amid the many storefront churches and dilapidated tenements, stands a soulful monument to African-American folk heroes past and present. Last summer, Billy Abernathy, his wife, and at least a score of other artists and draftsmen within the black community formed the Organization of Black American Culture (O.B.A.C.) and got the building's owner, who happens to be black, to consent to the creation of the revolutionary and historical hand-painted mural. Folk heroes who have made great contributions to the worlds of music, sports and literature adorn the Wall: men like Marcus Garvey, Malcolm X and Stokely Carmichael; men who have steered large masses of black people away from the "assimilation complex" bag that DuBois talked about and guided them to the positive course of *digging* themselves. The Wall is blessed with Dr. DuBois' image too. The great innovators of American music, Charlie Parker, Thelonious Monk, Max Roach, Ornette Coleman and the late John Coltrane, share a large portion of the Wall, along with Sassy Sarah Vaughn and Nina Simone. The mighty men, Muhammad Ali and Wilt Chamberlain, are there because they do their thing with a lot of style, and that's important. The real genius of the Wall is that it generates African-American self-pride. No matter what happens to Chicago, the Wall is sure to stand.

THE NITTY-GRITTY OF SOUL

There's a little piece of real estate in Harlem called Harlem Square, and on and about its four corners the curious, the intellectual and the political meet and exchange ideas. The center of activity there is one of Harlem's landmarks, Michaux's National Memorial African Bookstore. Marcus Garvey, Adam Clayton Powell Jr., Malcolm X and other soul heroes were heard by thousands at many a mass rally that took place in front of Michaux's. Inside the bookshop, every inch of available space is jammed with books by and about black folk. In the back room, where some of the soul heroes sat and wrote their speeches, the walls are crowded with photographs, paintings and drawings of great people of color. Every wall is a wall of respect. It is in Michaux's bookstore ("The House of Common Sense and Home of Proper Propaganda") that you learn about African musicians long ago who mastered the art of circular breathing and the simultaneous playing of instruments made out of elephant tusks and antelope horns. When you *see* the blind soul brother Roland Kirk playing his Manzello (the first saxophone), tenor sax and Stritch at the same time, and frequently blowing long sheets of sound without a breath, you are witnessing soul, baby. —One thing is certain: soul would be nowhere without the great savior, soul food. Black people brought to the Americas a tradition of how to make good food. Being close to the earth was their nature, and it was not difficult for them to find beans and greens that were good and to make good bread out of corn and crackling. It was a good thing that they knew this too, because *the man* would work them in the fields from sunup till dusk and sometimes they had other chores after that. On top of which they had to go all out for self, or the plantocracy would have starved them to death. When it came down to the hog, the planters didn't know anything except ham, bacon, spareribs and chops. The rest of it was no good, or so they thought, and the slaves copped it. They came up with pig tails, pig knuckles, ham hocks, hog maws, pig ears, snout, neck bones, chitlins, tripe and sowbelly. By the time fried or smothered chicken (The Gospel Bird) became a delicacy for special Sundays, black people were making candied yams, sweet-potato pie and fruit cobblers from the vegetables and fruits that they grew in their little patches or gathered from around. Traditionally, black people have congregated at the church for social and spiritual life, because church organization was (is) the only form allowed them. So when the sisters get together with those pots you can bet your life the food's going to be good. If you go into the Victory Restaurant on One Hundred Sixteenth Street in Harlem, you'll dig Bishop Shelton's sisters, with their natural hair and little caps and no makeup and floor-length gowns, serving soul food from eight in the morning till midnight. A plate of knuckles, black eyes and rice, a thick slice of corn bread, a glass of lemonade and a small home-made sweet-potato pie, and you're straight. If you really want to dig deep, get into Adam Powell's bag and cop a mess of chitlins and greens and soak them down with hot sauce. Soul food is why it is still chic to have a soul sister in the kitchen. Everybody digs the way she makes steaks, lobsters, roasts and *mmm* those rolls, pies and cakes.

THE STYLE OF SOUL

It is about nurturing creativity, being aesthetic in thought and action as much as possible. It permeates one's entire existence. In Harlem, as in all of America's urban black communities, the style is seen in the way a soul brother selects and wears his vines (suit, coat, tie, shirt, etc.). The hat and shoes are most important. If they are *correct*, it is certain that his whole thing is beautiful. You know that he's a cat who cares about himself. His hat will be a soft beaver, felt or velour, blocked in whatever way he may feel at any given time. He buys the best hat and while he's in his crib playing tunes and laying with his woman he may just let his hands go all over the hat like a potter does his clay. Thus, he creates his thing. A soul brother's shoes are always pointy-toed and so shined that he can almost adjust his hat while looking at them. The Sixties have ushered in a "new" mood among a significant number of soul brothers and sisters, causing a clean break with "anything other than what you really are." As reflected in manner of dress, a little stingy hat without the brim called a *ziki* is worn, or a free-form *fila* which is like a soft bag. The *kufe*, a small round headpiece, is also what's happening. Some soul brothers have gone all the way into a West African thing and are wearing *shokotos* (pants). The style of soul is getting back into the African folk bag. At the House of Ümoja (which means *unity* in Swahili), one of the many African shops in Harlem, soul brothers wear pieces of ivory in their ears and ornament their noses with gold like the Yorubas of West Africa. Wilt Chamberlain wears an African medallion around his neck and so does Jimmy Brown. Lew Alcindor wears *dasikis* and so does LeRoi Jones. —Soul is what, forever, has made black people hip. And it is what has enticed whites to imitate them without understanding it. Among black people, soul is a congenital understanding and respect for each other. It is the knowledge that one is but a segment of all that is, which is spatial, particled, like the colors in a rainbow; yet like when its colors are all rolled into one it is a deep purple haze . . . like morning . . . like dusk. It makes you humble, peaceful. That is why, above all, soul is wise and weary. It is the self-perception that informs you how and when to groove in your own way while others groove in theirs, and it is the sophistication that knows better than to ask, "Understand me," and settles instead for, "Don't mess with me; I'm in my own thing, baby."

CHAPTER 5

Bra Burners, Stonewallers, and Punk Rockers

Women's Issues, Gay Pride, and the End of the Counterculture

W omen's Liberation" and "Gay Liberation," as they were called at the time, were two distinctive ideas that arose in the late 1960s. Black civil rights movements of the early 1960s had demonstrated how unjust some laws and the social prejudices behind them were, and women and gays realized that they, too, could claim more civic and cultural equality using similar arguments. Susan Brownmiller's "The Enemy Within" reflects magazine articles of the times in which women question their traditional roles of wife and mother. The career woman, however, finds herself at odds with housewives and women lower on the social scale, a practice that continues to this day—in more affluent households, women who stay home with the children are congratulated for not "dumping their kids in daycare." As in the 1960s, today it is women, not men, who are judged for making a choice between career and family.

In areas as diverse as medicine and literature, the 1960s saw profound changes in women's issues. The Boston Women's Health Collective's *Our Bodies, Ourselves* sat out on coffee tables and was dragged into bathrooms everywhere, mirrors in hand, as women for the first time in U.S. history came to understand how their own bodies looked and functioned. One of the criticisms of the Women's Movement was that it was largely white and middle class. Frances M. Beal's "Double Jeopardy: To Be Black and Female" (see Chapter 4) expresses some of the early concerns of women from this time period that the mainstream magazines and media largely ignored.

Gay Liberation's impetus arose from the growing willingness to question received opinion that the Beats, hippies, war protestors, student radicals, and feminists had tapped into. What was once underground and hidden was soon coming out into the open, and the sexual liberation professed by the straights affected those who were not. Allen Ginsberg, several other Beats, and those who moved in their circles were openly gay at a time when such behavior could get you arrested. The Stonewall Riot of 1969, chronicled in this chapter by Jerry Lisker, came when a bar that had paid protection money to the police (as was the custom in those days for gay bars) was raided anyway. On the literary scene, Rita Mae Brown's *Rubyfruit Jungle* was the first bestselling novel by and about a lesbian. The humor Brown brought to the subject helped to dissipate some of the shock, but the publishing industry took notice and so did the academics. In the early 1970s came Andrew Holleran's *The Dancer from the Dance*, excerpted in this chapter, with scenes of sex, drugs, and parties in grand gay style. Well-received and reviewed by the mainstream press, it marked the beginnings of modern gay literature and represented, in many ways, the end of the 1960s as the party wound down.

What is "punk"? Is it music, fashion, an attitude, a lifestyle? Did it begin in America or England? In the late 1960s or middle 1970s? Once, to be punk meant searching thrift stores and putting together odds and ends for your look. Now, an eleven year old can go to the local mall and select safety-pinned items in all shades of black. Goths, an offshoot of punk culture, gather every year at Disneyland for an unofficial day to salute the evil queen from *Snow White* and their favorite villains. Skateboard culture overlaps with other countercultural elements to form subcultures that have now become mainstream. Music, t-shirts, and nihilistic attitudes are adopted by elementary school kids. But when it began, somewhere in America and England at the end of the hippie era, punk represented the more subversive, apolitical or anarchist elements of the counterculture from which it sprang.

Punk was not a literary movement, but it was much written *about*. Beat writer William Burroughs became *the* icon for a number of punk artists and Allen Ginsberg believed their rebellion and angst derived from the very beginning of the counterculture—the Beats themselves. Legs McNeil and Gillian Mc-Cain's *Please Kill Me: The Uncensored Oral History of Punk*, excerpted in this chapter, reminds us of the carnivalesque elements of rock music that would later be called punk in America, the MC5 (Motor City 5), who came from the heart of the Midwest—Detroit, Michigan. McNeil and McCain also write about the New York City scene with the Ramones, and others, but the MC5, who pre-dated the Sex Pistols by nearly ten years, reflect the origins of "anarchy in the U.S.A." that started in ballrooms with hippies and freaks dancing, taking drugs, and watching light shows.

Did punk signal the end of the counterculture? Some might view the 1970s underground cultures as mere extensions of the gritty, urban mean streets the Beats encountered in their travels. Allen Ginsberg's 1955 poem "Howl" begins with the lines "I saw the best minds of my generation destroyed by madness, starving and hysterical naked/dragging themselves through the negro streets at dawn looking for an angry fix"—could punk be nothing more than a manifestation of this nightmare? Gone are the optimistic dreams of a communal, racism-free, utopian world. Gone is any illusion about drugs opening the mind. The Vietnam War is over, but new conflicts, at home and abroad, had begun. Gone is the sexual revolution as herpes, AIDS, and new strains of sexually-transmitted diseases appear in younger and younger populations. Reproductive freedoms that the Women's Movement fought for begin to be challenged in the 1980s. The Counterculture was judged solely for its excesses, errors, and failed aspirations (see Chapter 6). The backlash had begun.

The Enemy Within

SUSAN BROWNMILLER

A frequent writer on feminist subjects, Susan Brownmiller wrote this piece, "The Enemy Within," in the heyday of what would become known as the "Women's Liberation Movement." Her most famous book, *Against Our Will: Men, Women and Rape* (1975), discusses the power structure of gender relations and views rape as "a conscious process of intimidation by which all men keep all women in a state of fear." Her latest, longer work, *In Our Time:*

Memoir of a Revolution (1999), reflects on the countercultural movements (largely male-centered) that led to women forming a movement of their own. Her criticisms of women's feigned "femininity" (she once said that "women are all female impersonators to some degree") can still be considered in light of twenty-first century media stereotypes of women.

———————————— ✦ ————————————

When I was 11 years old and talking in the schoolyard one day with a bunch of girlfriends from class, the discussion came around, as it did in those days, to "What are you going to be when you grow up?" At least three of us wanted to be actresses or models. Two had their sights already set on marriage, motherhood, and a house in the country. But one girl said *she* was going to go to medical school and be a doctor. This announcement was greeted with respectful silence (all those additional years of school!) until Martha, fat, bright, and at the head of the class, said solemnly, "I'd never go to a woman doctor. I just wouldn't have *confidence* in a woman doctor."

"Not even to deliver your baby?" I remember inquiring.

"Nope," Martha replied. "Especially not to deliver my baby. That's too important. Men doctors are better than women doctors."

It has been many years since that schoolyard discussion and I can't even recall the name or the face of the girl who had the ambitions, but I hope she wasn't sidetracked somewhere along the line. But I remember Martha. Calm, the best student, everybody's friend, more advanced physically than the rest of us—she had breasts, we didn't—and utterly positive at that tender age that men did things better than women. I will never forgive her for being the first person of my sex whom I ever heard put down women. I considered it traitorous then in the schoolyard, and I consider it traitorous now. Since that time, I have done a lot of observing of that strange phenomenon, have been guilty of it myself, I think, and have come to the conclusion that woman is often her own worst enemy—the enemy within.

5   One of the hardest things for a woman with aspirations to do in our society is to admit, first to herself and then to others, that she has ambitions that go beyond the routine—a good marriage, clever children. Early on, we learn that men don't take kindly to the notion of a woman entering the competitive lists. It is in the nature of power and position that those who have it do not relinquish it graciously, as all colonial peoples and all minority groups

discover at a certain stage in their development. Well, O.K., so be it. But infinitely more damaging to our psyche is the realization that our ambitions are met with equal hostility—pooh-poohed, sniffed at, scoffed at, ignored, or worse, not taken seriously—by mothers, sisters, cousins, aunts and friends, who won't believe that we have set our sights on a different sort of goal than *they* have envisioned, preferring instead to believe that our ambition is merely a "passing phase"—which, unfortunately, it often is because of lack of encouragement.

Psychologists talk a great deal about the importance of the approbation or approval of a peer group upon the individual. It is human nature to want to fit in. The senior at college who sends away for law-school catalogues while her dormitory mates down the corridor are sending away for catalogues of silver patterns is already conscious of swimming against the tide. (How different the atmosphere must be in a man's dormitory!) The magazine researcher who took her job as a stepping-stone to becoming a writer, but discovers that girl researchers are not encouraged to write by the magazine's male editors, will find little sympathy and understanding from other researchers who have taken the job to mark time until their proper engagements are properly announced in *The New York Times*. The peer-group pressure on a young woman in her 20s—as opposed to the pressure on a young man in his 20s—is decidedly against career.

I don't mean to imply that the force is necessarily insidious—although it sometimes is, and I intend to get around to discussing that aspect. I spent a wonderfully noncompetitive, warm, and friendly two years at *Newsweek* in the company of my "fellow" researchers in 1963–64 until I abruptly quit one day, wrenched myself out of the womb, because I finally realized that the warmth, the friendship, the long lunches, the joint shopping excursions to Saks Fifth Avenue, and the pleasant lack of direction among "the girls" had effectively smothered my own sense of direction. I was not the first *Newsweek* girl to break out of the researcher mold, and I will not be the last. But more heartening than individual breakthroughs is the news that has lately reached me from that sunny vineyard on Madison Avenue—the rumblings of insurrection among those very researchers who appeared so content with their lot just a few years ago.

There were two full-fledged women writers at *Newsweek* during the time I was there. One did her job quietly and went about unnoticed, but the other, an attractive, sexy young lady, was rather noticeable. We hated her. Among the grievances we held against this young woman was the fact that she never deigned to talk with us researchers. Considered herself superior, we thought. Got her job through unholy machinations, we believed. Dressed terribly, we agreed. *Couldn't really write,* we fervently hoped. It took me a few years after leaving the magazine to realize what this hostility toward someone we hardly knew was all about. *She* was where *we* wanted to be. When she walked through the halls she was L., the writer, not L., a researcher. There may have been 50 male writers who daily crossed our path at the magazine, but we spared them our collective resentment because, after all, they were men and we weren't. But L.—how dare she! She threatened our collective existence! Two years later, when I was working as a television newswriter at ABC (again, there were only two of us women writers), I experienced some of this collective cattiness from the ABC researchers and understood it perfectly. I also discovered that it's quite natural for writers to pal around with other writers and not with researchers. It has to do with field of interest and not with snobbery at all. L. knew it, and I discovered it.

There was a small item in the news not long ago about the first woman editor-in-chief of the University of Pennsylvania's daily student newspaper. The editor, Judith Teller, a junior at the University's Wharton School of Business, was quoted as saying, "I generally find women basically incompetent, and in general I deal with men." A harsh quote from Miss Teller, to be sure, and not designed to win her any women friends, but at the age of 20 Miss Teller, an obvious careerist, wants to be where the action is, and for that I can't blame her.

10   Women are *not* "basically incompetent," but so much of their energy goes into pretending incompetence when there are attractive men around who may be watching that the result is often the same. Schooled by their mothers to "let the man win" at Ping-pong or tennis, how can they develop a good game? They can't, of course, and the game becomes not an exercise of skill but a minuet of manners. The Ping-pong-and-tennis syndrome affects a woman's performance in practically all areas of her life. The idea is not to win. "Women is Losers," wails Janis Joplin in a repetitive, powerful lamentation. Losing has been equated with femininity for so long in our culture that it has become a virtual definition of the female role. The way to lose is not to try very hard to win, to convince oneself that personal achievement—if one is a woman—doesn't really matter at all. This peculiar attitude, which flies in the face of every success homily in *Poor Richard's Al-*

manack, is as unnatural as it is destructive. It has its parallels in the attitudes of the hard-core unemployed who have stripped away personal ambition and belief in their own abilities to a point where they are actually incapable of functioning. We are all familiar with the sexual double standards that men employ, but here is a sexual double standard that women hold on to for dear life: *admire individual achievement in men, but deny it for yourself.* The corollary to this dictum, by the way, is *marry the achiever.* Either way, it is a terrible denial of self-worth.

I have seen women who *admit* to small hankerings of personal ambition (usually expressed by a modest "I'd like to do more at work") throw up unbelievable psychological barriers to their own success. Two conversations I once had in the space of two days with a couple of young ladies who work in television will illustrate what I mean. Both women had neatly resolved their stymied careers with the oddest excuses I have ever heard. One thought she never could rise to a producer because she found the temperature in the film-editing rooms "too cold." The other said she never felt comfortable "near machines." To the first I answered, "Get a sweater." The second rendered me speechless. Of course, what these women were really saying was that their *femininity*—not the fact that they were female—somehow made them unfit for the tough world of television production.

The risk of losing that intangible called femininity weighs heavily on many women who are afraid to compete with men for better jobs. This sad state of affairs has come about because of arbitrary and rigid definitions of what is masculine and what is feminine that our culture has relied on for a variety of complex reasons. We can thank the hippie revolution for knocking down some of the old criteria, particularly external ones like the length of hair and form of dress. But as long as such qualities as self-assertion, decision-making, and leadership are considered masculine—and conversely, unfeminine—a woman who worries about her femininity will never make a go of it in terms of career.

It was men who made the arbitrary rules of masculine/feminine that we suffer under, but it is women who continue to buy the stereotypes. At the early women's-liberation meetings that I attended, I was struck with how all of us were unwilling to assume leadership roles, and how often a sensible comment or brilliant new insight was couched between giggles and stutters or surrounded by self-disparaging phrases and gestures. Clearly, we were women who were unused to speaking forthrightly—without the frills and furbelows of "feminine" roundabout logic designed to make a point as gently as possible for fear of offending. Since we had nobody to offend but ourselves, this namby-pambying ceased to some extent with the passage of time.

But a women's-liberation meeting is a very special crucible. In the world outside, the stereotype of the aggressive, castrating bitch is still posted as a warning to us. If a woman believes in the existence of this mythical creature—and believes in her own potential transmogrification—her case is hopeless. It astounds me that so many women remain convinced that a woman who functions in high gear in business, politics, or in the professions loses something intrinsic that is worth preserving. Personally, I have always felt that true femininity was rather indestructible. One look at the Irish revolutionary Bernadette Devlin should settle the matter once and for all. I suspect that this "castrating bitch" propaganda, a big lie, really, is perpetuated not only by insecure men but also by do-nothing women, the magpies who busy themselves with nothing more than nest-building. There is no getting around the uncomfortable truth that the militant stay-at-homes, the clinging vines, dislike and distrust their liberated sisters. I know exactly what I lost when I gave up pretending that passivity was a virtue and entered the competitive arena—some personality distortions which made me pirouette in concentric circles when I could have simply walked a straight line. And I know what I gained—self-esteem and a stretching of creative muscles and an exercising of a mind which had grown flaccid from disuse since the halcyon days of college.

15   A major tragedy of the female sex is that friendship and respect between women has never been highly regarded. During the dating years, girls are notoriously quick to ditch an appointment with a girlfriend at the sound of a male voice on the telephone. With marriage and family comes the suspicion that all other women are potentially "the other woman." In an early episode of *The Forsythe Saga* on TV, Irene the adulteress tells Young Jolyon's daughter, "Don't you know that women don't have friends? They have a lover, and they have people that they meet." How pathetic, but how historically accurate.

There is nothing in women's chemical or biological makeup that should preclude deep loyalty to those of the same sex. The sensitivity is certainly there, as is the capacity for warmth and love and fidelity. But until women cease to see themselves strictly in terms of men's eyes and to value men more highly than women, friendship with other women will remain a sometime thing, an expedient among competitors of inferior station that can be lightly discarded. I, for one, would much rather compete *with* men than for them. This affliction of competition between women for the attention of men—the only kind of women's competition that is encouraged by society—also affects the liberated women who manage to secure an equal footing with men in this man's world. Watch a couple of strong women in the same room and notice the sparks fly. Many women who reject the "woman is inferior" psychology for themselves apply it unsparingly to others of the same sex. An ambitious woman frequently thinks of herself as the only hen in the barnyard, to reverse a common metaphor. *She* is the exception, she believes. Women must recognize that they must make common cause with *all* women. When women get around to really liking—and respecting—other women, why then, we will have begun.

from *Our Bodies, Ourselves*
THE BOSTON WOMEN'S HEALTH COLLECTIVE

Our Bodies, Ourselves (1970) was a landmark book about women's health and sexuality. Begun in the spring of 1969 at a women's liberation conference held in Boston, the women collected questions and began to share medical information. This small, grassroots collective has evolved into a non-profit organization working at both the domestic and international levels over thirty years later, with the most recent edition of the book published in 1998. While the work began with issues about reproductive health and sexuality, more materials on environmental and occupational health, menopause, aging, and other topics are now included. The excepts here are from the preface to the 1973 edition.

———————————— ✦ ————————————

In the spring of 1969, a group of us met at a women's conference in Boston. The conference was one of the first gatherings of women meeting specifically to talk with other women. For many of us it was the first time we had joined together with other women to talk and think about our lives and what we could do about them. At one point, we took part in a small discussion group on "women and their bodies." Not wanting the discussion to end, some of us decided to keep on meeting as a group after the conference.

In the beginning we called ourselves "the doctors group." We had all experienced similar feelings of frustration and anger toward specific doctors and the medical maze in general, and initially we wanted to do something about those doctors who were condescending, paternalistic, judgmental and noninformative. As we talked and shared our experiences with one another, we realized just how much we had to learn about our bodies. So we decided on a summer project: to research those topics which we felt were particularly pertinent to learning about our bodies, to discuss in the group what we had learned, then to write papers individually or in groups of two or three, and finally to present the results in the fall as a course for women on women and their bodies.

As we developed the course we realized more and more that we really were capable of collecting, understanding, and evaluating medical information. Together we evaluated our reading of books and journals, our talks with doctors and friends who were medical students. We found we could discuss, question, and argue with each other in a new spirit of cooperation rather than competition. We were equally struck by how important it was for us to be able to open up with one another and share our feelings about our bodies. The process of talking was as crucial as the facts themselves. Over time the facts and feelings melted together in ways that touched us very deeply, and that is reflected in the changing titles of the course and then the book, from *Women and Their Bodies* to *Women and Our Bodies* to, finally, *Our Bodies, Ourselves*.

When we gave the course we met in any available free space we could get: in day schools, in nursery schools, in churches, in our homes. We wanted the course to stimulate the same kind of talking and sharing that we who had prepared the course had experienced. We had something to say, but we had a lot to learn as well; we did not want a traditional teacher-student relationship. At the end of ten to twelve sessions, we found that many women felt both eager and competent to get together in small groups and share what they had learned with other women. We saw it as a never-ending process always involving more and more women.

5   After the first teaching of the course, we decided to revise our initial papers and mimeograph them so that other women could

have copies as the course expanded. Eventually we got them printed and bound together in an inexpensive edition published by the New England Free Press. It was fascinating and very exciting for us to see what a constant demand there was for our book. It came out in several editions, a larger number being printed each time, and the time from one printing to the next becoming shorter. The growing volume of requests began to strain the staff of the New England Free Press. Since our book was clearly speaking to many people, we wanted to reach beyond the audience who lived in the area or who were acquainted with the New England Free Press. For wider distribution it made sense to publish our book commercially.

From the very beginning of working together, we have felt exhilarated and energized by our new knowledge. Finding out about our bodies and our bodies' needs, starting to take control over that area of our lives, has released for us an energy that has overflowed into our work, our friendships, our relationships with men and women, and for all of us to our marriages and our parenthood. In trying to figure out why this has had such a life-changing effect on us, we have come up with several important ways in which this kind of body education has been liberating for us and may be a starting point for the liberation of many other women.

First, we learned what we learned both from professional sources—textbooks, medical journals, doctors, nurses—and from our own experiences. The facts were important, and we did careful research to get the information we had not had in the past. As we brought the facts to one another we learned a good deal, but in sharing our personal experiences relating to those facts we learned still more. Once we had learned what the "experts" had to tell us, we found that we still had a lot to teach and to learn from one another. For instance, many of us had "learned" about the menstrual cycle in science or biology classes—we had perhaps even memorized the names of the menstrual hormones and what they did. But most of us did not remember much of what we had learned. This time when we read in a text that the onset of menstruation is a normal and universal occurrence in young girls from ages ten to eighteen, we started to talk about our first menstrual periods. We found that, for many of us, beginning to menstruate had not felt normal at all, but scary, embarrassing, mysterious. We realized that what we had been told about menstruation and what we had not been told—even the tone of voice it bad been told in—had all had an effect on our feelings about being female. Similarly, the information from enlightened texts describing masturbation as a normal, common sexual activity did not really become our own until we began to pull up from inside ourselves and share what we had never before expressed: the confusion and shame we had been made to feel, and often still felt, about touching our bodies in a sexual way.

Learning about our bodies in this way is an exciting kind of learning, where information and feelings are allowed to interact. It makes the difference between rote memorization and relevant learning, between fragmented pieces of a puzzle and the integrated picture, between abstractions and real knowledge. We discovered that people don't learn very much when they are just passive recipients of information. We found that each individual's response to information was valid and useful, and that by sharing our responses we could develop a base on which to be critical of what the experts tell us. Whatever we need to learn now, in whatever area of our lives, we know more how to go about it.

A second important result of this kind of learning is that we are better prepared to evaluate the institutions that are supposed to meet our health needs—the hospitals, clinics, doctors, medical schools, nursing schools, public health departments, Medicaid bureaucracies and so on. For some of us it was the first time we had looked critically, and with strength, at the existing institutions serving us. The experience of learning just how little control we had over our lives and bodies, the coming together out of isolation to learn from each other in order to define what we needed, and the experience of supporting one another in demanding the changes that grew out of our developing critique—all were crucial and formative political experiences for us. We have felt our potential power as a force for political and social change.

10   The learning we have done while working on *Our Bodies, Ourselves* has been a good basis for growth in other areas of life for still another reason. For women throughout the centuries, ignorance about our bodies has had one major consequence: pregnancy. Until very recently pregnancies were all but inevitable, and biology was our destiny: because our bodies are designed to get pregnant and give birth and lactate, that is what all or most of us did. The courageous and dedicated work begun by people like Margaret Sanger to spread and make available birth control methods that women could use freed us from the traditional lifetime of pregnancies. But the societal expectation that a woman

above all else will have babies does not die easily. When we first started talking to each other about this, we found that old expectations had nudged most of us into a fairly rigid role of wife-and-motherhood from the moment we were born female. Even in 1969, when we first started the work that led to this book, we found that many of us were still getting pregnant when we didn't want to. It was not until we researched carefully and learned more about our reproductive systems, about birth control methods and abortion, about laws governing birth control and abortion, and not until we put all this information together with what it meant to us to be female, that we began to feel we could truly set out to control whether and when we would have babies.

This knowledge has freed many of us from the constant energy-draining anxiety about becoming pregnant. It has made our pregnancies better because they no longer happen to us, but we actively choose them and enthusiastically participate in them. It has made our parenthood better because it is our choice rather than our destiny. This knowledge has freed us from playing the role of mother if it is not a role that fits us. It has given us a sense of a larger life space to work in, an invigorating and challenging sense of time and room to discover the energies and talents that are in us, to do the work we want to do. And one of the things we most want to do is to help make this freedom of choice, this life span, available to every woman. This is why people in the women's movement have been so active in fighting against the inhumane legal restrictions, the imperfections of available contraceptives, the poor sex education, the highly priced and poorly administered health care that keep too many women from having this crucial control over their bodies.

There is a fourth reason why knowledge about our bodies has generated so much new energy. For us, body education is core education. Our bodies are the physical bases from which we move out into the world; ignorance, uncertainty—even, at worst, shame—about our physical selves create in us an alienation from ourselves that keeps us from being the whole people that we could be. Picture a woman trying to do work and to enter into equal and satisfying relationships with other people when she feels physically weak because she has never tried to be strong; when she drains her energy trying to change her face, her figure, her hair, her smells, to match some ideal norm set by magazines, movies and TV; When she feels confused and ashamed of the menstrual blood that every month appears from some dark place in her body; when her internal body processes are a mystery to her and surface only to cause her trouble (an unplanned pregnancy or cervical cancer); when she does not understand or enjoy sex and concentrates her sexual drives into aimless romantic fantasies, perverting and misusing a potential energy because she has been brought up to deny it. Learning to understand, accept, and be responsible for our physical selves, we are freed of some of these preoccupations and can start to use our untapped energies. Our image of ourselves is on a firmer base, we can be better friends and better lovers, better people, more self-confident, more autonomous, stronger and more whole.

From,

Norma, Pam, Judy, Nancy, Paula, Ruth, Wilma, Esther, Jane, Wendy, and Joan.

Homo Nest Raided, Queen Bees Are Stinging Mad
JERRY LISKER

On Friday evening, June 27, 1969, the New York City tactical police force raided a popular Greenwich Village gay bar, the Stonewall Inn. Raids were not unusual, even as late as 1969; they were conducted regularly, despite payoffs to the police. That night, however, the street erupted into violent protest as the crowds at the bar fought back. For many, the Gay Liberation Movement began on that night when gay culture experienced its first truly countercultural moment since Allen Ginsberg read his poem "Howl" at the Six Gallery in 1955. Adopting many of the tactics of the politicals, gay influence on music, fashion, and dance intertwined with that of the hippies and other counterculturalists. Jerry Lisker's July 6, 1969, newspaper account depicts the actions of that evening.

———————— ✦ ————————

She sat there with her legs crossed, the lashes of her mascara-coated eyes beating like the wings of a hummingbird. She was angry. She was so upset she hadn't bothered to shave. A day old stubble was beginning to push through the pancake makeup. She was a he. A queen of Christopher Street.

Last weekend the queens had turned commandos and stood bra strap to bra strap against an invasion of the helmeted Tactical Patrol Force. The elite police squad had shut down one of their private gay clubs, the Stonewall Inn at 57 Christopher St., in the heart of a three-block homosexual community in Greenwich Village. Queen Power reared its bleached blonde head in revolt. New York City experienced its first homosexual riot. "We may have lost the battle, sweets, but the war is far from over," lisped an unofficial lady-in-waiting from the court of the Queens.

"We've had all we can take from the Gestapo," the spokesman, or spokeswoman, continued. "We're putting our foot down once and for all." The foot wore a spiked heel. According to reports, the Stonewall Inn, a two-story structure with a sand painted brick and opaque glass facade, was a mecca for the homosexual element in the village who wanted nothing but a private little place where they could congregate, drink, dance and do whatever little girls do when they get together.

The thick glass shut out the outside world of the street. Inside, the Stonewall bathed in wild, bright psychedelic lights, while the patrons writhed to the sounds of a juke box on a square dance floor surrounded by booths and tables. The bar did a good business and the waiters, or waitresses, were always kept busy, as they snaked their way around the dancing customers to the booths and tables. For nearly two years, peace and tranquility reigned supreme for the Alice in Wonderland clientele.

THE RAID LAST FRIDAY

Last Friday the privacy of the Stonewall was invaded by police   5
from the First Division. It was a raid. They had a warrant. After two years, police said they had been informed that liquor was being served on the premises. Since the Stonewall was without a license, the place was being closed. It was the law.

All hell broke loose when the police entered the Stonewall. The girls instinctively reached for each other. Others stood frozen, locked in an embrace of fear.

Only a handful of police were on hand for the initial landing in the homosexual beachhead. They ushered the patrons out onto Christopher Street, just off Sheridan Square. A crowd had formed in front of the Stonewall and the customers were greeted with cheers of encouragement from the gallery.

The whole proceeding took on the aura of a homosexual Academy Awards Night. The Queens pranced out to the street blowing kisses and waving to the crowd. A beauty of a specimen named Stella wailed uncontrollably while being led to the sidewalk in front of the Stonewall by a cop. She later confessed that she didn't protest the manhandling by the officer, it was just that her hair was in curlers and she was afraid her new beau might be in the crowd and spot her. She didn't want him to see her this way, she wept.

QUEEN POWER

The crowd began to get out of hand, eyewitnesses said. Then, without warning, Queen Power exploded with all the fury of a gay atomic bomb. Queens, princesses and ladies-in-waiting began hurling anything they could get their polished, manicured fingernails on. Bobby pins, compacts, curlers, lipstick tubes and other femme fatale missiles were flying in the direction of the cops. The war was on. The lilies of the valley had become carnivorous jungle plants.

10   Urged on by cries of "C'mon girls, lets go get 'em," the defenders of Stonewall launched an attack. The cops called for assistance. To the rescue came the Tactical Patrol Force.

Flushed with the excitement of battle, a fellow called Gloria pranced around like Wonder Woman, while several Florence Nightingales administered first aid to the fallen warriors. There were some assorted scratches and bruises, but nothing serious was suffered by the honeys turned Madwoman of Chaillot.

Official reports listed four injured policemen with 13 arrests. The War of the Roses lasted about 2 hours from about midnight to 2 a.m. There was a return bout Wednesday night.

Two veterans recently recalled the battle and issued a warning to the cops. "If they close up all the gay joints in this area, there is going to be all out war."

BRUCE AND NAN

Both said they were refugees from Indiana and had come to New York where they could live together happily ever after. They were in their early 20's. They preferred to be called by their married names, Bruce and Nan.

"I don't like your paper," Nan lisped matter-of-factly. "It's anti- 15
fag and pro-cop."

"I'll bet you didn't see what they did to the Stonewall. Did the pigs tell you that they smashed everything in sight? Did you ask them why they stole money out of the cash register and then smashed it with a sledge hammer? Did you ask them why it took them two years to discover that the Stonewall didn't have a liquor license?"

Bruce nodded in agreement and reached over for Nan's trembling hands.

"Calm down, doll," he said. "Your face is getting all flushed."

Nan wiped her face with a tissue.

"This would have to happen right before the wedding. The re- 20
ception was going to be held at the Stonewall, too," Nan said, tossing her ashen-tinted hair over her shoulder.

"What wedding?," the bystander asked.

Nan frowned with a how-could-anybody-be-so-stupid look. "Eric and Jack's wedding, of course. They're finally tying the knot. I thought they'd never get together."

MEET SHIRLEY

"We'll have to find another place, that's all there is to it," Bruce sighed. "But every time we start a place, the cops break it up sooner or later."

"They let us operate just as long as the payoff is regular," Nan said bitterly. "I believe they closed up the Stonewall because there was some trouble with the payoff to the cops. I think that's the real reason. It's a shame. It was such a lovely place. We never bothered anybody. Why couldn't they leave us alone?"

Shirley Evans, a neighbor with two children, agrees that the 25
Stonewall was not a rowdy place and the persons who frequented the club were never troublesome. She lives at 45 Christopher St.

"Up until the night of the police raid there was never any trouble there," she said. "The homosexuals minded their own business and never bothered a soul. There were never any fights or hollering, or anything like that. They just wanted to be left alone. I don't know what they did inside, but that's their business. I was never in there myself. It was just awful when the police came. It was like a swarm of hornets attacking a bunch of butterflies."

A reporter visited the now closed Stonewall and it indeed looked like a cyclone had struck the premises. Police said there were over 200 people in the Stonewall when they entered with a warrant. The crowd outside was estimated at 500 to 1,000. According to police, the Stonewall had been under observation for some time. Being a private club, plain clothesmen were refused entrance to the inside when they periodically tried to check the place. "They had the tightest security in the Village," a First Division officer said, "We could never get near the place without a warrant."

POLICE TALK

The men of the First Division were unable to find any humor in the situation, despite the comical overtones of the raid.

"They were throwing more than lace hankies," one inspector said. "I was almost decapitated by a slab of thick glass. It was thrown like a discus and just missed my throat by inches. The beer can didn't miss, though, it hit me right above the temple."

30   Police also believe the club was operated by Mafia connected owners. The police did confiscate the Stonewall's cash register as proceeds from an illegal operation. The receipts were counted and are on file at the division headquarters. The warrant was served and the establishment closed on the grounds it was an illegal membership club with no license, and no license to serve liquor.

The police are sure of one thing. They haven't heard the last from the Girls of Christopher Street.

from *The Dancer from the Dance*
ANDREW HOLLERAN

The Dancer from the Dance (1978), now considered a gay classic, was a groundbreaking work in gay fiction for both its bestseller status and the positive reviews it received from the mainstream press. Suddenly, the market for gay fiction expanded beyond the gay community. Holleran, who served drinks on Fire Island-bound buses in the 1970s in order to finance his writing career, based *Dancer* on his experiences of the seventies gay scene in New York. His other works of fiction include *Nights in Aruba* (1983) and *The Beauty of Men* (1991). This excerpt from *Dancer* depicts the gay version of the Counterculture's Summer of Love, embodied in the story of Malone, a party-circuit man looking for love and his urban-glitter guide Sutherland, "that tiny species of homosexual, the doomed queen."

———————— ✦ ————————

October on Fire Island was lovely partly because it had been abandoned by the crowd. And wasn't that the whole allure of love, and why Malone had been such a genius at it: our struggle, always, to isolate from the mob the single individual, having whom society meant nothing? There were lovers whose affair was purely public, whose union consisted of other people's considering them lovers, but the reason I loved the beach in autumn (besides the elegance of the weather, the enameled light that layered everything from carpenters to butterflies to the tips of the dune grass) was that now the false social organism had vanished and left it what Malone had always wished it to be: a fishing village, in which, presumably, no one lied to one another.

A sudden wish to feast on the past made me sit down on the steps leading to the beach for a moment, the steps where in the hot August sunlight we had rested our feet from the burning sand and shaded our eyes to look out at the figures in the dazzling light. There had been a dwarf that summer, a squat hydrocephalic woman who wandered up and down the beach among those handsome young men like a figure in an allegory. And there had been the Viet Nam veteran who had lost a leg, and walked along the water's edge in a leather jacket in the hottest weather, hobbling with a cane. He had drowned that Sunday so many swimmers had drowned. Not twenty feet from the steps on which I sat now, a corpse had lain all afternoon beneath a sheet because the police were too busy to remove it, and five feet away from the corpse, people lay taking the sun and admiring a man who had just given the kiss of life to a young boy. Death and desire, death and desire.

The whole long, mad summer came back in the warmth of that pale, distant sun burning high above the deserted sea. The summer gym shorts had become fashionable as bathing suits, the summer Frank Post (who each spring contemplated suicide because he could not rise to the occasion again—of being the most voluptuous, beautiful man on the Island, the homosexual myth everyone adored—but managed to go the gym, take his pills, and master yet another season) shaved his body and wore jockstraps to Tea Dance, and his lover died of an overdose of Angel Dust and Quaaludes. The summer "I'll Always Love My Mama" lasted all season and we never grew tired of it. The summer that began with the Leo Party and ended with the Pink and Green Party (which Sutherland had given, and from which Malone had vanished). The summer nude sunbathing began, the summer Todd Keller, from Laguna Beach, was the "hot number" and Angel Dust the favorite drug. The summer Kenny Lamar was arrested in the bar for sniffing a popper, the summer certain people got into piss, the summer his guests threw a birthday cake into Edwin Giglio's face, they all loathed him so, the summer Lyman Quinn's deck collapsed at the Heat Wave Party, with two thousand people on it; the summer a whale beached itself near Water Island in July, and a reindeer appeared swimming offshore in August. The summer Louis Deron dressed in gas masks, the summer Vuitton became pretentious, along with Cartier tank watches, and Lacostes were out. The summer the backpacking look began, the summer the grocery store changed hands, and people began to worry about the garbage floating three miles out in the Atlantic Ocean, the summer George Renfrew took the Kane House and built a new pool for the Esther Williams Party, the summer the new policeman drove everyone crazy, and Horst Jellaby began flying the flag of the country of his lover for one week: One only had to see the flag of Argentina to know he had snared the gorgeous physician visiting from Buenos Aires, or the flag of Colombia to know the coach of the national soccer team was in his bed at that moment. The summer the models moved to Water Island to get away from the mobs who had started to come to this place in greater numbers each summer. The summer two Cessnas collided in midair and the sky rained bodies into a grove of trees where everyone was in the middle of having afternoon sex. The summer some nameless ribbon clerk died trying to sniff a popper at the bottom of a pool . . . it was a blur, all of it, of faces, and parties, and weekends and storms; it vanished, as did all weeks, months, years in New York in one indistinguishable blur, life speeded up, life so crowded that nothing stood out in relief, and people waited, as they had one autumn weekend here, for a hurricane to provide some kind of sublime climax that never came. . . .

A single figure was walking along the ravaged beach frowning at the sand and then looking out to sea: alone with the late October sky, the coming storm. As we had watched so many figures approach, and pass, and disappear those furious summers given over to nothing more than watching figures like this one come near, and then finding them flawed or flawless, this late-autumn visitor assumed a face and body—and I recognized one of Malone's first lovers: a Hungarian nuclear physicist we had all adored one summer. This place, the city, was full of Malone's former lovers. He compared them once to the garbage of New York accumulating in a giant floating island off the coast of this very beach, floating nearer each year, as if accumulated loves, like waste, could choke us. The physicist passed by brooding over private sorrows. We had all of us wanted him with scant success. Which recalled a rule of Malone's, with which he used to comfort those who despaired of ever wedding their dreams, spoken with a rueful regret that it was true (for, if true lovers are either chaste or promiscuous, Malone belonged, in the end, to the first school): "Over a long enough period of time, everyone goes to bed with everyone else." And cheap as it was, that was the truth.

They had taken no notice of his disappearance, these people: no funeral pennants on the turrets of their houses, no black sash across the swimming pool. The Island waited now in bleak desuetude for next season; the very beach of that particular summer had been mercifully obliterated by autumn storms so that next summer's strand might assume its shape; and it was right. One came here for very selfish reasons; after all, it was a purely pagan place. Malone would be memorialized in gossip. He would be remembered at a dozen dinner parties next summer, or in those casual conversations after sex in which two strangers discover they know exactly the same people and live exactly the same lives. One would expect as much sentiment for the departure of an Island beauty as one would for the patron of a gambling casino who walks away from the roulette wheel. For such a private place, it was very public: Anyone could come here, and anyone did. If not this gypsy throng, who would mourn Malone? He lived perhaps in my memory: I would always think of this place, this sea, this sky, his face together, and wonder if he had wasted his life.

Can one waste a life? Especially now? "Well," Malone would say when some conceited beauty refused to even meet his eyes, "we're all part of the nitrogen cycle." Oh, yes, and the butterflies rising in golden clouds from the dunes on their way to Mexico, the deer lifting its head on a bluff to gaze down the beach, the silver fish suffocating in the back of the trucks, the very sky would not be subject to anything more. But in that narrower, human sense, of course it can. Malone worried that he had wasted his;

5

and many felt he had. Those smug people who had bought their own houses out here and arrived by seaplane with their Vuitton. Malone only wanted to be liked. Malone wanted life to be beautiful and Malone believed quite literally in happiness—in short, he was the most romantic creature of a community whose citizens are more romantic, perhaps, than any other on earth, and in the end—he learned—more philistine.

He wanted to be liked, and so he ran away to New York—away from his own family—and he vanished on Manhattan, which is a lot easier than vanishing in the jungles of Sumatra. And what did he do? Instead of becoming the success they expected him to be, instead of becoming a corporate lawyer, he went after, like hounds to the fox, the cheapest things in life: beauty, glamour . . . all the reasons this beach had once thrilled us to death. But the parties, the drugs, the T-shirts, the music were as capable of giving him his happiness as this sea I sat beside now was of stinging beneath the whips that Xerxes had his servants turn on the waves for swallowing up his ships.

from *Please Kill Me: The Uncensored Oral History of Punk*
Legs McNeil and Gillian McCain

In writing the "first oral history of the most nihilist of all pop movements," Legs McNeil credits himself with being the first person to coin the term "punk." Whether or not this is true, McNeil cofounded, in 1975, at age 18, *Punk* magazine in New York City. Gillian McCain, poet and author of *Tilt* (1996), a collection of prose poems, worked with McNeil to write *Please Kill Me: The Uncensored Oral History of Punk* (1996), the next best thing to being there. This excerpt from the book, "The Music We've Been Waiting to Hear," interviews all the major suspects in America's early punk days: John Sinclair (White Panther Party founder), Danny Fields (former "company freak" at Elektra Records and Atlantic Records executive, manager of the Stooges), Wayne Kramer (lead guitarist, MC5), Iggy Pop (a.k.a. James Osterberg, lead singer, the Stooges), Kathy Asheton (sister of Stooges members Ron and Scott Asheton), Dennis Thompson (drummer, MC5 and New Order), and Steve Harris (entrepreneur, former vice president of Elektra records).

———————— ✦ ————————

Steve Harris: With the success of the Doors' single, "Light My Fire," Elektra Records really became competitive, because we then had the leverage to sign other acts. We weren't just your nice little folk label anymore. . .

Danny Fields: Bob Rudnick and Dennis Frawley had a column in the *East Village Other* called "Kocaine Karma," and the two of them were relentless in loading me with propaganda about this band from Detroit, the MC5, which stood for "The Motor City Five."

Rudnick and Frawley would say, "You gotta see this band! You gotta sign this band! This is the greatest band! They're so popular! They sell out the Grande Ballroom! They sell out all over the Midwest! It's not just a band, it's a way of life!"

And the MC5 became legendary for being the only band that played at the riots at the Chicago Democratic National Convention. Norman Mailer had written about them.

Wayne Kramer: Being the young hustlers we were, the MC5 started to see that this hippie thing was gonna go, man. That it was gonna be big, because all these kids would come into Detroit from the suburbs, dressed like hippies on the weekend. So we figured the way to get the hippies to like us was to get the chief hippie to like us, who was John Sinclair.

Sinclair was doing six months for reefer in the Detroit House of Corrections and his getting-out-of-jail party was going to be the cultural event of the summer. We showed up and had to wait all day to play—there were all these poets reading and dancers dancing—so we didn't get to play until four in the morning. So we cranked up our fucking hundred-watt amps and were blasting away all the hippies and the beatniks. They didn't care what you played—hippies would dance to anything. So we were in the middle of our set, dedicating a song to this guy John Sinclair, and his wife pulls the plug on us.

Our relationship with John had started on a sour note. He had a column in the local underground paper, so he wrote about us saying, "What's with these jive rock & rollers? If only they'd pay attention to real music like Sun Ra and John Coltrane." I took exception with it, you know? I went over to his house and said,

5

"Hey man, what's up with all this? We're in the Community, too. And we know about John Coltrane and we need a place to rehearse and can't we use the Artist Workshop too?" So we smoked a joint and everything was cool.

Danny Fields: In 1968 the mood of the country was changing. The night President Lyndon Johnson announced, "I will not seek, I will not run," I couldn't believe it. I mean, who were you gonna hate now?

Of course, then came the Chicago Democratic National Convention. . . .

10   **John Sinclair:** We insisted we play at the Festival of Life outside the 1968 Democratic Convention in Chicago. We were this hungry band from Detroit—you know, we're trying to get over, we're trying to get recognized, we're trying to get a record contract. I mean, let's say it in so many words.

At the same time, we just wanted to be a part of it because it completely coincided with our world view. So on both of those fronts, we said, "Man, we can go there and be part of the Festival of Life and there'll probably be some people from the papers and shit." You know, "Maybe Norman Mailer will see us!"

Wayne Kramer: About an hour before we played, a couple of people came up to us and offered us some hash cookies. They said, "Just eat one, because they're very strong," so naturally we all ate one and then we all split four or five of 'em: "Oh yeah, take another bite, yeah, I'm not getting off, you getting off? No, man, I need some more."

So it came time to play and I started getting off, man. Getting off seriously. I think we were doing our song "Starship," and we're in this space-music thing and we're talking about the war and the human being—lawn mower and everything, and the Chicago police helicopters started buzzing above us.

They were coming down on top of us, and the helicopter sound fit in with what I was playing on the guitar—"Yeah, it's perfect man, waaaaahhhhh!"

15   There were all these police agent provocateurs in the audience starting fights and pushing people around—guys in army fatigue jackets with short hair and sunglasses. There were real bad vibes. And the whole thing just made absolutely perfect sense to me.

As high as I was, it all made perfect sense. It all fit.

Dennis Thompson: When I saw all those cops, the only thing I could think was, Jesus Christ, if this is the revolution, we lost. I was thinking, It's over, right now. I looked over my shoulder and didn't see any other band trucks.

"Hey, John Sinclair, where's everybody else?"

It was like Custer and the Indians, you know—"Where's the cavalry? There's no one here! I thought there was supposed to be all these other bands! Where's Janis Joplin? She was gonna be here, she was bringing the beer . . . Oh shit!"

There must have been four or five thousand kids all sitting in   20
Lincoln Park. We played about five or six songs, and then the police troopers came marching into the park with their three-foot batons.

The entire park was surrounded by cops. Literally surrounded—helicopters, everything, the whole nine yards.

John Sinclair: Abbie Hoffman came up onstage, grabbed the microphone, and started rapping about "the pigs" and "the siege of Chicago."

I said, "Oh dear, this does not bode well for us." So I kind of signaled to the guys, "Let's get the fuck outta here. . ."

All the equipment guys started packing everything away, everything except the one mike that Abbie was using. Finally they said, "Uh, Abbie, excuse me, we're gonna have to. . . get out of here."

Wayne Kramer: We just pulled the van right up and the   25
minute we stopped playing we threw the shit in the truck, man. I was so high, and I knew the minute we stopped playing there was gonna be a riot. We had seen it happen a lot of times before—we knew as soon as we stopped playing the crowd wouldn't have anything to focus on anymore and the riot would start. And it did.

John Sinclair: I looked back and saw these waves of cops descending on people. We were driving in the van across the field, we didn't bother with no road, we were just going the fastest way toward the exit. And there was the Up, they were in a van coming in from Ann Arbor, and we said "You gotta go back!"

Fortunately we escaped, ha ha ha. We headed right back home. But after that we were kind of *in* it, you know?

But I was always happy that we got out of Chicago with our gear intact, because we had to keep playing—you know, we weren't going to catch a plane to the next college to do a speech for five thousand bucks, we were going back to Michigan to play some teen club for two hundred dollars.

Dennis Thompson: Chicago was supposed to be the show of solidarity, goddamn it. This is the alternative culture? Come on. Where were all the other bands?

No one showed up but us. That's what pissed me off. I knew the revolution was over at that moment—I looked over my shoulder, and no one else was there. We were the ones who were gonna get hanged. I said, "This is it. There ain't no revolution. It doesn't exist. It's bullshit. The movement is dead."

Danny Fields: I went out to see the MC5 the first weekend of autumn 1968. They met me at the airport and took me back to their house. Of course I was just stunned. I'd never seen anything like it. John Sinclair, the MC5's manager, was bursting with charm, vigor, and intellect. Just the look and size of him—he was one of the most impressive people I had ever met—and that house!

Wayne Kramer: Before the Chicago riots, we moved from Detroit to Ann Arbor because of the 1967 Detroit race riots. It was real scary. I was living in an apartment at Second and Alexandrine, and the first couple of killings were right in that neighborhood. It was all police murders. The police just went insane and shot the place up for a week—killed forty or fifty people.

Shit started getting real tense after that. Some of our girlfriends got raped and our gear got ripped off a few times. I mean, we'd get to the place where we practiced and the door would be busted open and three more guitars would be gone. So we moved into two fraternity houses in Ann Arbor.

Danny Fields: It was sort of like a Viking commune on Fraternity Row. Each place had hundreds of bedrooms, and each bedroom was decorated by its inhabitants, sort of psychedelically. A lot of beds on the floor, draperies hanging from the ceiling, your typical sixties stuff. The basement was filled with printing presses, design studios, workshops, and darkrooms. A lot of their propaganda posters were produced in that factory downstairs. And there were Red Books everywhere. Mao's Red Books were everywhere. You had to have a Red Book. They came in all sizes, and they were all over the place.

Wayne Kramer: Self-righteousness flowed like water in that house. In fact, "righteousness" was an expression that we used all the time. "That's not righteous, man . . . No, this'll be really righteous, man. . . ."

We knew the world generally sucked and we didn't want to be a part of it. We wanted to do something else, which amounts to not wanting to get up in the morning and have a real job.

You know, it was "This sucks, that sucks, this is square" or "This isn't any fun." Working at Big Boy is not fun, playing in a band is *fun*, going to the drag strip is *fun*, riding around in the car drinking beer is *fun*. It was just on a gut level—that was the level of our politics—we wanted to make up different ways to be.

So our political program became dope, rock & roll, and fucking in the streets. That was our original three-point political program, which later got expanded to our ten-point program when we started to pretend we were serious. Then we started the White Panther party, which was originally the MC5's fan club. Originally it was called "The MC5's Social and Athletic Club." Then we started hearing about the Black Panthers and how the revolution was bubbling under, so it was, "Oh, let's change it to the White Panthers. Yeah, we'll be the White Panthers."

Danny Fields: On the one hand you had the politics of revolution and equality and liberation and on the other hand you had silent women in long dresses, gathered in the kitchen, preparing great meals of meat, which were brought out and served to the men—who ate alone.

The men and women didn't eat together. The men ate before a gig or after a gig. They'd come home and pound on the table like cavemen. And the women were very quiet. You weren't supposed to hear from them. Each one was supposed to service her man quietly.

Kathy Asheton: John Sinclair was a pig. He really took over the MC5 as far as instilling them with his political garbage. They got really into all that "brother and sister" kind of stuff, which was good for a live show, but . . .

I never took it seriously. Neither did my brothers or Iggy, so there was a parting of the ways between the Stooges and the MC5. The MC5 were still a good band, but they weren't as much fun anymore.

They were really chauvinistic. I definitely wasn't into this live-in maid thing and that's what they all gravitated toward. I wasn't friendly with any of the girls at Trans-Love. The girls were all big-time submissives, and I'd come over in the party mode, all primped to go out for the night, and they'd all be on their knees scrubbing the floor. I thought they were insane letting themselves be treated like that.

Wayne Kramer: We were sexist bastards. We were not politically correct at all. We had all the rhetoric of being revolutionary and new and different, but really what it was, was the boys get to go fuck and the girls can't complain about it.

And if the girls did complain, they were being bourgeois bitches—counterrevolutionary. Yep, we were really shitty about it. We tried free love and that didn't work so we went back to the traditional way—"No, honey, I didn't fuck nobody on the road, and by the way, I gotta go to the VD clinic."

I was the second runner-up in our band, I think I had the clap nine times. But Dennis beat me—he had it twelve times.

Danny Fields: Of course, I thought all that male bonding was sexy. It was a world I never knew. I mean, there was the myth of the Beatles living in adjoining rooms in *Help!* But everyone knew that was a myth, that bands didn't really live in the same house with the living rooms connected. But this band did!

So I thought that was wild. I just thought they were the sexiest thing I'd ever seen. I just thought it was quaint! I mean, there was a minister of defense carrying a rifle! Wearing one of those bullet things—a cartridge belt! With real bullets in it! I never saw a man wearing a cartridge belt. Even the girls were wearing these things. And they were serious!

Wayne Kramer: I was walking up to our house one day and I heard KABOOM! And then all these sirens, coming from just a couple blocks away. Just then, John Sinclair's buddy, Pun, came riding up on his bicycle and gave his girlfriend, Genie, a revolutionary hug.

Pun was a tough guy. He was just out of the penitentiary for reefer and was real surly. Pun really got into left-wing rhetoric and the ersatz politics of the day. He became the minister of defense of the White Panther party.

I said to Pun, "What did you just bomb?"

He whispered, "The CIA."

I said, "Right on! Power to the people!"

He had tossed a bomb at the CIA recruiting office at the University of Michigan. It didn't kill anybody. It just blew a hole in the sidewalk and freaked everybody out.

Iggy Pop: John Sinclair was always saying, "You've got to get with the People!"

I was like, "AWWWHHHH, THE PEOPLE? Oh man, what is this? Gimme a break! The People don't give a fuck."

Sinclair would say, "We are going to politicize the Youth!" But the kids were like, "WHAT? Just gimme some dope." They didn't care. That's how it really was.

John Sinclair: Lumpen hippies. Those were our people. That was the White Panther party. We were the voice of the lumpen hippie, just like the Black Panther party was the voice of the lumpen proletariat—which means working class without jobs.

My writing from the period was tailored precisely for the lumpen hippie, to the point where my work was ridiculed by the more erudite motherfuckers that came out of the SDS. Oh yeah, they thought we were a joke.

Iggy Pop: The MC5 went beyond having a sense of humor about themselves, they were a parody. They just acted like black thugs with guitars. In Detroit, if you were a white kid, your dream would be to be a black thug with a guitar and play like one.

I mean, the Stooges were the same way—a nasty bunch of people, but nice to each other. I can't say how political the MC5 really were, but I certainly didn't feel it. But on a basic level, would they share their peanut butter with me?

Yeah.

And sometimes I would have to walk two or three miles to the Trans-Love house to get a sandwich, because I didn't have any money, and they would never say, "Hey, don't eat that sandwich." And their girlfriends would sew my pants.

So they were a decent bunch of guys—a nice bunch of guys to have around to blow up your local CIA recruiting office.

Danny Fields: I don't know what they expected, or who they were going to fight off, but they had ministers of everything. Ministers of propaganda, ministers of defense. Of course they named themselves the White Panther party because their role models, musically and politically, were black radical musicians and politicians. Bobby Seale and Huey Newton and Eldridge Cleaver were their political heroes. Albert Ayler, Sun Ra, and Pharoah Sanders were their musical heroes.

It was a midwesternized version of anarchy. Tear down the walls, get the government out of our lives, smoke lots of dope, have lots of sex, and make lots of noise.

Wayne Kramer: The official party line from the Black Panther party in Oakland was that we were "psychedelic clowns." They said we were idiots and to keep the fuck away from us. But we got along well with the Ann Arbor chapter of the Black Panthers. They were neighborhood guys and they used to come to the house to hang out, and then we'd go have shooting practice.

We had all these M1s and pistols and sawed-off shotguns, so everyone would set up in the woods behind our house and blow the shit out of everything imaginable. Bla-bla-bla-bla-bla-pow-pow-pow-pow-pow-pow-bam-bam-bam-bam.

Then we'd drink this concoction the Black Panthers called the "Bitter Motherfucker." It was half a bottle of Rose's lime juice poured into a bottle of Gallo port. So we'd sit down, smoke reefer, drink that, and shoot guns. I guess we thought, We're all gonna end up in a shoot-out with the Man, you know, we'll shoot it out with the pigs.

Like we were gonna be trapped one day yelling, "WE'LL NEVER COME OUT, COPPER, YEAH? KKR! KKR! KKR! TAKE THAT, PIG! POW-POW-POW! POWER TO THE PEOPLE! KKR-KKR-KKR! TAKE THAT, OPPRESSOR!"

Danny Fields: Of course the MC5 sold out the Grande Ballroom the night I came to see them. They dressed up—they all wore satin—and they spun around really fast. It was a great show, but they weren't breaking the barriers of rock & roll. I had no criticism of it. It was fine blues-based rock & roll. The energy was great, and Wayne Kramer, who was very smart, must have sensed something, because the next day he said to me, "If you liked us, you will really love our little brother band, Iggy and the Stooges."

I think he knew something, intuitively, about my own taste in music. So that Sunday afternoon I went to see Iggy and the Stooges play at the student union on the campus of the University of Michigan. It was September 22, 1968. I can't minimize what I saw onstage. I never saw anyone dance or move like Iggy. I'd never seen such high atomic energy coming from one person. He was driven by the music like only true dancers are driven by the music.

It was the music I had been waiting to hear all my life.

Iggy Pop: It got to the end of our show, so I was just wandering around. I had this maternity dress on and a white face and I was doing unattractive things, spitting on people, things like that.

Danny Fields: I went up to Iggy when he came offstage and   75
I said, "I'm from Elektra Records."
He just said, "Yeah."
He didn't believe me. He thought I was like some janitor or
some weirdo, because no one had ever said "I'm from a record
company" to Iggy. So Iggy turned to me and said, "Yeah, see my
manager." And that was the beginning of our relationship.

Iggy Pop: So this guy, Danny Fields, says to me, "You're a
star!" just like in the movies. He said he worked for Elektra, so I
figured he cleaned up as a janitor or something. I didn't believe it,
you know, like, "Get away from me, man."

Danny Fields: I called New York on that Monday morning
from the kitchen of the MC5 house. I had John Sinclair and Jim
Silver, the manager of the Stooges, in the room with me while I
called Jac Holzman in New York and said, "I'm in Ann Arbor looking at that group the MC5 I told you about. Well, they're really
going to be big. They sold out four thousand tickets on Saturday
night; the crowd went wild, and there were crowds around the
street. They're also the most professional and ready-to-go act I've
ever seen."
And I added, "And what's more, they have a baby brother   80
group called Iggy and the Stooges, which is the most incredibly
advanced music I've ever heard. And the lead singer is a star—he's
really mesmerizing."
And Jac Holzman said, "So what are you telling me?"
I said, "I think we should take both groups."
He said, "See if you can get the big group for twenty grand
and the little group for five."
I put my hand over the mouthpiece and said to John Sinclair,
"Would you take twenty grand?"
Sinclair went white and fell backwards.   85
And I said to Jim Silver, "Would you take five?"
They both needed chairs or to have spirits brought to them.
And that was the deal. They were signed.

CHAPTER 6

Counterculture Legacies

This last chapter is probably the most controversial of all the parts of this reader for it aims to represent the range of views looking back at the countercultural legacies of the 1950s, 1960s, and 1970s. Negative, positive, shocking, angry, berating, but never indifferent, these readings express the mixed emotions the Counterculture still elicits. Joelle Fraser's harrowing account of walking alone to sell her drawings at the tender age of six on the streets of Sausalito reads more like an account from a hundred years ago than just thirty. (Compare this to Frank Conroy's "My Generation," from the post–World War II era in Chapter 1.) Danielle Pinchbeck's tales about his Beat writer mother, Joyce Johnson (whose book, *Minor Characters*, talks about her experiences with Jack Kerouac and other Beats) and numerous offspring of Beat movement writers is rather bitterly described in "Children of the Beats." How well one survived the Counterculture depends largely on one's age at the time, as well as a certain strength of character.

Reflections upon the Counterculture range from the nostalgic to repentant, as in Peter Collier and David Horowitz's *Destructive Generation*, in which two former radicals recant their youthful Marxist follies. Horowitz continues as an outspoken critic of what he views as crimes committed by liberal ideologies on our culture, particularly in the universities, where a number of former radicals have found tenure. His own autobiography, *Radical Son: A Generational Odyssey* (1997), is both a political memoir and discussion of his own painful estrangement from his radical parents and former political collaborators. His views have so infuriated some that at a recent lecture at the University of Michigan (where the Students for a Democratic Society was active in the 1960s), he needed bodyguards and dogs to protect him. Also in this chapter, Walter Berns chronicles the changes wrought by countercultural and radical left ideas upon our centers of higher learning in his angry "The Assault on the Universities: Then and Now." He outlines such currently rancorous issues as freedom of expression, affirmative action, gay and lesbian studies programs, ethnic studies programs, the critique of Eurocentrism, and requirements for college students to take classes examining race, class, and gender. In some universities these issues are taken for granted; in others, demands for more women's studies courses were not addressed until the mid-1990s. In a recent essay, "Reflections on Black Power," legal scholar Randall Kennedy addressed Walter Berns' concerns about the legacies of civil rights and black power movements. Kennedy chronicles the historical split between violent and non-violent protest, between racial integration and separatism, in America. Describing what he sees as the "creeping triumph of black powerite interpretation" of the Counterculture, he seeks to preserve the legacy of non-violent, non-exclusionary, non-racialized protest against racial oppression as expressed by leaders such as Martin Luther King, Jr.

In a famous essay "The White Negro," post–World War II writer Norman Mailer predicted the expression of "a disbelief in the socially monolithic ideas of the single mate, the solid family and the respectable love life." Although composed in the 1950s, Mailer anticipated the counterculture of the 1960s where "a psychically armed rebellion whose sexual impetus may rebound against the anti-sexual foundation of every organized power in America," where "every social restraint and category [would] be removed, and the affirmation implicit in the proposal is that man would then prove to be more creative than murderous and so would not destroy himself." In many ways, Mailer's prophecies have come true, with the exception that many critics have witnessed what they view as the destruction of many core values that they consider important to American life—replaced by a coarse and crass materialism, and a popular media full of vulgarity that was once considered transgressive. Censorship of films, books, and other media was virtually eliminated by the 1970s, and the internet seems to have removed all boundaries of what in Frank Conroy's generation would have been called decency.

The environmental legacy of the Counterculture, without which we might not have Earth Day, curbside recycling, wilderness areas, and more open spaces, takes off where people like John Muir and others, at the early part of the twentieth century, began. Those agrarian communes Iris Keltz and other hippies started in the 1960s have resulted in organic and health food supermarkets and a return to the home garden not seen in America since the Victory Gardens of World War II.

Probably the single most visible legacy of the Counterculture was the burgeoning of the conservative movements of the 1980s, which continue to this day. In books and on talk radio, many who would call themselves neo-conservatives (others leave the "neo" off or use the word "new") are often the most radical voices of the new millennium. Whatever was 'right' or 'wrong' with the ideas brought forward by the Counterculture is what makes up both American intellectualism and American popular culture these days. Whether you are listening to Rush Limbaugh complaining about the liberals on talk radio, signing up for the N.R.A., deciding who will stay home with your children, deciding what the U.S. role in world affairs should be, or joining the gay and lesbian student union on campus, remember the Counterculture. These were the questions they posed, and many are still left for us to answer.

Children of the Beats

DANIEL PINCHBECK

His writings have appeared in the *New York Times Magazine*, *Esquire*, and the *Village Voice*. He currently is editor of *Open City*, an art and literary journal. His mother, Joyce Johnson, served as muse and support system for Beat legend Jack Kerouac long before Daniel was born. Her book *Minor Characters* is one of the best memoirs of the Beat generation. As an editor, she was later responsible for the publication of numerous lost Beat works. This essay looks at the world of the Beats through the eyes of their offspring.

◆

As a child, browsing through the bookshelves in my mother's apartment on Manhattan's Upper West Side, I occasionally found strange pieces of paper and scrawled notes inside the pages of old books on Zen Buddhism and magazines with names like *Big Table* and *The Evergreen Review*. The notes were from Jack Kerouac, who had been involved with my mother, Joyce Johnson, for a few years in the late 1950s, long before I was born. These accidentally unearthed scraps provided me with insight into the ghostlike fragility of an artist's physical legacy. They also introduced me to the Beat Generation's work, which I began to read even before I entered high school.

From time to time, figures from my mother's mysterious past would appear in our living room—such as Allen Ginsberg, Abbie Hoffman or Lawrence Ferlinghetti. As a teenager, I felt somewhat shy in their presence, imagining a depth of history between them and my mother that I couldn't share. I also saw a certain wariness in these poets and avatars, a certain tension, similar to what soldiers might feel after a long military campaign. It later seemed to me that decades of public attention and media scrutiny—often negative or accusatory in tone, especially in the early years—had taken a toll on them, made them somewhat inflexible, alert to invisible dangers hidden in the air like radio frequencies.

Kerouac's insidiously catchy phrase "mad to live, mad to love, mad to be saved, desirous of everything at the same moment . . . " was the message that my mother paid to have inscribed in my high school yearbook upon graduation in 1984. I saw it, even then, as both an encouragement and a reproach—a reproach because I already suspected that something lodged in my consciousness, as well as in the world that I belonged to, didn't allow for such a fervent pursuit of experience and ecstasy. The cynicism of the Reagan years had seeped into the atmosphere. When my friends and I sought parallels to the 1950s counterculture, we found ourselves unsatisfied. What we wanted no longer existed, or continued to exist only as style, parody, pastiche.

My marginal relationship to Beat history made me wonder what became of the children of the group's central figures. From the safe vantage point of my middle-class adolescence, I loved the movement's original testimonies, but I had been spared the chaos of their creators. In 1995, I went on a journey to speak to their children to see how they had been shaped by the values of that distant era—had their parents' live-for-the-moment ethos inspired them? Had it hindered or harmed them? Some of both, I discovered.

The Gramercy Park Hotel is a gloomy place that attracts trav-   5
eling salesmen, rootless dowagers, tourists and low-level heavy-
metal bands. A hastily assembled press conference, held in a
plain, gray-carpeted suite, had been called by Jan Kerouac, the
forty-three-year-old only child of Jack Kerouac, to announce liti-
gation against her father's estate.

The meeting started late. Waiting around the coffee dispenser,
lawyers in shiny gray suits smelling of cologne and hair spray
chatted with frowzy-looking women journalists from the wire
services, while notebook-toting writers wearing beads and
T-shirts—most of them having no discernible press affiliation—
drank bitter coffee from plastic cups. Jack Micheline, a "street
poet" who had made something of a career based on his friendship
with Kerouac in the Fifties, held court in one corner. In another,
an enormously fat, brown-bearded man in a psychedelic jacket
and a priest's collar gave out photocopies of his own confused
manifesto. Finally, Jan appeared amid a small pack of journalists
and advisers; she looked terrified and fluttery in a white linen
dress. She walked to the front of the room and joined her support-
ers seated behind a cafeteria-style table and a microphone.

Jan's lawyer, Thomas A. Brill, a stiff-faced, blond-haired man
in pinstripes, spoke first at the conference. "We hope to demonstrate," he said, "that the signature of Gabrielle Kerouac, Kerouac's mother, was forged on her last will in 1973, while she lay
dying in a nursing home." That will left sole title of the estate to
Kerouac's last wife, Stella Sampas Kerouac, who died in 1990,
and not to his daughter, whom Gabrielle Kerouac never really
knew. Jan received royalty checks from her father's estate. But his
physical property—manuscripts, letters, clothes—belonged to the
Sampas family. The scroll on which Kerouac wrote *On the Road*
during a three-week breakthrough into spontaneous prose might
sell for more than one million dollars at auction, with each of his
other manuscripts worth perhaps a third of that price. Everything
that Kerouac touched or wrote has become sanctified with value.

In his work, Kerouac often avowed a horror of procreation,
of "the wheel of the quivering meat conception" that turns in the
void, "expelling human beings, pigs, turtles, frogs. . . . " He could
never accept Jan as his own contribution to "that slaving meat
wheel." He once showed my mother a photograph of a little girl in
pigtails. Even in the snapshot, my mother could see that the girl
looked like him, sharing his tan skin and solid jaw. "This isn't my
daughter," said Kerouac, explaining that a former wife, Joan

Haverty—Jan's mother—had been impregnated by another man while they were married.

Jan had met her father only twice before his death in 1969: when she was nine and a court ordered blood tests to determine whether Kerouac should pay child support, and when she was fifteen and had run away from home. She had published two novels, *Baby Driver* and *Trainsong*, chronicling her early life, before she became seriously ill. Alcoholism led to kidney failure, and she now had to administer dialysis to herself four times each day.

10   When Jan spoke, she told of her final meeting with her father. She had driven to his house in Lowell, Massachusetts, on her way to Mexico with her boyfriend, pregnant with a child that would be stillborn. In his dreary, desperate drunkenness, Kerouac said to her: "Yeah, you go to Mexico. Write a book. You can use my name." Her voice breaking and her eyes often failing so that she frequently stalled in mid-sentence, Jan also described her life on the road after she left home, living on a commune in California, then working as a stablehand and a waitress. As the audience shifted uneasily, she discussed her drinking, her years of poverty, her unhappy relationships. "For some reason," she said, "I kept being attracted to men who would abuse me."

When we met for breakfast a few days later at the Gramercy, Jan wore blue jeans and a baseball cap backward. "I hope to live for another ten years," she said to me.

Her small hands were thick and tough, like the hands of a farm laborer. Her eyes, however, were clear blue and guileless, almost childlike. "My dream is to buy my own house in New Mexico, but at the moment, I'm broke, almost completely penniless," she said. "The checks from the estate seem to arrive very erratically." (In fact, it turned out that royalty checks came regularly from Kerouac's agent, Sterling Lord.)

The huge bearded man who wore a priest's collar at the press conference hovered protectively at a nearby table.

"Who's that?" I asked.

15   "Oh, that's Buddha," Jan said, and waved at him.

"He calls himself Buddha?"

"Yeah. Buddha's a fan of my work. He lives in Lowell and visits my father's grave every day. He offered to act as my bodyguard while I'm in New York."

Jan said that she received about $60,000 a year from the Kerouac estate, and had another lawyer investigating to see whether she deserved more. "I didn't even know I was entitled to any royalties until 1985, and Stella fought tooth and nail to stop me from getting them. But this case is not about getting more money for me." Her dream was to have a Kerouac house "like the Hemingway house in Florida, where people can visit and scholars can go to examine my father's manuscripts, letters and books."

On the Road closed with Kerouac's alter ego Sal Paradise musing on his lost friend and hero: "I think of Dean Moriarty, I even think of old Dean Moriarty, the father we never found, I think of Dean Moriarty." For Jan, Kerouac was also "the father we never found," his absence sentencing her to a kind of permanent exile.

Speaking to her, I thought of William Burroughs Jr.—the son of Burroughs and Joan Vollmer, whom Burroughs killed in Mexico in 1951 when he drunkenly tried to shoot a glass off her head and missed—who had also endured a childhood in exile. While his father traveled the world, searching for the mystical drug yage in South America and then living in Tangier, Billy grew up with his grandparents in Florida. He followed his father into drug addiction, writing two autobiographical novels, *Speed* and *Kentucky Ham*, before a liver transplant failed. "I've always wanted to continue beyond X point," Billy wrote in *Speed.* "That is, I've always been kind of dumb." He died in 1981, at the age of thirty-four. Jan Kerouac would die a year after I met her of liver and kidney failure. 20

Unlike the Kerouac legacy, the estate of the Beat poet Bob Kaufman is not exactly a money machine. "We get a check for around $200 a year in royalties," said Parker Kaufman, the poet's thirty-six-year-old son, named after Charlie Parker. I met Parker in San Anselmo, a sunny suburban town at the foot of the mountains outside San Francisco, where he lived in a small residential hotel—what a hard-boiled writer in a previous era would have unhesitatingly called a "fleabag," with ratty carpets on the floor, bathrooms in the hallway and a laminated tree stump lodged in the dingy downstairs lobby instead of a bench.

He had a long, fine-featured face with a jagged scar running along one edge of his jaw. Tall and thin, wearing a Paula Abdul T-shirt and blue jeans, he carried a knapsack filled with schoolbooks over his slumped shoulders—he had just begun attending a small college nearby. As we shook hands, I noticed his faint grimace of reluctance. Several people, including Parker's mother, Eileen Kaufman, had warned me that he hated to talk about his father; setting up a meeting at all had been a delicate matter.

"They tell me that my dad's world-renowned and famous, but I can't see any reason to be interested in him," said Parker. "I never thought he amounted to much. Most of the times that I remember, he was totally incoherent."

Bob Kaufman was a legendary figure on the West Coast and in Europe, where he was known as the "American Rimbaud." The term "beatnik" was originally adopted to describe Kaufman after one of his spontaneous readings in the Coexistence Bagel Shop in San Francisco during the late Fifties. A street in North Beach was named after Kaufman, and his face was painted next to Baudelaire's on the mural against the wall of City Lights Books, which faces Jack Kerouac Alley. Part black, part Jewish, Kaufman was less well-known on the East Coast and in academic circles, perhaps because he had been ignored by what Lawrence Ferlinghetti, the poet and publisher of City Lights Books, has called "the East Coast Beat establishment." Other people ascribe his exclusion from the canon to racism.

25 It is also true that Kaufman chose to be obscure. Not long before his death in 1989, he told a scholar who sought him out in a bar around North Beach: "I don't know how you get involved with uninvolvement, but I don't want to be involved. My ambition is to be completely forgotten." Some of his poems reflect this desire, including "I Am a Camera," one of his last:

THE POET NAILED ON
THE HARD BONE OF THIS WORLD
HIS SOUL DEDICATED TO SILENCE
IS A FISH WITH FROG'S EYES,
THE BLOOD OF A POET FLOWS   5
OUT WITH HIS POEMS, BACK
TO THE PYRAMID OF BONES
FROM WHICH HE IS THRUST
HIS DEATH IS A SAVING GRACE
CREATION IS PERFECT.   10

Kaufman's life story suggests a certain chaotic helplessness. Invited to read at Harvard in 1960, he got waylaid instead in the underground world of New York City, where he became addicted to amphetamines, served time in prison and received shock therapy. When he returned to San Francisco in 1963, he began a ten-year vow of silence during which he wrote nothing. His silence lasted until the end of the Vietnam War.

"I don't really remember the silent treatment thing too well," Parker said. "The main thing I remember is when I was like fourteen, we went out to the park together and it took Dad somewhere between a half hour and forty-five minutes to hit a ball out to me. He was so wasted from all of the years of self-abuse that he couldn't swing a bat."

After his initial reluctance faded, Parker was eager to talk—his San Anselmo life, it seemed, was isolated and friendless. He led me to a coffee shop decorated in imitation of a Fifties diner, its shiny tin walls adorned with photographs of Elvis. "In San Francisco, everyone identifies me as Bob Kaufman's son," he told me. "I only want to be known for myself." Most of his early childhood was spent in North Beach where, as a toddler, he appeared with his parents and Taylor Mead in Ron Rice's experimental film *The Flower Thief*. His parents split up during Kaufman's decade of speechlessness, and Parker traveled with his white hippie mother to Mexico, Morocco and Ibiza, Spain. In Ibiza, Eileen let Parker, who was then ten, go off with a wealthy English family that was traveling around the world. She was not to hear from him again for more than two years.

"I was with my second family in the mountains of Afghanistan near Kabul when war broke out and we couldn't get across the Khyber Pass," Parker recalled. "We were trapped in this house, under two hundred feet of snow. We had to tunnel out to buy vegetables or food; we had no heat. If we were out in the streets after 5:00 p.m., starving attack dogs would chase us. This situation lasted for one and a half years."

In North Beach in the early Seventies—before Parker and his second family were rescued by a scouting party—Eileen was reunited with her husband. When Kaufman found out that Parker was missing, he broke his vow of silence only once, to say: "You lost our son." After Parker returned home, his parents were remarried in a ceremony on Mount Tamalpais, in California. But Parker found it impossible to relate to his father.

"It's frustrating when everyone's telling you, 'How dare you talk back to your dad? He's a genius,'" Parker said. "Meanwhile, it's okay for him to sleep on the sofa all day, drinking beer and smoking four packs of cigarettes."

Parker opened up a leather portfolio of his modeling and acting photographs, most of them at least a decade old. He had appeared in a few movies, including *The Right Stuff*, and in some television shows, including *Midnight Caller*, and was working on his acting career—"it was getting to the point where I was beginning to get paid"—when he was beat up and knifed at a club where he was working.

"Sometimes I just think I have bad karma," he said. He told me that he and his mother were currently destitute. "I don't know where my next meal is coming from. It's *that* bad." His elderly mother rode the bus to see him every few days, wearing a bright blue cape and bringing him lunch meat and bread. He was out of cigarettes, and I guiltily got him a couple of packs of Marlboros at a convenience store.

"Right now, I'm like this close to ending it all," he said between bites of a cheeseburger I bought him. "I was walking across the Golden Gate Bridge and I looked over and thought how easy it would be just to leap over the ledge." He sighed. "I am trying to come to terms with the possibility that I won't do anything spectacular with my life. My main goal at this point is just to be able to provide for my family someday. I want to have what we never had."

35   Although he never published his own creative writing, Lucien Carr was an important and original member of the Beats. He rolled the young Kerouac home in a beer barrel one drunken night, and introduced Kerouac and Ginsberg to William Burroughs. In an incident that is part of the peculiarly violent pre-history of the Beat movement, Carr stabbed David Kammerer to death in Riverside Park in New York in 1944. An older man who had fallen obsessively in love with Carr as his Boy Scout master in Missouri, Kammerer had pursued Carr to Columbia, even taking a job as a janitor at the university to be near him. Carr was found guilty of manslaughter and was sent to a state reformatory in Elmira, New York, for two years before he was pardoned by the governor. (He later became an assistant managing editor of United Press International, and is now retired.) Two of Carr's sons are Caleb Carr, the best-selling author of *The Alienist* and *Angel of Darkness*, and Simon Carr, an abstract painter.

I visited Simon Carr in his Lower East Side studio, crowded with abstract paintings of swirls rendered with a Cézanne-like palette. Slender and handsome, with brown hair going gray, Simon wore round gold-framed intellectual-style glasses, and his eyes looked gentle behind the lenses. He showed me a catalogue from his last SoHo exhibition, "Chromaticism and Joy."

Simon credited his father with giving him and his siblings "the sense that you were definitely going to do something—that you had to express it to say it. My dad was a great talker—he and his friends would talk all night." But he said he gravitated to fine art because "it's the opposite of talking: The bottom line of great painting is silence."

Simon's wife Cristina worked as a conservator at the Metropolitan Museum of Art; they had three children in private schools in the city. He made a living teaching at various colleges and art schools around New York; he was also running a special studio class for unwed mothers at Manhattan Community College. "I associate the Beats with the more difficult times we had as a family," he said. "There was a lot of wild drinking, a lot of people disappearing and then coming back. It was a difficult time for a ten-year-old trying to hold his world together. You might have a wild time one night and then wake up the next morning and you don't know what to eat for breakfast because there's no food around and everyone's asleep."

His brother Caleb agreed: "What's extremely romantic for adults may be disruptive and frightening for children," he said when I reached him by phone. "The Beats were so concerned with breaking molds and creating new lifestyles that they threw the baby out with the bathwater—they threw out the social framework needed to maintain a family. If any element got lost in the Beat equation, it was the idea of children."

Caleb's novel *The Alienist* was about as un-Beat a book as it is   40
possible to imagine—as clammy as the Beats were heated—and I wondered if this was intentional. I saw personal messages in lines like this: "He probably had a troubled relationship with one or both parents early on, and eventually grew to despise everything about them—including their heritage."

"I think the Beats were extremely dysfunctional people who basically had no business raising children," said Christina Mitchell, the daughter of John Mitchell—a Beat entrepreneur who started many of the original coffeehouses in Greenwich Village, including the Fat Black Pussy Cat and the Figaro. Christina was also the daughter of Alene Lee. Part black, part Cherokee Indian, Lee appeared in Kerouac's novel *The Subterraneans* as Mardou Fox, the gorgeous dark-skinned woman that Leo Percepied loved and lost and mourned for: "No girl had ever moved me with a story of spiritual suffering and so beautifully her soul showing out radiant as an angel wandering in hell." Lee was the only woman and the only black person included in an early essay by Kerouac, defining the Beat movement by the spiritual epiphanies that the group experienced: "A.L.'s vision of everything as mysterious electricity."

During the years Christina was growing up, she and her mother lived with Lucien Carr. Her mother's relationship with Carr, Christina recalled in a voice filled with incantatory rage, was "ten years of fighting, screaming, hitting, going to the police station in the middle of the night, going to Bellevue, wandering the streets, watching Mom and Lucien beat each other to a pulp." Their narcissism was all-consuming, she thinks now. "I was basically a nonperson to them. I don't think they knew I was there."

She said she never read *The Subterraneans* or any of the other manifestoes of the group. The only Beat she really respected was Allen Ginsberg. "Most of the Beat people disappeared from our lives, but when my mother died, Allen was by her bedside. He was one of the few people to value a human being beyond their fame or status."

Christina stumbled out of her adolescence—"I was either shy or catatonic"—and joined the Reverend Sun Myung Moon's Unification Church. "I spaced out for five years. I entered the group because I wanted the stability of a family—what they talked about—one happy world. The whole time I was with them my mother never told me to come back." She finally left the Moonies and resurfaced in Denver, where she attended a community college and began to rebuild her life.

45   When I spoke to her, Christina was thirty-seven, living in Upstate New York and majoring in English literature. As a reaction to the horror that she feels was her own childhood, she admitted to being perhaps overly protective of her six-year-old son and infant daughter: "I am compulsive with my kids. I feel that it is a really shitty world and I want to keep the shit off of them." She accompanied her son to the first day of his first-grade class, despite the teacher's objections. "I hope my compulsion to protect them won't destroy them."

Despite her anger at her mother, Christina believed that Lee was an extraordinary person. "She went out with all of them, didn't she? Kerouac, Corso, Lucien. But she never capitalized on her involvement with the beatniks. She had no interest in having her fifteen minutes of fame. My mother was a woman who could not be typecast, stereotyped or dismissed. I think they were all a little bit in awe of her."

"I see that generation as kind of like a brilliant child," said Tara Marlowe, the twenty-seven-year-old daughter of the anarchist Beat poet Diane di Prima. "They did whatever they wanted."

Di Prima, a ferocious individualist, was the mother of five children by four different men. She reared her brood in San Francisco's rough Fillmore district. "We got chased a lot," Tara recalled the day I met her in the East Village, where our mothers had once lived. Tara's father, Alan Marlowe, was a former male model who spent his last years at the Rocky Mountain Buddhist Center. "Dad thought women were for breeding and men were for fucking." Tara didn't visit him when he was dying. "I don't regret that decision," she said. "A dying asshole is still an asshole."

Tara was short and stocky—she resembled her mother except for her long, polished fingernails and the silver chain around her neck. Frank and eloquent about her past, she said she grew up "like a kid in a potato patch. I've never met anyone poorer than we were. When I was a kid, my mother once told us that she was going on strike—she wasn't going to be the mother and cook for us anymore. She's still on strike."

"What did that mean to you?"

50

"It meant that no one ever taught me table manners," she said, "or how to dress or that I should clean myself, so I walked around like a filthy ragamuffin with matted hair." At thirteen, Tara left home and moved to Mendocino, where she met a seventeen-year-old coke-dealer boyfriend. "I got involved in sexual relationships that to me weren't sexual. I was basically in a rage most of the time. Now I'm sort of a born-again virgin." She lived as an "emancipated minor" in a converted chicken coop near the alternative school she was attending. Eventually, she returned home. "At our house, the drug dealers were the good guys," she recalled. "They brought Christmas presents—the whole Robin Hood thing. The poets were these icky guys with foam at the side of their mouths."

In college, Marlowe wrote poems and even published her own poetry magazine, *Dissociated Press*. She said as an adult she drinks only occasionally, noting that when she does drink, "there's not enough alcohol in the world to make me feel better." She lived in the Williamsburg section of Brooklyn, working as a freelance graphic artist. "For the first time, I'm beginning to enjoy my life," she said. "I still feel like some kind of space alien, a complete outsider from middle-class culture. It sometimes seems as if the world is this big office party and I'm the uninvited guest."

Some of my earliest memories are of visiting Hettie Jones, my mother's best friend from her blackstocking days, and her daughters, Kellie and Lisa, on the Bowery. When I was a child, Hettie's creaky, crooked and labyrinthine apartment seemed almost organic to me, as if it had grown outward from her vibrant personality to fill the space around her. I faintly recall crowded holiday parties with a cheerful mix of poets, painters and jazz musicians drinking and laughing, jammed up against each other in the narrow hallways. Growing up, I regretted that my mother put that bohemian world behind us, moving away from downtown to the more bourgeois boundaries of the Upper West Side.

"I don't know much about the Beat period," said Lisa Jones, the daughter of Hettie and the poet LeRoi Jones. "I never read the books—the writers of the Harlem Renaissance had a much greater influence on me. I guess I was trying to divorce myself from that history, from my parents' story."

55   A *Village Voice* columnist, Lisa had published a book of essays called *Bulletproof Diva*. She had also worked with Spike Lee and written movie and television scripts. Her older sister, Kellie, had become a curator and art historian. Lisa's father left the family early in her childhood to join the Black Nationalist movement, changing his name to Amiri Baraka. "People like my mom were already talking about a different idea of family back then," Lisa said. "We belonged to a tight community. I hate the idea that growing up with one parent automatically means you have to be dysfunctional. Though my parents weren't together, we spent time with both of them and were loved and nurtured by both of them. My grandparents were always there and they were a strong force.

"As a kid, it never struck me that we were that bohemian," Lisa said emphatically. "We had chores and curfews—although my mom might disagree. I always referred to myself as a B.A.P.— a Bohemian American Princess."

Some people found in the Beat quest for personal freedom not an excuse for nihilism or bad behavior, but a way to develop new models of commitment. For instance, the Beat poet Michael McClure's daughter, Jane McClure, followed the thread of her father's interest in naturalism to study molecular biology and eventually became a doctor. Of her life on Haight-Ashbury she recalled "nothing was scary—everything was interesting." Her father's friendships with Jim Morrison and the Hell's Angels caused no injury and seemed to leave no particular impression.

Allen Ginsberg's life demonstrated his Buddhist-Beat ethos of compassion and responsibility. Although he never had his own kids, he continued to help members of his huge community as well as their children. Many of the children I spoke to had memories of Allen's generosity. At various times, he bailed Burroughs's son, Billy, out of jail, let Jan Kerouac live at his house in Boulder, and put up Cassady's son Curtis Hansen at his apartment in New York. Treating the Beats as an extended family, Allen nursed his friends back to health when they were sick, put them up when they ran out of money, supported their work and used his influence to help whenever possible. His empathetic behavior offers a contrast to the self-centered concerns of most artists today.

The children of Neal Cassady, the Beat Generation's most famous icon of perpetual adolescence and sexual craving, grew up as well. Cassady and his "wild yea-saying over burst of American joy" inspired some of Kerouac's and Ginsberg's best work in the Fifties. A decade later, he led the Merry Pranksters psychedelic charge across the continent. The son of a Denver wino, Cassady wasn't much of a writer, but he played the role of Socrates to the counterculture, inspiring others by his manic example.

I met John Allen Cassady, the son of Neal and Carolyn Cassady, for several pints of beer at a bar in the North Beach section of San Francisco. John Allen told me that he found *On the Road* dull going. "A lot of that Beat stuff is so obtuse," he said. He was an expansive man with a white beard and bright blue eyes, friendly and talkative. "My friends used to call me the albino wino." He was living in San Jose, California, working for a computer company that manufactured optical scanners; he answered customers' queries about the product. Years before, he had made dulcimers and sold them at country fairs; he was also something of a Deadhead.

"Neal had such a capacity for everything," John Allen said. "I think he was a very evolved soul. I've inherited his wheel karma. Dad had eighteen cars in the back of our yard; I've got about six in mine. We must have been charioteers in ancient Rome." As John Allen spoke, I sensed that he had told some of his stories many times in other pubs, for other occasions, and I began to suspect that sadness lurked beneath his surface gregariousness.

John Allen said that his father wrote other books besides *The First Third*, an early childhood memoir published by City Lights. He added: "There was a *Second Third* and a *Third Third*, Neal told me. He wrote them on reams and reams of yellow notebook paper but, unfortunately, he had all of the papers in the backseat of this old jalopy, which he left at Ken Kesey's place. He went away for a couple of weeks, and when he came back he found that some punk kids had stolen the car. That was it—his whole life's work gone. He was really upset about that."

John Allen also told me that Billy Burroughs, the son of William, had lived with him in Santa Cruz, California, for three months in 1976, after he received a liver transplant. "That guy was hell-bent on self-destruction. His attitude was, 'Hey, I got a new one to burn.' Toward the end, he started getting pretty unintelligible." John Allen was glad when Billy moved on—he had already witnessed his own father's unraveling a decade earlier.

"By the Sixties, Dad was so burned out, so bitter," John Allen said. "He told me once that he felt like a dancing bear, that he was just performing. He was wired all the time, talking nonstop. I remember once, after a party, about 2:00 a.m., he went in the bathroom, turned on the shower and just started screaming and didn't stop. I was about fifteen then and I knew he was in deep trouble, that he was really a tortured soul. He died not too long after that."

65   "Maybe you can explain what all the fuss was about," said Curtis Hansen, John Allen's half-brother and Neal Cassady's other son. Curtis, forty-five when I met him, never really knew his father. Curtis's mother, Diana Hansen, was a Barnard graduate who fell in love with Cassady while working at an advertising agency in the late Forties; she ended up with a walk-on in *On the Road*. "What did those guys do that was so amazing?"

"Um, well, I suppose they offered some kind of antidote to the repression of the Cold War period," I said, hesitating at the English-lit-class banality of the phrases. "They encouraged people to find new ways of living, to rediscover America."

Curtis paused thoughtfully. "Cassady had a great public-relations department, I guess," he said, "always surrounding himself with all those phenomenal writers and so on."

A former disc jockey, Curtis was programming director for WICC-AM, a radio station in Bridgeport, Connecticut, and for WEBE-FM in Fairfield County. We drove in his Japanese compact through the city's rainy, eerily empty streets to the radio station's impersonal glass office tower. Solidly good-looking in a jungle-print tie and tan pants—he looked like a somewhat stockier version of Cassady—Hansen gave off a strong positive vibe that suggested a disposition inherited from his father. The only thing of

Neal's that he owned was a sheaf of yellowing handwritten letters that Cassady wrote to Diana Hansen in the early Fifties, when he was trying to convince her to move to one town away from his wife, Carolyn, so he could continue the sexual triangulation that was one of his life's driving obsessions.

"The letters have some pretty wild stuff in them," Curtis said. "He talks about cunt hair and all the sex they're going to have when they get together. You can tell they had a real good sexual relationship."

"What did your mom tell you about Cassady?" I asked.   70

"Oh, she said that he was a jailbird—that I should stay away from him. I was real embarrassed when he went to prison in the late Fifties—that's why we changed my name to Hansen."

"What did you think of *On the Road?*"

"That book they wrote together?" he said. "I thought it was *boring,*" he says. "I never really understood what that whole shtick was about."

Yet Hansen was inspired by the father he never knew and the book he didn't care for to go on the road himself, driving across country in 1969, after he was "invited to leave" college on suspicion of selling mescaline and for having a girl in his room. "That trip across the country is one of the things I'm proudest of in my life," he said. "Cassady had just died, I got laid for the first time, got high and took off. It was definitely a symbolic journey."

"I imagine that it must have been difficult to be Cassady's   75 son," I offered.

"Well, I used to feel I had a lot to live up to," he said in his effusive, former-DJ voice. "I wish my dad had been around so I could have asked him about girls. I used to have a lot of trouble in that area. . . ."

Listening to the drone of a Michael Bolton song in Hansen's office, where windows overlooked the gray panorama of Bridgeport, I thought about how radio once encouraged the outsider expression of someone like Alan Freed, who promoted rock & roll in its early days. In the Forties and Fifties, Symphony Sid's shows of jazz and bebop had inspired Kerouac and Cassady on their manic jaunts across the continent.

"Does it bother you that radio has become so corporate?" I asked Hansen.

"No, that's what's so great about our time," he said. "What I think has happened is that the counterculture and the mainstream have merged." He waved his hands excitedly in the air as he continued. "You don't have to listen anymore to the songs you don't like—you only listen to the songs that the *majority* of the people like. You see what I mean? The mainstream has become the new frontier." From his desk, he turned up the volume on the live feed from the soundstage down the hall, and the voice of Michael Bolton grew louder and louder until it momentarily seemed to envelop us.

from *The Territory of Men: A Memoir*
JOELLE FRASER

"Any man, every man, could be my father," writes Joelle Fraser in the preface to her recent memoir, *The Territory of men: A memoir* (2002), about growing up in the Counterculture and beyond. "I was loved," she recalls. "I had no bedtime. I fell asleep on laps and couches and on piles of coats, and sometimes a dog or another kid slept beside me. I was never alone." Many reviewers of the book have focused on what they view as negative images of raising children in the Counterculture, although Fraser believes the work is neither in praise of or a condemnation of her parents. Reviewer Janet Maslin of *The New York Times*, however, exemplifies the strong reactions to her candid account: "When Joelle Fraser was a little girl, she understood that late at night was the time when the grow-ups got in the hot tub. Her favorite aunt and the aunt's friends wore high boots and long coats and dangling jewelry as they inhaled white powder off the kitchen table. Houses smelled like meat and bread and marijuana." The first excerpt, "Summertime: Mother's Day, 1966," is about the day she was born. In the second, "Miss America," six-year-old Joelle sells her artwork on the streets of Sausalito, California.

————————— ◆ —————————

SUMMERTIME

Mother's Day, 1966

Watch us as we barrel across that bright bridge toward San Francisco, the gray waves of the ocean seething and crashing below. It's a warm May day, the windows are wide open, and my mother's black hair flies wildly around her sweating face.

We're late for the hospital, but traffic is light—and this is a party, after all, one that began in the morning and lasted all night and hasn't stopped for years. In the backsent, my father sits between two friends, smoking a cigarette, lips stained dark from gin and grape juice. He grins at my mother in front, tells her to hold on. He says wouldn't it be a great story if they had a baby on the Golden Gate Bridge.

The Mamas and the Papas' "California Dreamin' " comes on the radio, and everyone sings, the words swept up by scarves of fog and spread over the sea. They're drunk, all of them, all but my mother, who leans back to ease the pain, belly swollen, legs braced because it's almost time and I'm pushing to get out.

That summer my mother's twenty-four and broke, living in a small flat in Sausalito with an infant, and my father's away somewhere trying to earn money. He's lost jobs, as a shoe salesman, as a ranger in Muir Woods—he was let go for not keeping the latrines clean enough. This last job, at a landscaping company, they fired him for pulling out the jasmine instead of the weeds. He's been away from home for weeks.

She reads my father's letter, which says he's lost his fourth   5
job, and it's his fourth job in half a year. Life is much harder now with a baby, and she suspects that it will not ease up soon, or ever. She remembers those wonderful evenings after they were first married, living here in Sausalito, drinking Red Mountain wine at three dollars a gallon, feet dangling over the water as the fog lifted and the small boats floated by on the bay, with San Francisco's lights beyond. She thinks of the late nights at *Contact*, the art magazine they worked at in the city, and the concerts at the Fillmore. She has all the memories of the year before, in New York, when he worked at *Look* and she at *Mademoiselle*. In New York, the party began Wednesday and ended late Monday night: their home was an open invitation to visit anytime but Tuesday. They made jokes about their lifestyle, how it was like the title from Hemingway's book *A Moveable Feast*. Almost every night they drank, and in the morning woke to friends passed out on their floor.

They were both dreamers, but my mother had a practical side, and it was mostly this concern for the future and for a sense of security that came between them. When they argued, it was about money, which fell through the cracks of their lives, emptied on booze and parties and books. But they had loved each other while it was just the two of them, and that was all that really mattered.

Then she got pregnant with me and they headed back west.

My mother tries not to think about the way her life has turned, how somewhere along the way the wheel jerked and took a hard left onto a road she didn't want to go down or wasn't ready for. The pregnancy had not been planned; it was a ridiculous thing—a baby!—when they were so poor, and so full of dreams of being writers, and there was this sense of promise that was inspired partly by their youth, but also by something beyond them, a firey optimism that surrounded them in California in the sixties. . . .

MISS AMERICA

In the June mornings I painted Hawaiian flowers, watercolors of red hibiscus and yellow plumeria, my mother's favorites. The watercolor set was a gift from my grandmother, for my sixth birthday the month before. I liked the rhythm of my days, the early hours spent with brushes, their wet cold tips, the first splash of color on white paper, the shades I discovered when yellow touched red, then seeped into blue. I loved the smell of chalky paint, which got thin and watery and washed away if I wasn't careful.

10   Each painting was of a single flower, and it would fill the paper, the petals wide open and reaching.

My mother would kneel beside me, smiling at the artwork and also at my ability to entertain myself. This was the way she liked me best: content, engrossed in an activity. When I finished, I'd lay the paintings out to dry in rows on the deck, placing a stone on each corner to keep the paper flat. The deck was then covered with giant flowers. From the kitchen window, I proudly watched this garden.

After lunch I rolled the stiff paintings, and my mother helped me tie each one with a ribbon. I'd say goodbye to her and my new father, Mac, and carry them in a bag to Bridgeway Street. There I sold them for fifty cents apiece, and spent the money on bubblegum ice cream and red licorice.

We lived on a hill, and there was no direct way to Bridgeway, but instead an intricate maze of narrow, curving roads that often led to dead ends and short streets that stopped at parks or driveways. Heading downward, I would eventually find Princess Street, which spilled out onto Bridgeway at the bottom, but the opposite was not true: as I worked my way upward from Princess, the streets didn't all lead home, so I had to be careful to follow the right path. One wrong turn could greatly lengthen my walk or leave me utterly lost, and I would have to retrace my way to the bottom and begin again.

Even so, I loved the walks. Every time was different. The streets were quiet, just the sound of birds, and I kicked acorns that scattered like marbles. The pavement was crisscrossed with tar, lightning-bolt strips that made no sense but whose random patterns were pretty and reminded me of macramé designs. Sometimes I squatted down next to one, my knees making a tent of my sundress, and touched the smooth, sunwarmed tar. On some streets, I could see through breaks in fences and, through windows, the bay and San Francisco beyond.

Bridgeway had always been my favorite place. It was never too 15 far of a walk, though we had lived in a few different places in Sausalito. A necklace of a street, Bridgeway swooped for almost a mile along the edge of Sausalito. One side of the street was lined with stores and restaurants and bars, the other by People's Park and a long stretch of boulders, against which the bay heaved and splashed. I sat on a bench by these boulders, where I could watch the birds—the seagulls, and the pigeons with their satiny green throats. Across the bay, San Francisco looked like a saucer piled with toy buildings. The Golden Gate Bridge was just around the corner, though I couldn't see it. Seagulls crawled up the sky and then plunged to the ground, strutting and squawking along the rocks.

On Bridgeway Street, every day was a street fair, a carnival, and I was part of it. Musicians played on street corners and in doorways, their songs surrounding me, then fading as I passed, replaced by others farther on. I moved through music as if swimming in and out of warm ocean currents.

In the park, people sat cross-legged on blankets. Like me, they sold things they'd made, beaded necklaces and medicine bags and carvings. Someone would call me over, give me a handful of beads, a leather ribbon. Another would trade me a drawing for one of my paintings. Most knew my name, were happy to see me. Some got too close, touched my face, kissed my cheek, smelled my hair. I would pull away gently. I was used to the way strangers seemed to love me, though I was always a little surprised at first, and overwhelmed. It was something about my face, my hair, my smallness. I didn't seek it out, not directly, but maybe that was one reason I came to Bridgeway so often that summer, for the affection I found there. I gathered the attention, stored it inside me. I always moved on, though, because I didn't belong with these people, friendly as they were. Despite all the people around me, there was never any doubt that I belonged to my mother. My attachment to her was fierce. Still, I never insisted that she come with me—I didn't whine or plead. The most certain way to her heart was to be self-sufficient, as grown-up as possible.

So in my mind I carried my mother's image with me as surely as I carried my paintings that made her proud, and along with her image, I brought the love and longing I felt for her.

People offered me hits off their joints, but I smiled and walked on. I was like the dogs that traveled solo up and down this street. Seen and not seen. People gave us food, petted us, called to us. Yet we were free and answered to no one.

20   My mother told me to be good each time I left, but she had faith in me. She trained me to think for myself. She thought it was creative and enterprising that I sold my paintings on Bridgeway. My independence cultivated as a reflection of her own. Mac told me all the time that children should be seen and not heard, and he liked that I never raised my voice. I loved him, and his praise, the way it wrapped itself around me, kept me warm.

One day I notice a man is following me, from one end of the street to the other. There's something wrong with him, I can tell. Suddenly he's beside me. He's too friendly, too close. He takes my hand. I look at people who no longer see me. I'm invisible to everyone but this man, and I am all that he sees. He wants to look at my paintings, the few I have left. In here, he says, and pulls me up to sit with him in a stairwell, a small, dark opening between buildings. He says it's his step, and now it's mine, too.

He puts the paintings down and sets me on his lap; with one arm he circles me and with the other strokes my hair, which he claims is as beautiful as my flowers, even more. Under my dress, my knees poke out round and white, and I hold them tight in each hand like apples. Beneath, my feet dangle in their dirty gray Keds with no shoelaces. Leaning in this close to my face, he calls me "Miss America." I smell the sour-wine stink of his breath as it rides the back of his words.

People walk by, but no one looks up far enough, not when I cry, not when he kisses me, his mouth warm and wet. My face in his huge, huge hands. I don't know what he wants from me. He touches me, and though it doesn't hurt, I hate it. He touches me like the grown-ups who lie together in the park or on blankets on the grass. I can tell he's drunk, but there's something else, something worse. His words are loud, crowding one another. His shivering hands.

There is a place inside that I pull into when I need to, a safe place where I hope he can't reach me. I pretend I don't feel his mouth or see his face. Instead I listen, I nod when I'm supposed to, because if I'm good and quiet enough he might go away. Then, very softly, I tell him I have to go home. My mother. She's waiting for me, please. But, he says, you won't come back. I can't let you go, Miss America. This goes on for a long time. He makes me swear that I'll come back. I have to promise again and again.

I want my mother, want to scream for her. She would tear   25 and claw this man to pieces.

I'm crying hard now, and my nose runs, and he lets me go. I leave the flowers, and with them my days of painting, my love of Bridgeway, on the concrete step.

I run faster and faster up the steep, curving streets, over the dried tar that looks like spilled black paint. I try not to get lost because we live in a new place, and I'm not sure I can find it just now.

The Assault on the Universities: Then and Now

WALTER BERNS

Reflecting the conservative views of the American Enterprise Institute, Berns' discussion of the state of higher education in America denounces a number of events spawned by the Counterculture that changed university policies forever. This excerpt from "The Assault on the Universities: Then and Now" addresses both the physical violence and media attention that forced university faculties and administrations to create new schools, and government to create affirmative action programs. He also critiques new ways of looking at texts and history, pointing to the critical stance known as deconstruction for what he views as its absurd claims. He views his complaints as similar to those leveled at college life in the sixties: "the irrelevance of the curriculum." He sees this remaking of "the university into a kind of countercultural welfare agency," at the root of this irrelevancy.

———————— ✦ ————————

The assault on the university began with the student revolt at the Berkeley campus of the University of California in December

1964. Berkeley was followed by Columbia in 1968, Harvard and Cornell in 1969, and Yale and Kent State in 1970; during this same period some three hundred universities were the scenes of student sit-ins, building takeovers, strikes, riots, and other forms of rebellious behavior. In addition to its violent character, what distinguishes this assault from those of the past is that it came from within the university itself and that it met little resistance from professors and administrators.

The issue at Berkeley, initially at least, was free speech, but free speech had little or nothing to do with the subsequent campus disruptions; here the issues were, or were said to be, university involvement in neighborhood deterioration, in the draft and the Vietnam War, in racism, as well as in university governance, especially in disciplinary matters, and the alleged irrelevance of the curriculum. Except for the neighborhood issue (so prominent at Columbia), all these figured in the events at Cornell, which, under pressure from gun-bearing students, proceeded to jettison every vestige of academic integrity. In this respect the Cornell of the sixties became the prototype of the university as we know it today.

Shortly after he was installed as Cornell's president in 1963, James A. Perkins formed a Committee on Special Educational Projects charged with recruiting black students whose SAT scores were substantially below (as it turned out, 175 points below) the average of Cornell's entering class. Subsequently it was revealed that many of these students were to be recruited from the slums of the central cities, and perhaps not surprisingly, they proved incapable of being, or were unwilling to be, integrated into or assimilated by the Cornell student body; assimilation, they said, threatened their identity and needs as blacks.

In 1966 they formed an Afro-American Society, which in short order demanded separate living quarters, an Afro-American studies program—and seized a university building to house it— and ultimately an autonomous degree-granting college. To justify it, they issued a statement saying that "whites can make no contribution to Black Studies except in an advisory, non-decision making or financial capacity" and therefore that the program must be developed and taught by blacks and, as it turned out, only to black students.

5   This demand for an autonomous, degree-granting college took the form of an ultimatum, to which President Perkins responded by saying that he was "extremely reluctant to accept this idea of a college exclusive to one race, but [that he was] not fi-

nally opposed to it; it would involve a lot of rearranging of [his] own personality." To head this college, or as it came to be known, this Center for Afro-American Studies, the university, without the consent of the faculty, hired a twenty-eight-year-old graduate student in sociology at Northwestern University who, despite repeated requests, failed to submit a statement explaining the center's purpose and operation. (The closest thing to a statement of purpose came from the Afro-American Society, which said that the aim of the center "would be to create the tools necessary for the formation of a black nation.") To teach the first course in the program (on "black ideology"), the university, over the objection of two (and only two) faculty members of the appropriate committee, hired a twenty-four-year-old SNCC (Student Nonviolent Coordinating Committee) organizer who had completed a mere two years of college.

This jettisoning of academic standards, respecting the courses to be taught and the faculty to teach them, was largely the work of various members of the administration, only one of whom (the vice provost) was honest enough to admit that it was being done under pressure from the Afro-American Society—but, he assured the few dissenting members of the faculty, "it would never be done again." To refuse to accommodate the black "moderates," he said, would only strengthen the hands of the "militants."

Within a few months these "moderates" were burning buildings; joining with the SDS (Students for a Democratic Society) to barricade Chase Manhattan bank recruiters; removing furniture from a women's dorm and placing it in a building taken over by the Afro-American Society; disrupting traffic; overturning vending machines; trashing the library; grabbing President Perkins and pulling him from a podium (and, when the head of the campus police rushed to Perkins's aid, driving him off with a two-by-four); harassing campus visitors with toy guns; and, at five or six o'clock of a cold morning, seizing the student union building, driving visiting (and shivering) parents from their bedrooms—it was Parents Weekend—out into the street. Justification for this seizure was said to be the burning of a cross on the lawn of a black women's dorm, which, the university now implicitly admits, was done by the "moderate" blacks themselves. They then brought guns—real, not toy, guns—into the student union and, two days later, at gunpoint, forced the university to rescind the mild (very mild) punishment imposed on the blacks found guilty of these various offenses by the student-faculty

Committee on Student Affairs; in effect, they took control of the university. Photographs of the arms-bearing blacks, led by Thomas W. Jones, and of Vice President Steven Muller signing the surrender document appeared on the covers of the leading national newsmagazines.

All that remained to be done was to get the faculty to agree to the surrender terms, but this proved to be easy. Jones went on the radio to say that Cornell had only "three hours to live" and that the "racist" professors—by which he meant those professors who opposed the surrender—would be "dealt with." (But Cornell's most famous philosophy professor was speaking for the majority of the faculty when he said, "You don't have to intimidate us.") The final act took place at a Nuremberg-like faculty-student rally at which one famous professor after another pledged his allegiance to the new order. As Allan Bloom put it, the students "discovered that pompous teachers who catechized them about academic freedom could, with a little shove, be made into dancing bears."

No one should have been surprised by the faculty's willingness to capitulate to the armed students; the stage had been set for it a year earlier, when black students brought a charge of racism against a visiting professor of economics—he had made the mistake of employing a "Western" standard to judge the economic performance of various African countries—and, not satisfied with the professor's subsequent apology (which the administration required him to make), took possession of the Economics Department office, holding the chairman and the department secretary prisoner for some eighteen hours. The students were never punished, and much to the relief of the dean of the College of Arts and Science, the accused professor left Cornell. On the basis of the findings of a special faculty-student commission, the dean then pronounced the professor innocent of racism but went on to announce that the university and faculty were guilty of "institutional racism" and were obliged to mend their ways.

10   Nor should anyone have been surprised by the faculty's willingness to "reform" the curriculum, which is to say, to obliterate whatever differences there might still have been between the purposes of higher education and what were perceived to be the immediate, and pressing, concerns of the world outside. In the years immediately preceding the "crisis," one requirement after another of the old "core curriculum" had been dropped in favor of what can best be called consumer freedom or, in the jargon of the

day, of allowing the students "to do their own thing." One of the university's most famous professors, Paul de Man (of whom more later), argued that nothing of value would be lost by doing away with these requirements.

Begun as an assault on university "racism," the Cornell student uprising quickly became an assault on the integrity of the academic enterprise, an assault that was bound to succeed because it was met with only nominal resistance on the part of the faculty and none at all from the administration. Although university rules were broken left and right, the dean of the law school supported the president and voted for peace (to paraphrase Shakespeare's Hamlet, "What was law to him or he to law that he should weep for it?"); at a special meeting of the Arts College (in which, for the first time in its history, students were allowed to participate), the so-called humanists confessed their sins and called upon the president to do what he was not legally entitled to do—namely, nullify all the penalties imposed on black students "since the beginning of [the] spring term"; and the natural scientists, in the spirit of "better them than us," confident that none of it would reach the doors of their laboratories, remained aloof from the battle. On the whole, just as George Orwell's Winston Smith came finally to love Big Brother, so the typical Cornell professor came to admire the student radicals and sought their approval. From his perspective, theirs was the only moral game in town.

The black students, while threatening the lives of named members of the faculty, claimed to be putting "their [own] lives on the line"; others, inspired by Cornell's resident priest, Father Daniel Berrigan, insisted that they had "the moral right to engage in civil disobedience" and proceeded ceremoniously to burn their draft cards; the SDS, the vanguard of the New Left, led the assault on the "irrelevant" curriculum, insisting that the university could not remain disengaged from the great moral issues, war, racism, and the rank injustice of "bourgeois society." The largely bourgeois faculty agreed, thereby demonstrating that Andy Warhol was right when he said that "nothing is more bourgeois than to be afraid to look bourgeois."

With the faculty acquiescent and the students either triumphant or confused, Perkins had only to deal with the university trustees. They had been willing to fund the black studies program with a million dollars and had remained quiet when Perkins placed the university airplane at the disposal of black students, enabling them to go to New York City to purchase, with two thousand dollars in university funds, a set of bongo drums for Malcolm X Day. The one thing they could not abide was negative publicity—could not abide and, as it turned out, could not prevent. Covering the Cornell story for the *New York Times* was a Pulitzer Prize war reporter, Homer Bigart, who had learned to distrust official press releases, in this case those issuing from Muller's public relations office. Bigart's stories provided *Times* readers with a vivid account of what was in fact going on at Cornell, and when, despite Perkins's efforts to have it suppressed, the *Times* eventually ran on its front page a particularly damaging story, summarizing the events (the *Cornell Alumni News*, a publication with forty thousand subscribers and over which Perkins and Muller had no control, hurried into print with its own damaging account), the trustees called for Perkins's resignation, or according to the story handed out, he chose to resign.

But Perkins and his friends survived, their reputations (at least in some circles) unblemished. Muller became president of Johns Hopkins University; in 1993 Thomas Jones, the erstwhile black revolutionist, having been named president of TIAA-CREF (Teachers Insurance and Annuity Association—College Retirement Equities Fund, the world's largest pension fund), was appointed to the Cornell Board of Trustees, and in 1992, by way of recognizing "his outstanding leadership and extraordinary contributions to [the] University," Cornell established the James A. Perkins Professorship of Environmental Studies. In 1995 Jones "made a large contribution to the University," enabling it to endow an annual Perkins Prize of five thousand dollars "for the student, faculty, staff member or program that has done the most during the preceding year to promote interracial understanding and harmony on campus."

15   To say the least, not everyone thought Perkins deserved this recognition—Bayard Rustin, the great civil rights leader, called him "a masochistic and pusillanimous university president"—but even his critics would have to admit that Perkins left his mark on the university, and not only on Cornell. By surrendering to students armed with guns, he made it easier for those who came after him to surrender to students armed only with epithets ("racists," "sexists," "elitists," "homophobes"); by inaugurating a black studies program, Perkins paved the way for Latino studies programs, women's studies programs, and multicultural studies programs; by failing to support a professor's freedom to teach, he paved the

way for speech codes and political correctness; and of course he pioneered the practice of affirmative action admissions and hiring. In a word, while it would exaggerate his influence to hold him responsible for subsequent developments, he did provide an example that other institutions found it convenient to follow. . . .

Although a legacy of the sixties, affirmative action—for women or even for blacks—was not the principal cause for which the students took to the barricades in those turbulent times. True, they accused the universities of racism (as well as complicity in the draft and Vietnam War), but like their counterparts in France and Germany—remember Rudi Dutschke?—they fancied themselves part of a mass movement against the "repressive system" or the "technological culture" being imposed on them by the universities. According to the chroniclers of the Berkeley "rebellion," the students of the sixties were searching for "authentic values" and could not find them in the courses available to them. The same complaints were heard at Cornell (as well as at Columbia, Harvard, Yale, and the rest), where students paraded as New Left "revolutionists," all the while expressing their contempt for "bourgeois society."

The antibourgeois sloganizing, so popular, so easy at the time, was mostly cant, as Richard Nixon demonstrated when he put an end to the draft and, with it, the so-called student movement. The radical students of the sixties may have hated bourgeois society (and despised its representatives), but having no clear idea of what to put in its place, they abandoned politics for the drugs and sex of Woodstock. They should find the university much more to their liking today.

For the others, the sort of student who took no part in the sixties' rebellions, the universities continue their bourgeois ways. According to a recent report, more than 50 percent of the baccalaureate degrees now being awarded in our colleges and universities are in those most bourgeois of subjects: engineering, business, and other professional programs (excluding education).

There is of course nothing despicable about learning how to make a living; on the contrary, providing for oneself (and for one's family) is, as Tocqueville points out, one of the things that distinguishes a free man from a slave. But the radical students were justified in thinking that vocational training is not the proper business of the university. Americans have never had to be encouraged to look after the practical side of things; they do that for themselves. As Tocqueville said, "people living in a democratic age are quite certain to bring the industrial side of science to perfection anyhow," which is to say, without being encouraged to do so. This explains why the taxpayers and alumni who pay the piper are disposed to call an industrial or vocational tune. Yet, perhaps uncharacteristically, they continue to support the universities even though so much of vocational training—basic economics, business, accounting, computer science, and the like—could be provided at less than half the cost by the community colleges. (Less than 18 percent of Maryland's higher education budget is allocated to community colleges, even though they enroll 57 percent of the state's undergraduates.) They probably support the universities because they think it important that students—even prospective engineers, bankers, lawyers, doctors, accountants, and the like—should have some acquaintance with the humanities, or, as they might say (but with only the vaguest idea of what they mean by it), with "culture." Before contributing to the annual fund drives, however, they would do well to learn how these "culture" courses are being taught these days.

20   Although not the first to define the term as it is used in this context, Thomas Carlyle (in the 1860s) spoke of culture as the body of arts and learning separate from the "work" or "business" of society. This definition has the merit of reflecting (and that very clearly) the problem that gave rise to the culture movement in the nineteenth century. Carlyle was preceded by Coleridge, Keats, and Wordsworth (who, in his role as poet, saw himself as an "upholder of culture" in a world that had come to disdain it); by Shelley (who said that society could do without John Locke "but not without Dante, Petrarch, Chaucer, Shakespeare"); and by John Stuart Mill, for whom culture meant the qualities and faculties that characterize our humanity or those aspects of humanity that he, like Tocqueville, foresaw might be absent in a utilitarian or commercial society. Carlyle was followed by Matthew Arnold, for whom culture meant not only literary pursuits but—in a sentence that became familiar, if not famous—the pursuit of "the best which has been thought and said in the world."

These critics and poets had a concern for the sublime (or the aesthetic) and a complaint against the modern commercial and bourgeois society in which the sublime, they feared, would have no firm place. The philosophical founders of this new society—particularly John Locke and Adam Smith—promised to provide for the needs of the body (and in this they surely succeeded); culture was intended to provide for the needs of the soul. Coleridge made this the business of his "clerisy," an official body—originally (as in the case of the Church of England) but not necessarily a religious corporation—set apart and publicly endowed for the cultivation and diffusion of knowledge. America assigned this task to the universities.

Of course no American university, or at least no public university, can ignore the task Jefferson assigned to the University of Virginia, that of paying "especial attention to the principles of government which shall be inculcated therein." He believed that students have to be prepared to live in a free society, to know what is required of citizens in that society. But one of the things required of them is to criticize it, for example, to call it to account for its racism or, as Coleridge and Company were doing in the nineteenth century, for its failure to inculcate respect for "the best which has been thought and said in the world." Unable, for constitutional reasons, to establish a clerisy, we assigned this task to the universities and, more precisely, to their humanities faculties. Unfortunately, as Allan Bloom wrote, "the humanities are now failing, not for want of support but for want of anything to say." Or, as he might have said, what the humanities are now saying is a sophisticated version of what the radical students used to say.

Shortly after Bloom published *The Closing of the American Mind*, a trenchant account of the state of the humanities in this country, and especially in the universities, the American Council of Learned Societies assembled a group of distinguished humanities professors and charged them with writing a response to it. Their report acknowledges the book's "disturbingly popular" success but insists that the attacks on the humanities (by Lynne Cheney and William Bennett, as well as by Bloom) "would be comic in their incongruity if they were not taken so seriously by so many people, with such potentially dangerous consequences." It goes on to say that "such attacks mislead the public [and] give students quite the wrong impression about what the humanities are doing." Contrary to what the critics are alleged to be saying, students are reading the great books (or, as the report puts it by way of casting doubt on their greatness, the "great books"), but they have "to learn to think about them in ways that do not suppress the challenges of contemporary modes of analysis." But in making that statement about the humanities having nothing to say, Bloom was referring to deconstructionism, the most prominent of those "contemporary modes of analysis," the mode of analysis then favored by—to quote the ACLS report—"the best scholars in the humanities today." . . .

The assault on the universities, begun by the radical students of the sixties, was continued in a more subtle fashion by the deconstructionists in the eighties. Unlike the students, they did not strike, riot, occupy buildings, or take up arms, nor, as one of the Berrigan brothers was accused of doing—even as he was nominated for a Nobel Peace Prize—did they engage in a plot to kidnap Henry Kissinger and blow up the heating system of federal buildings in Washington. (The case ended in a mistrial.) All they did is teach (and teach the next generation of teachers), but what they taught is that the universities have nothing of importance to teach. Matthew Arnold would have had the universities teach the books containing the best that has been thought and said in the world, and Thomas Jefferson wanted them to teach the Declaration of Independence and *The Federalist*, the "best guides [to the] distinctive principles of the government of the United States." But, according to Paul de Man, there is no best thought and no best guide because there is no text; there is only interpretation. As he said, "the distinctive curse of all language" is that it cannot convey meaning in any objective sense. Thus, about those things that mattered most to Arnold and Jefferson—all the things written about by poets, playwrights, philosophers, historians, statesmen, and founders—the humanities, indeed the universities, would have nothing to say.

25   In a way this is what the students were complaining about in the sixties: the irrelevance of the curriculum. For some of them the solution was to remake the university into a kind of countercultural welfare agency, and the extent of their success is evident in the prevalence of black studies, women's studies, and multicultural programs. For the others—the ones searching for "authentic values," in which phrase there is, perhaps, a hint of a longing for an education of the sort proposed by Coleridge and Company—what does the university offer? In the humanities it offers a politicized curriculum, the core of which is antirationalist, antihumanist, and antiliberal.

It used to be thought (and in some quarters is still thought) that Shakespeare is the greatest of our poets, the playwright who shows us, for example, the meaning of love and friendship, envy and jealousy, the character of good rulers and the fate of tyrants. In a word, he shows us human beings just as they are, a mixture of the high and the low, or as someone said, "his poetry gives us the eyes to see what is there." The political plays especially meant something for Abraham Lincoln. "Some of Shakespeare's plays I have never read," he said, "while others I have gone over perhaps as frequently as any unprofessional reader. Among the latter are

Lear, Richard Third, Henry Eighth, Hamlet, and especially Macbeth. It is wonderful." But for the New Historicism, currently the dominant movement in the field of Shakespeare studies, his plays simply reflect the prejudices of his day. They are said to be worthy of study only because in them can be found the seeds of racism, sexism, capitalism, classism, all the evils that are said to characterize bourgeois society. Reading Shakespeare in this way has the effect of reducing his stature in the eyes of the students. "Safely entrenched in their politically correct attitude," writes Paul Cantor, a critic of the New Historicism, "students are made to feel superior to Shakespeare, to look down patronizingly at his supposedly limited and biased view of the world."

For the students looking for something "wonderful," for something not available to them in the bourgeois world from which they come and to which they must, willy-nilly, return, these antihumanists have nothing to say.

from *Destructive Generation: Second Thoughts About the Sixties*

PETER COLLIER AND DAVID HOROWITZ

Once leading members of the more radical elements of the Counterculture, editors of *Ramparts* magazine, and die-hard Marxists, Collier and Horowitz's, *Destructive Generation: Second Thoughts About the Sixties* (1989) represented a new wave of neo-conservative reflection about the era. Embracing what they called the "conservative counterculture against the radical counterculture" Collier and Horowitz—heralded by conservative victories in American politics with Ronald Reagan's two terms in office and Newt Gingrich's election in 1994—their book provides insights into many of the negative legacies of the times. Billed as "an inside look at the 'lost generation' of the 1960s," Collier and Horowitz take on the Weathermen, the Black Panther Party, and several of the most notorious countercultural icons, as well as the general reckless hedonism, sexism, and violence of their generation.

———————————— ✦ ————————————

A while back, we were on a radio talk show about former Sixties radicals. At one point, the host asked us what we thought was the "summary moment" of the decade. The question begged a certain kind of answer: Selma, the Free Speech Movement, the March on the Pentagon, Chicago. But we had discussed the issue before and agreed that the interesting truths about that era were to be found in the small moments rather than in the grand ones. We told the interviewer about one such moment that took place in the summer of 1969.

It was that magic instant when the auguries all seemed to point toward revolution. Tom Hayden, a leading Movement figure facing conspiracy charges in Chicago, was calling for the creation of "liberated zones" in American cities. Weatherman, the faction that had seized control of the Students for a Democratic Society, was planning to begin "guerrilla warfare" before the year was out. But most radicals had fixed their attention on the Black Panther Party, which Hayden had called "America's Vietcong."

Others were talking, the Panthers were doing. Their membership had been involved in shootouts with the police which were widely regarded by the radical community as dress rehearsals for the coming Armageddon. Because the Party leadership had been decimated (Huey Newton was in jail for killing a policeman, Eldridge Cleaver in exile, and Bobby Seale under indictment), "Field Marshal" David Hilliard had taken charge of the effort to keep the Party together and build support among whites. Learning that the celebrated French writer Jean Genet was infatuated with the Panthers, Hillard convinced him to come to the Bay Area to speak in behalf of the Party.

One of the stops was an appearance at Stanford University sponsored by the French Department, whose higher-ups had convinced eminent historian Gordon Wright to host a cocktail party before the speech. The Panthers arrived early in the afternoon in their uniforms of black leather jackets and sunglasses, looking like some lost Nazi legion whose skin color had changed during their diaspora. The small Frenchman with bad teeth and shabby clothes spoke through a young woman translator on loan from *Ramparts* magazine. He praised the Panther's *authenticity* (a characteristic he said he also admired in the Marquis de Sade, whom he called "the greatest revolutionary of all, greater even than Marx"). The Panthers milled around in sullen incomprehension as he talked. Discovering that Wright's son, an Army draftee, had brought a black Army friend home with him on leave, Panther Elmer "Geronimo" Pratt confronted the young man in the kitchen, spitting in his face and calling him an "Uncle Tom" and "enemy of the people." When Geronimo reappeared in the living room, the white guests pretended not to notice.

Not long after the cocktail party began, an unexpected guest 5 dropped in. It was Ken Kesey. He had been on the fringes of the Stanford scene since getting his start as a novelist in one of Wallace Stegner's creative writing seminars. Oblivious to the Panthers, Kesey, his eyes cloudy with drugs and an out-of-plumb smile on his face, said that he had come because he had heard that a great French writer was there; since he was a great writer too it seemed a good thing that they should meet.

The guests sensed that a portentous moment was approaching as Sartre's St. Genet, *deracine* homosexual outlaw, and Tom Wolfe's St. Kesey, picaresque hero of the acid test, shook hands. In what seemed an act of semiotics, Kesey flashed a smile which showed that one of his front teeth had a cap in the form of an American flag. Genet, self-conscious because of his own chipped and discolored teeth, was delighted by the desecration and laughed out loud. Kesey pointed down at his feet. "I'm wearing green socks," he said with a beatific look on his face. Genet frowned uncomprehendingly as Kesey kept on talking: "Green socks. Can you dig it? Green socks. They're heavy, man, very heavy." Trying to keep up, the young woman translator rendered the remarks with awkward literalness: "*Les chausettes vertes, elles sont très, très lourdes.*" Genet looked down at Kesey's feet with the beginnings of sympathy. But before he could commiserate with him over the fact that he had somehow been condemned to wear heavy green objects around his ankles, Kesey's attention had lurched off in another direction. Pointing at the Black Panthers, he said to Genet: "You know what? I feel like playing basketball. There's nothing better than playing basketball with Negroes. I could go for a little one-on-one with some of these Negroes right now."

So taken aback by the boyish innocence of Kesey's manner that they momentarily failed to assess the implications of the words, the Panthers stared at him. Then one of them moved forward threateningly. David Hilliard stopped him: "Stay cool, man. This motherfucker is crazy." He repeated the words to everyone else in a louder voice: "This motherfucker is crazy and we're getting the fuck out of here."

The Panthers left, pulling Genet along with them. The diminutive Frenchman turned and glanced at Kesey, shrugging slightly as if to indicate that left to his own devices he would just as soon stay with him and exchange bizarre comments through a translator. Kesey watched him go. "Wonder what's wrong with those Negroes?" he asked, as the entourage moved away. "Don't they like basketball? I thought Negroes *loved* basketball."

In another era this would have been seen simply as an odd moment—two men from different worlds trying to communicate across a vast cultural divide and winding up in a fatuous contretemps. But this brief encounter, widely discussed in Bay Area Movement circles, was regarded as an "epiphany." Self-identified radicals like ourselves were fond of this word during the Sixties because it tended to elevate life's commonplaces and to infuse a sense of portent into situations whose *heaviness*, like that of Ken Kesey's socks, was not otherwise discernible to the inquiring eye.

10   *Epiphanies*: they made the world worthy of us. We searched for them like stargazers. This was part of the decade's transcendental conviction that there was something apocalyptic lurking behind the veil of the ordinary, and that just a little more pressure was needed to pierce the last remaining membrane—of civility, bourgeois consciousness, corporate liberalism, sexual uptightness, or whatever else prevented us all from breaking through to the other side.

From its earliest battle cry—"You can't trust anyone over thirty"—until the end of its brief strut on the stage of national attention, the Sixties generation saw itself as a scouting party for a new world. The "cultural revolution" it was staging would free inmates from the prison of linear thought. It was the social horticulturalist whose "greening of America" would allow the postindustrialist age finally to break through the crust of the Puritan past. It was the avenging angel that would destroy the evil empire of "Amerika" and free the captive peoples of the world.

It is hard to believe in epiphanies now, and it is hard not to wince at these homemade hankerings for Armageddon. Yet while the Sixties, that age of wonders, is over in fact, it is still with us in spirit. Nostalgia artists have made it into a holograph that creates beguiling images of the last good time—a prelapsarian age of good sex, good drugs, and good vibes. For unreconstructed leftists, the Sixties is not just an era of good fun but of good politics too—a time of monumental idealism populated by individuals who wanted nothing more than to give peace a chance; a time of commitment and action when dewy-eyed young people in the throes of a moral passion unknown in our own selfish age sought only to remake the world.

There is truth in the nostalgia. It is the *memory* of the era that is false. The vision we see when we look into the glass of Sixties narcissism is distorted. It may have been the best of times, but it was the worst of times as well. And by this we do not simply mean to add snapshots of the race riots at home and war in Vietnam to the sentimental collage of people being free. It was a time when innocence quickly became cynical, when American mischief fermented into American mayhem. It was a time when a gang of ghetto thugs like the Black Panthers might be anointed as political visionaries, when Merry Pranksters of all stripes could credibly set up shop as social evangelists spreading a chemical gospel.

The Sixties might have been a time of tantalizing glimpses of the New Jerusalem. But it was also a time when the "System"— that collection of values that provide guidelines for societies as well as individuals—was assaulted and mauled. As one center of authority after another was discredited under the New Left offensive, we radicals claimed that we murdered to create. But while we wanted a revolution, we didn't have a plan. The decade ended with a big bang that made society into a collection of splinter groups, special interest organizations and newly minted "minorities," whose only common belief was that America was guilty and untrustworthy. This is perhaps the enduring legacy of the Sixties. The political philosopher Michael Walzer expressed this adversarial sensibility when he confessed, in a recent article in *The New Republic*, "It is still true that only when I go to Washington to demonstrate do I feel at home there."

The Sixties are still with us, therefore, as a nostalgic artifact 15
that measures our more somber world and finds it wanting, and also as a goad to radical revival. It has become the decade that would not die, the decade whose long half-life continues to contaminate our own. The Sixties are the green socks around our ankles: heavy, man, very heavy.

This book is about the Sixties and also about that phenomenon—there's really no name for it—that might be termed the Sixties-within-the-Eighties. It is also about the two of us and our understanding of the weight of Kierkegaard's observation that life may be lived forward but can only be understood backward.

By the mid-Seventies, our own path had begun to diverge from the one taken by other New Leftists who wanted to maintain the struggle and keep the faith. For both of us the withdrawal from radicalism involved an interplay between the personal and political which we have tried to describe in detail in the explicitly autobiographical part of this book. Broadly speaking, however, if there was one event that triggered our reevaluations (and those of others who began to have second thoughts about the Leftism of the Sixties), it was the fate of Vietnam. There was no "new morning" as radicals had predicted, no peasant utopia. Instead, there was a bloodbath greater than the one we set out to oppose and a government worse than the one we had wanted to replace.

Coming out of Southeast Asia in bits and pieces (the flow of information impeded by the Left itself), these facts slowed our forward political motion rather than throwing it immediately into reverse. That was accomplished a few years later when the Soviet Union invaded Afghanistan and the reformed Left reacted not by denouncing the genocide but by denouncing tenuous U.S. efforts to impose sanctions on the U.S.S.R. and to help the mujahideen as the beginning of a "new cold war."

By the early Eighties, we felt it was time to try for an honest inventory of our generation's impact. Some of the accomplishments were undeniably positive. There *was* an expansion of consciousness, of social space, of tolerance, of prospects for individual fulfillment. But there was a dark side too. In the inchoate attack against authority, we had weakened our culture's immune system, making it vulnerable to opportunistic diseases. The origins of metaphorical epidemics of crime and drugs could be traced to the Sixties, as could literal ones such as AIDS.

20   As we began to write episodically about some of the people we had known and events we had experienced, we encountered considerable resistance from our former comrades. They made it clear that for them there were two categories of truth—the "progressive" truths which aided the cause, and subversive truths which were best left unsaid. We watched them pick up the mothballed banners once again and revive the old slogans, these middle-aged activists with gray sideburns and sagging bellies now agitating for a new anti-Americanism despite the change in what we had once called the "objective conditions" of global power. And we began to realize that one of the strongest holds the Sixties had on our generation was its promise of eternal youth, a state of being that would never require a balance sheet of one's prior acts, let alone a profit-and-loss statement. It was as Lionel Trilling had written in his classic novel of ideas *The Middle of the Journey:* "To live the life of promises was to remain children."

The contents of this book, then, mirror our attempt to understand the movement of which we were a part, to understand the lost boys and girls of the Sixties who never grew up, and to understand ourselves as well. Our approach utilizes memoir, documentary reconstruction, commentary, adumbration. But the overall spirit of these pieces is interrogatory—of ourselves and our past, of our old comrades who chose to keep to the revolutionary road. "Pieces," that journalistic code-word for essays, is indeed an appropriate term for the chapters of this book. Not the "picked up pieces" that usually comprise collections of occasional writings but pieces of the past and pieces of the present that past has influenced; pieces of the puzzle of the way we were and the way we have become. Writing this book was an act of discovery for us which is not over yet.

EXPLORING *THE* COUNTERCULTURE *READER*

The Counterculture Reader is a sampling of readings from the 1950s through 2002. It is meant as a starting point for you in your countercultural explorations. The following are suggestions for ways to approach the reader, select outside materials, formulate discussions, and construct writing assignments. Look for films of the eras, books, academic articles, and the hundreds of web sites of varying quality on the Beats and the Counterculture, including rotating virtual museums.

CHAPTER 1: CAPTURING THE BEAT SPIRIT

Discussion

1. Discover jazz recordings of the era, recorded poetry, film, and web sites. Include these in your discussions.
2. Of the writers featured in Chapter 1, who do you think best captures the idea of Beat?
3. Compare and contrast the writing advice of Jack Kerouac to that of William Burroughs.
4. How is a "dharma bum" like a saint, according to Jack Kerouac?
5. How does Frank Conroy's generation compare to that of your parents, or to your own? Have an older person read the piece. Does the America Conroy depicts appear more or less desirable than our own?

Ideas, Projects, Writing

1. Keep a Beat journal. As much as possible, try to record events in the style Jack Kerouac recommends in "Essentials of Spontaneous Prose." What are the strengths and weaknesses of this style of writing?
2. Read the poetry of Gary Snyder, Diana di Prima, and Lawrence Ferlinghetti, and then compare their work to a current piece of popular music. Do you see any similarities? Any

differences? Do they appear to be writing in the Kerouac style? Can you find a current poet or songwriter that has been influenced by the Beats?

3. Research one or more of the Beat writers and conduct a mock interview (like the Burroughs' interview) with one class member playing the Beat and another the interviewer. Or, locate another interview with one of the Beat writers.

4. Research the reading at Six Gallery and stage a reading of your own. Or, have class members read their works written in the Beat style for the class. Include a variety of genres if possible—poetry, fiction, and an essay.

CHAPTER 2: HOW TO BE A HIPPIE—OR NOT

Discussion

1. Using several of the readings combined, describe how you would characterize hippies. Can one still be called a hippie, even if he or she was not part of the 1960s?

2. According to Robert Pirsig, what is the problem with the "groovy dimension" or fear of technology? Using some of the other readings, speculate as to why the Counterculture flees from "the Machine"?

3. What are some of the pros and cons to living in communes, according to Iris Keltz, David Lee Pratt, and Peter Coyote?

4. Examine the use of profanity in the readings. Discuss what cultural factors contributed to the relaxing of censorship laws.

5. Looking at several of the readings and incorporating David Felton and David Dalton's piece on Charles Manson's Family, how might hippies be targets for cults?

Ideas, Projects, Writing

1. Construct a collage or write a paper collaboratively discussing how the images of the Counterculture depicted in Chapter 2 remain in popular music (album covers, videos, concerts), drug use, film, fashion, and literature.

2. If you know someone who lived in a commune (or does now), interview and write an article about these experiences.

3. Research several well-known or obscure American cults. Read psychologists' and commentators' findings about the similarities among these groups.

4. Conduct a Diggers free experiment on your campus. (You may need permission from your institution, first.) In a group, collect clothing, shoes, books, housewares, and non-perishable food items and attempt to give them away. Make signs reflecting the Digger Papers' philosophy. Record the observations you make as people walk by.
5. Utilizing several of the readings, write a paper comparing and contrasting negative and positive views of the Counterculture.

CHAPTER 3: DRUGS AND VIOLENCE

Discussion

1. Using photographs, film, and music from the era, discuss how drugs were portrayed in the 1950s, 1960s, and 1970s. Look online for exhibits about the drug culture. You may also want to compare them with the turn of the nineteenth century.
2. Although revered as a countercultural icon known for his drug writings, look at some of William Burroughs' other writings and write a paper about how he actually depicts drug abuse.
3. What did former professor Timothy Leary hope to achieve by "turning on the world"? Write a paper examining his arguments.
4. Discuss how the style and tone of Hunter S. Thompson and Tom Wolfe's works attempt to capture the feel of the Counterculture, usually through humor, in writing.
5. How does Dennis Hopper defend the film *Easy Rider*?
6. Using several readings to support your argument, why did young people take hallucinogens despite their illegality, the health warnings, and the lack of substantial research about their effects? Why was this such a strong Countercultural trend?
7. What did violent protests do to the left, according to several of the writers? (See also the readings by Walter Berns, and David Horowitz and Peter Collier in Chapter 6.)

Ideas, Projects, Writing

1. Show the film *Easy Rider* in class and have everyone write a response to the film and L. M. Kit Carson's interview with actor and director Dennis Hopper.
2. Research and trace the use of hallucinogens in the 1960s and 1970s as compared with the 1990s. Do you think drug use by young people is affected by countercultural images from the past?

3. Compare the style and tone of Jean Genet's depiction of the Chicago Convention with Walter Berns' response to student unrest.
4. Describe the style and tone of "Communique #2 From the Weatherman Underground."

CHAPTER 4: CRITIQUING THE NEW AGE

Discussion

1. Using several of the readings, compare the Countercultural views of Native Americans.
2. How do Eldridge Cleaver, Frances M. Beal, and Al Calloway describe the Counterculture's interest in images of black culture?
3. Why is Wendy Rose critical of "white poets"?
4. How does Leslie Marmon Silko describe "Indian lovers" in the excerpt from *Almanac of the Dead*?
5. How does Mary Crow Dog view the American Indian Movement and the white Counterculture?

Ideas, Projects, Writing

1. View two films about Native Americans from the last thirty years, *Little Big Man* (1970) and *Dances with Wolves* (1990). Write brief comparisons of the movies' depictions of "Indians and white people." How did the Counterculture change America's way of viewing history?
2. Research Eldridge Cleaver and other Black Power figures, male and female, of the1960s and 1970s. Write a paper describing the images, fashions, and language they used that defined the movement.
3. Does your university have an ethnic studies program? Or separate programs in Native American studies and African American studies? Write a paper or present a project discussing how and why these programs were started. Include interviews, if possible, and incorporate Walter Bern's essay from Chapter 6.
4. Present a panel representing a number of ethnicities that came to be recognized during Countercultural movements of the 1960s, 1970s, and 1980s. Open the discussion to how people identify themselves today in our culture.
5. Write a paper or present a project or collage that defines New Age ideas and the Counterculture.

CHAPTER 5: FEMINISM, GAY ISSUES, AND PUNKS

1. Does Susan Brownmiller's essay have relevance today?
2. What were the women in Boston attempting to accomplish with their Women's Health Collective?
3. What did the Stonewall Riots represent for gay culture?
4. What elements of the Counterculture can be found in Andrew Holleran's *The Dancer from the Dance?*
5. Are punks a part of the Counterculture? Why or why not?

Ideas, Projects, Writing

1. Find a 1970s copy of *Our Bodies, Ourselves* in the library (or go to the Boston Women's Collective web site) and compare it with the 1998 edition. Present your findings to the class.
2. Research and read contemporary reviews of *The Dancer from the Dance* and Rita Mae Brown's lesbian novel *Rubyfruit Jungle.* Write a paper summarizing reactions to the books. Why did such works not appear until the 1970s?
3. Present a panel about women's issues then and now.
4. Trace the origins of courses in women's studies and gay studies on your campus or elsewhere. Write a paper or present a project describing how these programs or courses came to be.
5. Listen to some punk music from the late 1970s or view the film *Sid and Nancy* and then comment on the images punk conveys in opposition to what they perceived as the "peace and love" generation of the 1960s.
6. Research and compare English and American punk music from the late 1970s and early 1980s. Who came first and why?
7. Write a paper or present a project that compares the punk era of the late 1970s to current interpretations of punk. Focus on music, fashion, philosophy, and commodification.

CHAPTER 6: BACKLASH—THE RIGHT, THE LEFT, AND THE LEGACIES

Discussion

1. Have everyone in the class come up with five legacies of the Counterculture based on their readings, observations, and experiences.

2. Discuss Walter Bern's points about the "assault on the universities" and compare them with Peter Collier and David Horowitz's critiques of their generation.
3. Read the accounts Daniel Pinchbeck and Joelle Fraser, and compare some of the experiences of the children who grew up in the Counterculture.

Ideas, Projects, Writing

1. Interview several professors on your campus about changes in American universities over the last thirty years. Write a paper presenting their views of these changes.
2. Present a project tracing the development of the conservative backlash against the Counterculture. Based on your readings and further research, present a panel discussing whether the Countercultures of the 1950s, 1960s, and 1970s produced more or less dissent and fragmentation in American culture.
3. Write a paper comparing and contrasting descriptions of life in the Counterculture depicted in the readings by Walter Berns and Peter Collier and David Horowitz. View NBC's film *The Sixties* and look for depictions of the era.
4. Look for current alternative technologies in use or development that arose from Countercultural ideas about the environment. Would Robert Pirsig (*Zen and the Art of Motorcycle Maintenance*) approve of these new machines?
5. Research web site depictions of the Counterculture, including conservative responses such as David Horowitz's. Write a paper or present a project describing how the internet influences the way we view history.

CREDITS

Beal, Frances M. "Double Jeopardy: To Be Black and Female." from *Double Jeopardy: To Be Black and Female* by Frances M. Beal. Copyright © 1969 by Frances M. Beale. Reprinted by permission of Frances M. Beal.

Berns, Walter. "The Assault on the Universities: Then and Now," from *Reassessing the Sixties: Debating the Political and Cultural Legacy*, edited by Stephen Macedo. Copyright © 1997 by W.W. Norton & Company, Inc. Used by permission of W.W. Norton & Company, Inc.

The Boston Women's Health Collective (Judy Norsigian, Vilunya Diskin, Paula Doress-Worters, Jane Pincus, Wendy Sanford, and Norma Swenson). "Our Bodies, Ourselves," from "The Boston Women's Health Book Collective and *Our Bodies, Ourselves: A Brief History and Reflection*," *Journal of the American Medical Women's Association*, Winter 1999, Vol. 54, No. 1. Copyright © American Medical Women's Association. Reprinted by permission of American Medical Women's Association.

Brownmiller, Susan. "The Enemy Within," from *Apocalypse: Dominant Contemporary Forms*, edited by Joe David Bellamy, J. B. Lippincott Company, 1972. Copyright © Susan Brownmiller 2003. This article first appeared in *Mademoiselle* in 1970.

Burroughs, William. "Burroughs After Lunch," from *Burroughs Live: The Collected Interviews of William S. Burroughs 1960-1997*, by William Burroughs, edited by Sylvere Lotringer. Semiotext(e), 2002, pp. 47-50.

Carson, L. M. Kit. "*Easy Rider*: A Very American Thing: An Interview with Dennis Hopper," in *Apocalypse: Dominant Contemporary Forms*, edited by Joe David Bellamy, J.B. Lippincott Company, 1972. "*Easy Rider*: A Very American Thing: An Interview with Dennis Hopper," copyright © L. M. Kit Carson. Reprinted by permission of L. M. Kit Carson.

Cleaver, Eldridge. "Soul on Ice," from *Soul on Ice* by Eldridge Cleaver. Copyright © 1968 by McGraw-Hill. Used by permission of McGraw-Hill.

Collier, Peter, and David Horowitz. "Destructive Generation: Second Thoughts About the Sixties," from *Destructive Generation: Second Thoughts About the Sixties* by Peter Collier and David Horowitz. Copyright © 1989, 1990, 1996 by Peter Collier, Inc., and David Horowitz. Reprinted with permission from Georges Borchardt, Inc., for the authors.

Conroy, Frank. "My Generation," from *Smiling Through the Apocalypse: Esquire's History of the Sixties*, Crown Publishers, Inc., 1987, pp. 301-305. "My Generation" reprinted by permission of Donadio & Olson, Inc. Copyright © 1968 by Frank Conroy.

Coyote, Peter. "Sleeping Where I Fall," from *Sleeping Where I Fall: A Chronicle* by Peter Coyote. Copyright © 1998 by Peter Coyote. Reprinted by permission of Counterpoint Press, a member of Perseus Books, L.L.C.

Crow Dog, Mary. "Lakota Woman," from *Lakota Woman* by Mary Crow Dog with Richard Erdoes. Copyright © 1990 by Mary Crow Dog and Richard Erdoes. Used by permission of Grove/Atlantic, Inc.

The Diggers. "The Digger Papers," from Digger Archives (online), http://www.diggers.org.

di Prima, Diane, "Revolutionary Letter #1" from *City Lights Pocket Poets Anthology*, edited by Lawrence Ferlinghetti, City Lights Books, 1995, pp. 128-130. "Revolutionary Letter #1" copyright © 1971, 1974, and 1979 by Diane di Prima. Used by permission.

Felton, David, and David Dalton. "Year of the Fork, Night of the Hunter," from *Mindfuckers* by David Felton and David Dalton, a Rolling Stone Press book published by Quick Fox Inc. © 1972 Rolling Stone Press. All rights reserved. Reprinted by permission.

Ferlinghetti, Lawrence. "Pictures of the Gone World #21: [The world is a beautiful place]," from *City Lights Pocket Poets Anthology*, edited by Lawrence Ferlinghetti, City Lights Books, 1995, pp. 2-4. Copyright © 1955 by Lawrence Ferlinghetti. Reprinted by permission of City Lights Books.

Fraser, Joelle. "The Territory of Men: A Memoir," from *The Territory of Men: A Memoir* by Joelle Fraser. Copyright © 2002 by Joelle Fraser. Used by permission of Villard Books, a division of Random House, Inc.

Holleran, Andrew. "The Dancer from the Dance," from *The Dancer from the Dance* by Andrew Holleran, pp. 30-34. Copyright © 1978 by Andrew Holleran. Reprinted by permission of HarperCollins Publishers Inc., William Morrow.

Kapur, Tribhuwan. "Hippies: A Study of Their Drug Habits and Sexual Customs," from *Hippies: A Study of Their Drug Habits and Sexual Customs.* Copyright © Dr. Tribhuwan Kapur. Reprinted by permission of Dr. Tribhuwan Kapur.

Keltz, Iris. "Close Encounters with New Buffalo" and "The Founding of Morningstar Commune" from *Scrapbook of a Taos Hippie: Tribal Tales from the Heart of a Cultural Revolution* by Iris Keltz. Copyright © 2000 by Cinco Puntos Press. Reprinted by permission of Cinco Puntos Press.

Kerouac, Jack. "Dharma Bums," from *The Dharma Bums* by Jack Kerouac. Copyright © 1958 by Jack Kerouac, © renewed 1986 by Stella Kerouac and Jan Kerouac. Used by permission of Viking Penguin, a division of Penguin Group (USA) Inc.

Kerouac, Jack. "Essentials of Spontaneous Prose" and "Belief & Technique for Modern Prose." Reprinted by permission of Sterling Lord Literistic. Copyright by Jack Kerouac.

Leary, Timothy. "Turning on the World," from *The Blueprint to Turn-on the World: Ecstatic Politics.* Copyright © 1968, 1995 by Timothy Leary, Ph.D. High Priest, Ronin Publishing. Used by permission. All rights reserved.

Lisker, Jerry. "Homo Nest Raided, Queen Bees Are Stinging Mad," from *New York Daily News*, July 6, 1969. Copyright © New York Daily News, L.P. Reprinted with permission.

Marmon Silko, Leslie. "Almanac of the Dead," from *Almanac of the Dead* by Leslie Marmon Silko. Reprinted with the permission of Simon & Schuster Adult Publishing Group. Copyright © 1991 by Leslie Marmon Silko.

McClure, Michael. "Scratching the Beat Surface," excerpt from *Scratching the Beat Surface* by Michael McClure, Penguin, 1994. Copyright © Michael McClure. Reprinted by permission of Michael McClure.

McNeil, Legs, and Gillian McCain. "Please Kill Me: The Uncensored Oral History of Punk," from *Please Kill Me: The Uncensored Oral History of Punk*, Chapter 3 "The Music You've Been Waiting to Hear," by Legs McNeil and Gillian McCain, Copyright ©1996 by Legs McNeil and Gillian McCain. Used by permission of Grove/Atlantic, Inc.

Pellerin, Cheryl. "Trips," from *Trips: How Hallucinogens Work in Your Brain.* Copyright © 1998 by Seven Stories Press. Used by permission of Seven Stories Press.

Pinchbeck, Daniel. "Children of the Beats," from *The Rolling Stone Book of the Beats and American Culture*, edited by Holly George-Warren, Hyperion Books, 1999. "Children of the Beats" copyright © by Daniel Pinchbeck. Reprinted by permission of Daniel Pinchbeck.

Pirsig, Robert. "Zen and the Art of Motorcycle Maintenance," from *Zen and the Art of Motorcycle Maintenance: An Inquiry into Values* by Robert Pirsig. Reprinted by permission of HarperCollins Publishers Inc. (William Morrow).

Rose, Wendy. "For the White Poets Who Would Be Indian," from *Lost Copper: Poems* by Wendy Rose. Copyright © 1980. Reprinted by permission of Malki Museum, Inc.

Sinclair, John. "Rock and Roll Is a Weapon of the Cultural Revolution," from *Guitar Army: Sheet Writings/Prison Writings*. Copyright © 1972, 2003 John Sinclair.

Snyder, Gary. "Note on the Religious Tendencies." Copyright © Gary Snyder, 1960. Reprinted by permission of Gary Snyder.

Snyder, Gary. "I Went into the Maverick Bar," from *Turtle Island.* Copyright © 1974 by Gary Snyder. Reprinted by permission of New Directions Publishing Corp.

Thompson, Hunter S. "Fear and Loathing in Las Vegas," from *Fear and Loathing in Las Vegas* by Hunter S. Thompson. Copyright © 1972 by Hunter S. Thompson. Used by permission of Random House, Inc.

The Weathermen. "Communique #2 From the Weatherman Underground," from *Weathermen*, edited by Harold Jacobs, Ramparts Press, 1971. Copyright © Harold Jacobs. Reprinted by permission of Harold Jacobs.

Wolfe, Tom. "The Electric Kool-Aid Acid Test," from *The Electric Kool-Aid Acid Test* by Tom Wolfe. Copyright © 1968, renewed 1996 by Tom Wolfe. Reprinted by permission of Farrar, Straus and Giroux, LLC.